Readings in
American Government
Fifth Edition

Steffen W. Schmidt
Iowa State University

Mack C. Shelley, II
Iowa State University

Erica Merkley
Iowa State University

Printed in the United States of America

1 2 3 4 5 6 7   09 08 07 06 05

Printer: Thomson West

0-534-63171-1

Cover image: ©PhotoDisc

Thomson Higher Education
10 Davis Drive
Belmont, CA 94002-3098
USA

For more information about our products, contact us at:
Thomson Learning Academic Resource Center
1-800-423-0563

For permission to use material from this text or product, submit a request online at
http://www.thomsonrights.com.
Any additional questions about permissions can be submitted by email to **thomsonrights@thomson.com.**

Dedication

This book is dedicated to:

Lisel Suspiro de Schmidt & Walter Schmidt T.

Sarah F. Shelley & Mack C. Shelley

David, Donna, & Leah Merkley

CONTENTS

Chapter 11: The Media

Chapter 12: The Congress

Chapter 13: The Presidency

Chapter 14: The Bureaucracy

Chapter 15: The Judiciary

Chapter 16: Domestic Policy

INTRODUCTION

As we began to select material for this current, fifth edition of *Readings in American Government*, we reflected on how much has changed in American society and how some things continue to hold up over time.

Reflections

In the Introduction to the third edition of this book, written in 2000, we noted the following:

> *President Clinton survived impeachment and we hardly know Monica Lewinsky anymore. The greatest crisis of the Millennium was to be the Y2K computer problem that, possibly, might have brought a collapse of civilization as we know it. It has gone the way of Monica. On the other hand, the "new economy" and the continued explosion of computers, the World Wide Web, e-democracy, and dot com companies have raised many issues of great significance. We also now have a more divided and partisan politics with liberals and conservatives injecting more extreme radicalism into the national agenda on all issues including gun control, abortion, the globalization of the world religion, and the general social agenda of the country. At the same time, the two major candidates for president, George W. Bush and Al Gore, are trying very hard to hug the political center (while not alienating their conservative and liberal core base, respectively).*

In 2004 the new economy, outsourcing of jobs overseas, and the place of information technology and the Internet remained hot political buttons. Sen. John Kerry made job losses to China and other low-wage countries a major theme of his campaign. Democratic presidential wannabe former Vermont governor Howard Dean and his campaign adviser Joe Trippi honed the Internet into a sharp tool for fundraising and for bringing together Dean supporters through "Meet Up" get-togethers. On the other hand, the "dot com" companies, which were such a buzz during the Clinton years, had, by 2004, become a major part of the unemployment and economic slowdown during the four years of the Bush administration. The unemployment and decline in revenue caused by the burst of the dot com "bubble" was another major campaign issue for John Kerry.

The division between liberals and conservatives, observed by us years ago, became more intense.

On the other hand, terrorism, homeland security, Osama Bin Laden, and war in Iraq were not words on anyone's lips. In particular, the terrorist attacks of September 11, 2001 were unthinkable and have infused all of American society and American government and politics. Concerns about energy and Enron were not on our list of interests, and missile defense was a historical memory of the Reagan era.

Anti-globalization seemed more like a radical fringe group, not a serious player in the international centers of power as it has become in the past few years. *Bush v. Gore* was, as far as we knew then, an impending election, not a landmark U.S. Supreme Court case that would determine the outcome of a presidential election.

Almost no one reading our book would have heard of "military tribunals" in which to try foreign terrorists plotting against the United States. There were as yet no "Lessons from the Election of 2000" one of the most interesting and contentious in American political history.

Some of the other topics described in the introduction to the third edition still ring true and are very relevant and some have even risen to the top of the agenda again in the past few years, as the following paragraph suggests:

> *Other salient issues include affirmative action, which is under attack everywhere, and race relations, which are still very bad. Moreover, gender discrimination continues, school violence is of enormous concern, while the poor performance of public schools has raised all kinds of suggestions including vouchers and other remedies. Other issues that are of current interest are gun control* [actually the right to own guns], *privacy (possibly threatened by both the Internet and government intrusion), and the concern that Americans have become more apathetic politically than at any other time in our country's history.*

Senator John Kerry was so worried about being painted as anti gun that he dressed up in a camouflage suit and went goose hunting in Ohio just days before the presidential election. Congress, under pressure from gun owners and the National Rifle Association let the "assault weapons ban" law expire. This law had prohibited the sale of certain "assault rifles" such as modified AK-47s.

The privacy issue, noted in the previous introduction to this book gained intensity after the 9-11 terrorist attacks against the U.S. The Patriot Act, passed in the aftermath of the terror attacks and giving government much more expansive powers of surveillance and arrest (and thus intrusion into American's privacy), was hotly debated. The Bush administration argued that it was necessary to prevent further attacks, which civil liberty groups and many Democrats argued that it should be allowed to expire or be seriously modified.

> *Public opinion polls have taken an unprecedented importance, almost overshadowing elections (while their accuracy is increasingly questioned), and campaign money is out of control. However, while campaign finance is on everyone's lips, there seem few prospects of meaningful reform in the near future.*

These observations hold up amazingly well over the years! In the 2004 election, public opinion polls proliferated—there were more polls and more frequent polling results reported in the media than ever in American history. At the same time, serious questions were raised about the accuracy of polls in a time of cell phones (these numbers are usually not available to pollsters), call screening, and "polling fatigue"—people refusing to talk to pollsters calling during dinner. Moreover, on November 2, 2004, election day, the exit polls (polls taken of people as they leave the polling place) became a huge controversy because information was leaked about those polls early on election day. The early polls showed Senator Kerry ahead of Bush, and Internet "bloggers" as well as electronic media began to report this information. As the day wore on, Bush caught up. This produced paranoia about the election being stolen. It also triggered a demand for the exit polling organization, which was hired by all the networks, to hold their information longer in the next election cycle so that the polling numbers would not become an active part of the election again.

As to our observation about campaign money being out of control, little did we know that the 2004 election would become the most expensive in history with estimates that over $1.5 billion would be spent on the presidential election alone. Campaign finance reform (mentioned in our earlier edition) was again one of the most salient issues even though Congress passed the so-called McCain-Feingold law that was supposed to regulate money. As one would expect, the lawyers found loopholes, and in the latest presidential election independent groups spent a record amount of money on negative campaign ads (these were not officially coordinated with the campaigns but appeared to be so closely parallel to the Kerry and Bush campaigns that clearly something did not work).

The last version of this book, the fourth edition, which came out shortly after the 9-11 terrorist attacks on the U.S., has held up well. We wrote:

> *The issue of privacy is rising to perhaps an all time high as a result of counter terrorist security concerns, especially the proposals for a national identity card. The appropriate role for the government, always a hot topic, has now come under new and different scrutiny as the nation faces renewed fears about national security (and as the role of the armed forces has been suddenly propelled to the role of airport security and protecting water supplies and power stations within the United States). Gun ownership has become an even more relevant topic with millions of Americans (even college students at liberal, East coast institutions) forming gun clubs and towns once again requiring citizens to be armed. The terrorist attacks of September 11, 2001, as we said above, have changed everything.*

We were correct in assuming that 9-11 would be a huge and lasting factor in American society and certainly politics. In exit polls from the 2004 election, terrorism was almost tied with moral issues as the top reason why people voted for the reelection of Bush-Cheney.

Some of the following that was covered in the fourth edition also holds up fairly well, although the hate crimes issue has faded and environmental issues have been completely overshadowed by other hot button topics.

> *We have also addressed the "crisis" of Social Security, the rights of patients, the new reality of the media in America, and the terribly difficult issue of whether juveniles should be tried as adults as more and more horrific crimes (adult crimes) are committed by America's children. We also explore several environmental issues. The environment continues to grow as a very salient and intense topic in American electoral politics and regulatory regimes, hate crimes are in the news, and, as you might have expected, the use*

of high technology as tools for combat in the military of the future (and present) are all hot topics.

Of course, in 2004 Social Security actually rose very high as a concern. Americans were aware that this system will eventually run out of money as fewer workers pay into the fund and a huge generation of over 70 million retirees draw down the fund. The debate was whether the Bush plan to provide for "individual personal accounts" for younger workers was an appropriate way to repair the system or whether, as Kerry and the Democrats argue, propping up the system with further funding (i.e., leaving it untouched) was the only acceptable way to manage this important part of American old-age security.

We also wrote that,

This reader reflects the massive changes in mood and in priorities that have shaken the United States since 9-11, 2001. Never in our wildest dreams would we have guessed that the American government would, within a few short years of our last and fourth effort at producing a reader, be on a crash program to produce enough Smallpox vaccines to immunize every American in case of a germ warfare attack. It never crossed our minds that Americans would be demanding that airport security be federalized and that we would be happy when we are asked to take off our shoes at the airport to check for "sneaker bombs."

Some of the nuances of anti-terrorism such as smallpox vaccines have diminished in the public eye but is the focus of intensive activity by policymakers seeking to develop protection against such potential attacks in the future. Concerns about the lack of flu vaccines in 2004 because a British supplier to the U.S. was shut down due to contamination also became an important discussion. Sneaker bombers are also much less of a concern than the unfolding network of terrorist around the world who are now using car bombs as weapons. And the concern about ground-to-air missiles that could be used to shoot down civilian aircraft became a new security problem.

New Fifth Edition 2005

The readings in this new, fifth edition of the book bring us to the present and to new, complex issues facing Americans. We think these readings are enlightening, interesting, and will allow you to engage in a vigorous discussion.

The war in Iraq and terrorism have been front and center in the American political scene and is a new issue no one could have imagined the last time this book was edited. Other issues that are of interest include the cost of healthcare and prescription drugs, gay marriage, "values" (including the role of religion and morality), and policy issues related to development along the Eastern coast (especially Florida and the Gulf of Mexico coast) with the renewal of intense hurricane seasons that may expose this area to great disasters such as the spate of deadly storms in 2004. The reliability of electronic voting machines and questions about the legitimacy of the 2004 election also erupted after the voting was done.

More generally, America in 2004 was a deeply divided country and American politics contentious and harsh.

Mack C. Shelley II
Erica Merkley
Steffen W. Schmidt

P.S. If you are interested in **environmental issues,** we suggest you visit Prof. Schmidt's innovative World Wide Web based course "The Policy and Politics of Coastal Areas." Did you know that 80% of Americans live within one hour's drive of a coast? Did you know that the coastal areas are highly vulnerable to natural disaster and are under intense environmental stress? Did you follow the hurricane season of 2004 that caused the most expensive national disaster in U.S. history?

The course can be accessed from anywhere in the world by going to:
http://www.public.iastate.edu/~sws
E-mail Professor Schmidt at sws@iastate.edu

CHAPTER 1
THE DEMOCRATIC REPUBLIC

In his televised speech at the Democratic National Convention, in Boston, Massachusetts, on July 27, 2004, Illinois Senator Barack Obama lays out his version of the dreams of the huge numbers of immigrants from extremely diverse backgrounds who have contributed so much to the growth and development of the United States over more than two centuries. That immigrant tide gave rise to power centers for the Democratic Party, particularly in urban areas, throughout the country. His progressive vision of equality is contrasted with the conservative views of California Governor Arnold Schwarzenegger that are laid out in the text of his speech delivered at the Republican National Convention, in New York City, on September 1, 2004. Schwarzenegger, who rode a Hollywood career away from his own immigrant origins, became governor of California following the recall of Democratic Governor Gray Davis, as a moderate Republican in a party increasingly dominated by its conservative wing. These presentations provide an intriguing contrast of views regarding what the United States has been about in the past and where it might be headed in the future.

Speech by Illinois Senator Barack Obama at the Democratic National Convention, Boston, MA, July 27, 2004

On behalf of the great state of Illinois, crossroads of a nation, land of Lincoln, let me express my deep gratitude for the privilege of addressing this convention. Tonight is a particular honor for me because, let's face it, my presence on this stage is pretty unlikely. My father was a foreign student, born and raised in a small village in Kenya. He grew up herding goats, went to school in a tin-roof shack. His father, my grandfather, was a cook, a domestic servant.

But my grandfather had larger dreams for his son. Through hard work and perseverance my father got a scholarship to study in a magical place; America which stood as a beacon of freedom and opportunity to so many who had come before. While studying here, my father met my mother. She was born in a town on the other side of the world, in Kansas. Her father worked on oil rigs and farms through most of the Depression. The day after Pearl Harbor he signed up for duty, joined Patton's army and marched across Europe. Back home, my grandmother raised their baby and went to work on a bomber assembly line. After the war, they studied on the GI Bill, bought a house through FHA, and moved west in search of opportunity.

And they, too, had big dreams for their daughter, a common dream, born of two continents. My parents shared not only an improbable love; they shared an abiding faith in the possibilities of this nation. They would give me an African name, Barack, or "blessed," believing that in a tolerant America your name is no barrier to success. They imagined me going to the best schools in the land, even though they weren't rich, because in a generous America you don't have to be rich to achieve your potential. They are both passed away now. Yet, I know that, on this night, they look down on me with pride.

I stand here today, grateful for the diversity of my heritage, aware that my parents' dreams live on in my precious daughters. I stand here knowing that my story is part of the larger American story, that I owe a debt to all of those who came before me, and that, in no other country on earth, is my story even possible. Tonight, we gather to affirm the greatness of our nation, not because of the height of our skyscrapers, or the power of our military, or the size of our economy. Our pride is based on a very simple premise, summed up in a declaration made over two hundred years ago, "We hold these truths to be self-evident, that all men are created equal. That they are endowed by their Creator with certain inalienable rights. That among these are life, liberty and the pursuit of happiness."

That is the true genius of America, a faith in the simple dreams of its people, the insistence on small miracles. That we can tuck in our children at night and know they are fed and clothed and safe from harm. That we can say what we think, write what we think, without hearing a sudden knock on the door. That we can have an idea and start our own business without paying a bribe or hiring somebody's son. That we can participate in the political process without fear of retribution, and that our votes will be counted—or at least, most of the time.

This year, in this election, we are called to reaffirm our values and commitments, to hold them against a hard reality and see how we are measuring up, to the legacy of our forbearers, and the promise of future generations. And fellow Americans—Democrats, Republicans, Independents—I say to you tonight: we have more work to do. More to do for the workers I met in Galesburg, Illinois, who are losing their union jobs at the Maytag plant that's moving to Mexico, and now are having to compete with their own children for jobs that pay seven bucks an hour. More to do for the father I met who was losing his job and choking back tears, wondering how he would pay $4,500 a month for the drugs his son needs without the health benefits he counted on. More to do for the young woman in East St. Louis, and thousands more like her, who has the grades, has the drive, has the will, but doesn't have the money to go to college.

Don't get me wrong. The people I meet in small towns and big cities, in diners and office parks, they don't expect government to solve all their problems. They know they have to work hard to get ahead and they want to. Go into the collar counties around Chicago, and people will tell you they don't want their tax money wasted by a welfare agency or the Pentagon. Go into any inner city neighborhood, and folks will tell you that government alone can't teach kids to learn. They know that parents have to parent, that children can't achieve unless we raise their expectations and turn off the television sets and eradicate the slander that says a black youth with a book is acting white. No, people don't expect government to solve all their problems. But they sense, deep in their bones, that with just a change in priorities, we can make sure that every child in America has a decent shot at life, and that the doors of opportunity remain open to all. They know we can do better. And they want that choice.

In this election, we offer that choice. Our party has chosen a man to lead us who embodies the best this country has to offer. That man is John Kerry. John Kerry understands the ideals of community, faith, and sacrifice, because they've defined his life. From his heroic service in Vietnam to his years as prosecutor and lieutenant governor, through two decades in the United

States Senate, he has devoted himself to this country. Again and again, we've seen him make tough choices when easier ones were available. His values and his record affirm what is best in us.

John Kerry believes in an America where hard work is rewarded. So instead of offering tax breaks to companies shipping jobs overseas, he'll offer them to companies creating jobs here at home. John Kerry believes in an America where all Americans can afford the same health coverage our politicians in Washington have for themselves. John Kerry believes in energy independence, so we aren't held hostage to the profits of oil companies or the sabotage of foreign oil fields. John Kerry believes in the constitutional freedoms that have made our country the envy of the world, and he will never sacrifice our basic liberties nor use faith as a wedge to divide us. And John Kerry believes that in a dangerous world, war must be an option, but it should never be the first option.

A while back, I met a young man named Shamus at the VFW Hall in East Moline, Illinois. He was a good-looking kid, six-two or six-three, clear eyed, with an easy smile. He told me he'd joined the Marines and was heading to Iraq the following week. As I listened to him explain why he'd enlisted, his absolute faith in our country and its leaders, his devotion to duty and service, I thought this young man was all any of us might hope for in a child. But then I asked myself: Are we serving Shamus as well as he was serving us? I thought of more than 900 service men and women, sons and daughters, husbands and wives, friends and neighbors, who will not be returning to their hometowns. I thought of families I had met who were struggling to get by without a loved one's full income, or whose loved ones had returned with a limb missing or with nerves shattered, but who still lacked long-term health benefits because they were reservists. When we send our young men and women into harm's way, we have a solemn obligation not to fudge the numbers or shade the truth about why they're going, to care for their families while they're gone, to tend to the soldiers upon their return, and to never ever go to war without enough troops to win the war, secure the peace, and earn the respect of the world.

Now let me be clear. We have real enemies in the world. These enemies must be found. They must be pursued and they must be defeated. John Kerry knows this. And just as Lieutenant Kerry did not hesitate to risk his life to protect the men who served with him in Vietnam, President Kerry will not hesitate one moment to use our military might to keep America safe and secure. John Kerry believes in America. And he knows it's not enough for just some of us to prosper. For alongside our famous individualism, there's another ingredient in the American saga.

A belief that we are connected as one people. If there's a child on the south side of Chicago who can't read, that matters to me, even if it's not my child. If there's a senior citizen somewhere who can't pay for her prescription and has to choose between medicine and the rent, that makes my life poorer, even if it's not my grandmother. If there's an Arab American family being rounded up without benefit of an attorney or due process, that threatens my civil liberties. It's that fundamental belief—I am my brother's keeper, I am my sisters' keeper—that makes this country work. It's what allows us to pursue our individual dreams, yet still come together as a single American family. "*E pluribus unum*." Out of many, one.

Yet even as we speak, there are those who are preparing to divide us, the spin masters and negative ad peddlers who embrace the politics of anything goes. Well, I say to them tonight, there's not a liberal America and a conservative America—there's the United States of America. There's not a black America and white America and Latino America and Asian America; there's the United States of America. The pundits like to slice-and-dice our country into Red States and Blue States; Red States for Republicans, Blue States for Democrats. But I've got news for them, too. We worship an awesome God in the Blue States, and we don't like federal agents poking around our libraries in the Red States. We coach Little League in the Blue States and have gay friends in the Red States. There are patriots who opposed the war in Iraq and patriots who supported it. We are one people, all of us pledging allegiance to the stars and stripes, all of us defending the United States of America.

In the end, that's what this election is about. Do we participate in a politics of cynicism or a politics of hope? John Kerry calls on us to hope. John Edwards calls on us to hope. I'm not talking about blind optimism here—the almost willful ignorance that thinks unemployment will go away if we just don't talk about it, or the health care crisis will solve itself if we just ignore it. No, I'm talking about something more substantial. It's the hope of slaves sitting around a fire singing freedom songs; the hope of immigrants setting out for distant shores; the hope of a young naval lieutenant bravely patrolling the Mekong Delta; the hope of a millworker's son who dares to defy the odds; the hope of a skinny kid with a funny name who believes that America has a place for him, too. The audacity of hope!

In the end, that is God's greatest gift to us, the bedrock of this nation; the belief in things not seen; the belief that there are better days ahead. I believe we can give our middle class relief and provide working families with a road to opportunity. I believe we can provide jobs to the jobless, homes to the homeless, and reclaim young people in cities across America from violence and despair. I believe that as we stand on the crossroads of history, we can make the right choices, and meet the challenges that face us. America!

Tonight, if you feel the same energy I do, the same urgency I do, the same passion I do, the same hopefulness I do—if we do what we must do, then I have no doubt that all across the country, from Florida to Oregon, from Washington to Maine, the people will rise up in November, and John Kerry will be sworn in as president, and John Edwards will be sworn in as vice president, and this country will reclaim its promise, and out of this long political darkness a brighter day will come. Thank you and God bless you.

Public Domain: accessed at
http://www.dems2004.org/site/apps/nl/content3.asp?c=luI2LaPYG&b=125925&ct=158769

T hank you.

What a greeting!

This is like winning an Oscar! ...As if I would know! Speaking of acting, one of my movies was called "True Lies." It's what the Democrats should have called their convention.

My fellow Americans, this is an amazing moment for me. To think that a once scrawny boy from Austria could grow up to become Governor of California and stand in Madison Square Garden to speak on behalf of the President of the United States that is an immigrant's dream. It is the American dream.

I was born in Europe ...and I've traveled all over the world. I can tell you that there is no place, no country, more compassionate more generous more accepting and more welcoming than the United States of America.

As long as I live, I will never forget that day 21 years ago when I raised my hand and took the oath of citizenship.

Do you know how proud I was? I was so proud that I walked around with an American flag around my shoulders all day long.

Tonight, I want to talk about why I'm even more proud to be an American - why I'm proud to be a Republican and why I believe this country is in good hands.

When I was a boy, the Soviets occupied part of Austria. I saw their tanks in the streets. I saw communism with my own eyes. I remember the fear we had when we had to cross into the Soviet sector. Growing up, we were told, "Don't look the soldiers in the eye. Look straight ahead." It was a common belief that Soviet soldiers could take a man out of his own car and ship him off to the Soviet Union as slave labor.

My family didn't have a car - but one day we were in my uncle's car. It was near dark as we came to a Soviet checkpoint. I was a little boy, I wasn't an action hero back then, and I remember how scared I was that the soldiers would pull my father or my uncle out of the car and I'd never see him again. My family and so many others lived in fear of the Soviet boot. Today, the world no longer fears the Soviet Union and it is because of the United States of America!

As a kid I saw the socialist country that Austria became after the Soviets left. I love Austria and I love the Austrian people - but I always knew America was the place for me. In school, when the teacher would talk about America, I would daydream about coming here. I would sit for hours watching American movies transfixed by my heroes like John Wayne. Everything about America seemed so big to me so open, so possible.

I finally arrived here in 1968. I had empty pockets, but I was full of dreams. The presidential campaign was in full swing. I remember watching the Nixon and Humphrey presidential race on TV. A friend who spoke German and English, translated for me. I heard Humphrey saying things that sounded like socialism, which is what I had just left. But then I heard Nixon speak. He was talking about free enterprise, getting government off your back, lowering taxes and strengthening the military. Listening to Nixon speak sounded more like a breath of fresh air.

I said to my fried, "What party is he?" My friend said, "He's a Republican." I said, "Then I am a Republican!" And I've been a Republican ever since! And trust me, in my wife's family, that's no small achievement! I'm proud to belong to the party of Abraham Lincoln, the party of Teddy Roosevelt, the party of Ronald Reagan and the party of George W. Bush.

To my fellow immigrants listening tonight, I want you to know how welcome you are in this party. We Republicans admire your ambition. We encourage your dreams. We believe in your future. One thing I learned about America is that if you work hard and play by the rules, this country is truly open to you. You can achieve anything.

Everything I have my career my success my family I owe to America. In this country, it doesn't make any difference where you were born. It doesn't make any difference who your parents were. It doesn't make any difference if, like me, you couldn't even speak English until you were in your twenties.

America gave me opportunities and my immigrant dreams came true. I want other people to get the same chances I did, the same opportunities. And I believe they can. That's why I believe in this country, that's why I believe in this party and that's why I believe in this President.

Now, many of you out there tonight are "Republican" like me in your hearts and in your beliefs. Maybe you're from Guatemala. Maybe you're from the Philippines. Maybe Europe or the Ivory Coast. Maybe you live in Ohio, Pennsylvania or New Mexico. And maybe just maybe you don't agree with this party on every single issue. I say to you tonight I believe that's not only okay, that's what's great about this country. Here we can respectfully disagree and still be patriotic still be American and still be good Republicans.

My fellow immigrants, my fellow Americans, how do you know if you are a Republican? I'll tell you how.

If you believe that government should be accountable to the people, not the people to the government...then you are a Republican! If you believe a person should be treated as an individual, not as a member of an interest group... then you are a Republican! If you believe your family knows how to spend your money better than the government does... then you are a Republican! If you believe our educational system should be held accountable for the progress of our children ... then you are a Republican! If you believe this country, not the United Nations, is

11

the best hope of democracy in the world ... then you are a Republican! And, ladies and gentlemen ...if you believe we must be fierce and relentless and terminate terrorism ... then you are a Republican!

There is another way you can tell you're a Republican. You have faith in free enterprise, faith in the resourcefulness of the American people ... and faith in the U.S. economy. To those critics who are so pessimistic about our economy, I say: "Don't be economic girlie men!"

The U.S. economy remains the envy of the world. We have the highest economic growth of any of the world's major industrialized nations. Don't you remember the pessimism of 20 years ago when the critics said Japan and Germany were overtaking the U.S.? Ridiculous!

Now they say India and China are overtaking us. Don't you believe it! We may hit a few bumps - but America always moves ahead! That's what Americans do!

We move prosperity ahead. We move freedom ahead. We move people ahead. Under President Bush and Vice President Cheney, America's economy is moving ahead in spite of a recession they inherited and in spite of the attack on our homeland.

Now, the other party says there are two Americas. Don't believe that either. I've visited our troops in Iraq, Kuwait, Bosnia, Germany and all over the world. I've visited our troops in California, where they train before they go overseas. And I've visited our military hospitals. And I can tell you this: Our young men and women in uniform do not believe there are two Americas!

They believe we are one America and they are fighting for it! We are one America - and President Bush is defending it with all his heart and soul!

That's what I admire most about the President. He's a man of perseverance.

He's a man of inner strength. He is a leader who doesn't flinch, doesn't waiver, does not back down. My fellow Americans, make no mistake about it terrorism is more insidious than communism, because it yearns to destroy not just the individual, but the entire international order. The President didn't go into Iraq because the polls told him it was popular. As a matter of fact, the polls said just the opposite. But leadership isn't about polls. It's about making decisions you think are right and then standing behind those decisions. That's why America is safer with George W. Bush as President.

He knows you don't reason with terrorists. You defeat them. He knows you can't reason with people blinded by hate. They hate the power of the individual. They hate the progress of women. They hate the religious freedom of others. They hate the liberating breeze of democracy. But ladies and gentlemen, their hate is no match for America's decency.

We're the America that sends out Peace Corps volunteers to teach village children. We're the America that sends out missionaries and doctors to raise up the poor and the sick. We're the America that gives more than any other country, to fight aids in Africa and the developing world. And we're the America that fights not for imperialism but for human rights and democracy.

You know, when the Germans brought down the Berlin Wall, America's determination helped wield the sledgehammers. When that lone, young Chinese man stood in front of those tanks in Tiananmen Square, America's hopes stood with him. And when Nelson Mandela smiled in election victory after all those years in prison, America celebrated, too.

We are still the lamp lighting the world especially for those who struggle. No matter in what labor camp, they slave no matter in what injustice they're trapped - they hear our call ... they see our light ... and they feel the pull of our freedom. They come here as I did because they believe. They believe in us.

They come because their hearts say to them, as mine did, "If only I can get to America." Someone once wrote - "There are those who say that freedom is nothing but a dream." They are right. It's the American dream.

No matter the nationality, no matter the religion, no matter the ethnic background, America brings out the best in people. And as Governor of the great state of California - I see the best in Americans every day ... our police, our firefighters our nurses, doctors and teachers, our parents.

And what about the extraordinary men and women who have volunteered to fight for the United States of America! I have such great respect for them and their heroic families.

Let me tell you about the sacrifice and commitment I've seen firsthand. In one of the military hospitals I visited, I met a young guy who was in bad shape. He'd lost a leg had a hole in his stomach ... his shoulder had been shot through.

I could tell there was no way he could ever return to combat. But when I asked him, "When do you think you'll get out of the hospital?" He said, "Sir, in three weeks." And do you know what he said to me then? He said he was going to get a new leg ... and get some therapy ... and then he was going back to Iraq to serve alongside his buddies! He grinned at me and said, "Arnold ... I'll be back!"

Ladies and gentlemen, America is back! Back from the attack on our homeland - back from the attack on our economy, back from the attack on our way of life. We're back because of the perseverance, character and leadership of the 43rd President of the United States, George W. Bush.

My fellow Americans ...I want you to know that I believe with all my heart that America remains "the great idea" that inspires the world. It's a privilege to be born here. It's an honor to become a citizen here. It's a gift to raise your family here to vote here and to live here.

Our president, George W. Bush, has worked hard to protect and preserve the American dream for all of us. That's why I say ... send him back to Washington for four more years!

Thank you, America - and God bless you all!

Public Domain: accessed at http://www.gopconvention.com/News/Read.aspx?ID=4593

Chapter 1
Questions

1. Which vision—Obama's or Schwarzennger's—do you think is closer to your own views? Why?

2. What would Obama have to do to see his views become reality? What would Schwarzenegger have to do to put his views into practice?

CHAPTER 2
THE CONSTITUTION

The readings in Chapter 2 address three aspect of the issue of marriage for gay males and lesbians—which we will refer to as "gay marriage," for short. "The Politics of Gay Marriage" presents a legal brief about the possible impact of the 2003 decision by the Massachusetts Supreme Judicial Court legalizing same-sex marriage. This is followed by the text of a proposed amendment to the constitution of the state of Massachusetts that would provide for same-sex civil unions, which would provide many of the same legal protections for partners as a formal marriage but still would fall short of marital rights. We also present the official statement of President George W. Bush calling for an amendment to the United States Constitution that would ban gay marriage, invoking the congressional Defense of Marriage Act of 1996.

The Politics of Gay Marriage
SEAS Consulting, "Briefing Paper #38," © 2004

On November 18, 2003 the highest court in the state of Massachusetts ruled that gay couples have the right to marry under the state's Constitution. The court also ordered the state legislature to make same-sex marriages possible in no more than 180 days of the ruling.

Gay rights groups and liberal politicians and interest groups applauded the ruling and saw it as a civil rights issue similar to the civil rights of blacks. Conservatives and churches as well as traditional religious interest groups condemned the ruling declaring it to be a challenge to American values and to a basic institution with ancient historical roots. Interestingly, many African Americans also rejected the parallel between the black civil rights struggle and gay marriage, often noting that "you can't change your color" when discriminated against.

The governor and legislature of Massachusetts were opposed to same sex marriage. On February 11, 2004 the joint legislative leadership of the Massachusetts legislature wrote and proposed an amendment to the constitution (reproduced below) that would limit marriage to a man and a woman. By law, this could not become effective in 180 days and therefore proved to be a symbolic gesture.

The court (in a 4-3 decision—i.e. only four people favored this ruling) made Massachusetts the first state in the country in which a high court ruled that homosexual couples are constitutionally entitled to marry. The ruling proved to be the launching point for a national debate on this issue, prompted many states to either write laws defining marriage as a union of a man and a woman or passing constitutional amendments prohibiting gay marriage. In the 2004 national elections, eleven states had such amendments on the ballot and all passed. The anti-gay marriage amendments were may have brought voters with traditional values to the polls nationwide. The issue may also have helped the Republicans (who are generally opposed to same sex marriage) achieve a major election victory.

"The question before us is whether, consistent with the Massachusetts Constitution, the commonwealth may deny the protections, benefits and obligations conferred by civil marriage to two individuals of the same sex who wish to marry," Chief Justice Margaret H. Marshall of the state's Supreme Judicial Court wrote in her opinion. "We conclude that it may not. The Massachusetts Constitution affirms the dignity and equality of all individuals. It forbids the creation of second-class citizens."

The court did not tell the state legislature how to carry out the ruling but most agree that the court intended to extend full marriage rights to gay men and lesbians and would not permit "same sex partnerships" or other intermediate legal steps.

Unofficial Synopsis Prepared by the Reporter of Decisions
(Editors Note: This information comes from the Massachusetts Court System)

The Supreme Judicial Court held today [Nov 18, 2003] that "barring an individual from the protections, benefits, and obligations of civil marriage solely because that person would marry a person of the same sex violates the Massachusetts Constitution." The court stayed the entry of judgment for 180 days "to permit the Legislature to take such action as it may deem appropriate in light of this opinion."

"Marriage is a vital social institution," wrote Chief Justice Margaret H. Marshall for the majority of the Justices. "The exclusive commitment of two individuals to each other nurtures love and mutual support; it brings stability to our society. For those who choose to marry, and for their children, marriage provides an abundance of legal, financial, and social benefits. In turn it imposes weighty legal, financial, and social obligations." The question before the court was "whether, consistent with the Massachusetts Constitution," the Commonwealth could deny those protections, benefits, and obligations to two individuals of the same sex who wish to marry.

In ruling that the Commonwealth could not do so, the court observed that the Massachusetts Constitution "affirms the dignity and equality of all individuals," and "forbids the creation of second-class citizens." It reaches its conclusion, the court said, giving "full deference to the arguments made by the Commonwealth." The Commonwealth, the court ruled, "has failed to identify any constitutionality adequate reason for denying civil marriage to same-sex couples."

The court affirmed that it owes "great deference to the Legislature to decide social and policy issues." Where, as here, the constitutionality of a law is challenged, it is the "traditional and settled role" of courts to decide the constitutional question. The "marriage ban" the court held, "works a deep and scarring hardship" on same-sex families "for no rational reason." It prevents children of same-sex couples "from enjoying the immeasurable advantages that flow from the assurance of 'a stable family structure in which children will be reared, educated, and socialized.'" "It cannot be rational under our laws," the court held, "to penalize children by depriving them of State benefits" because of their parents' sexual orientation.

The court rejected the Commonwealth's claim that the primary purpose of marriage was procreation. Rather, the history of the marriage laws in the Commonwealth demonstrates that "it is the exclusive and permanent commitment of the marriage partners to one another, not the begetting of children, that is the sine qua non of marriage."

The court remarked that its decision "does not disturb the fundamental value of marriage in our society." "That same-sex couples are willing to embrace marriage's solemn obligations of exclusivity, mutual support, and commitment to one another is a testament to the enduring place of marriage in our laws and in the human spirit," the court stated.

The opinion reformulates the common-law definition of civil marriage to mean "the voluntary union of two persons as spouses, to the exclusion of all others. Nothing that "civil marriage has long been termed a 'civil right,'" the court concluded that "the right to marry means little if it does not include the right to marry the person of one's choice, subject to appropriate government restrictions in the interests of public health, safety, and welfare."

Justices John M. Greaney, Roderick L. Ireland, and Judith A. Cowin joined in the court's opinion. Justice Greaney also filed a separate concurring opinion.

Justices Francis X. Spina, Martha B. Sosman, and Robert J. Cordy each filed separate dissenting opinions.

Justice Greaney concurred "with the result reached by the court, the remedy ordered, and much of the reasoning in the court's opinion," but expressed the view that "the case is more directly resolved using traditional equal protection analysis." He stated that to withhold "relief from the plaintiffs, who wish to marry, and are otherwise eligible to marry, on the ground that the couples are of the same gender, constitutes a categorical restriction of a fundamental right." Moreover, Justice Greaney concluded that such a restriction is impermissible under art. 1 of the Massachusetts Declaration of Rights. In so doing, Justice Greaney did not rely on art. 1, as amended in 1976, because the voters' intent in passing the amendment was clearly not to approve gay marriage, but he relied on well-established principles of equal protection that antedated the amendment.

Justice Cordy, with whom Justice Spina and Justice Sosman joined, dissented on the ground that the marriage statute, as historically interpreted to mean the union of one man and one woman, does not violate the Massachusetts Constitution because "the Legislature could rationally conclude that it furthers the legitimate State purpose of ensuring, promoting, and supporting an optimal social structure for the bearing and raising of children." Justice Cordy stated that the court's conclusions to the contrary are unsupportable in light of "the presumption of constitutional validity and significant deference afforded to legislative enactments, and the 'undesirability of the judiciary substituting its notion of correct policy for that of a popularly elected legislature' responsible for making it.' Further, Justice Cordy stated that "[w]hile 'the Massachusetts Constitution protects matters of personal liberty against government intrusion at least as zealously and often more so than does the Federal Constitution,' this case is not about government intrusions into matters of personal liberty," but "about whether the State must endorse and support [the choices of same-sex couples] by changing the institution of civil marriage to make its benefits, obligations, and responsibilities applicable to them." Justice Cordy concluded that, although the plaintiffs had made a powerful case for the extension of the benefits and burdens of civil marriage to same-sex couples, the issue "is one deeply rooted in social policy" and 'that decision must be made by the Legislature, not the court."

Justice Spina, in a separately filed dissenting opinion, stated that "[W]hat is at stake in this case is not the unequal treatment of individuals or whether individuals rights have been impermissibly burdened, but the power of the Legislature to effectuate social change without interference from the courts, pursuant to art. 30 of the Massachusetts Declaration of Rights." He emphasized that the "power to regulate marriage lies with the Legislature, not with the judiciary."

Justice Sosman, in a separately filed dissenting opinion, stated that "the issue is not whether the Legislature's rationale behind [the statutory scheme being challenged] is persuasive to [the court]," but whether it is "rational" for the Legislature to "reserve judgment" on whether changing the definition of marriage "can be made at this time without damaging the institution of marriage or adversely affecting the critical role it has played in our society." She concluded that, "[a]bsent consensus on the issue (which obviously does not exist), or unanimity amongst scientists studying the issue (which also does not exist), or a more prolonged period of observation of this new family structure (which has not yet been possible), it is rational for the Legislature to postpone any redefinition of marriage that would include same-sex couples until such time as it is certain that redefinition will not have unintended and undesirable social consequences."

Full text of the ruling can be found at:
http://www.mass.gov/courts/courtsandjudges/courts/supremejudicialcourt/goodridge.html

Reprinted with permission from © SEAS Consulting, 2004.

**Massachusetts Constitutional Amendment on Gay Marriage
February 11, 2004**

Amendment proposed by joint leadership

Proposed jointly by leaders of the House and Senate, which would ban gay marriage and establish civil unions:

This article shall ensure that the people, not the courts, define the unique relationship of marriage.

It being the public policy of this commonwealth to protect the unique relationship of marriage, only the union of one man and one woman shall be valid or recognized as a marriage in Massachusetts. Two persons of the same sex shall have the right to form a civil union, if they meet the requirements set forth by law for marriage between a man and a woman.

Civil unions for same sex couples are established hereunder and shall provide entirely the same benefits, protections, rights and responsibilities that are afforded to couples married under Massachusetts law. All laws applicable to marriage shall also apply to civil unions.

This article is self-executing, but the General Court may enact laws not inconsistent with anything herein contained to carry out the purpose of this article.

Public Domain

President Calls for Constitutional Amendment Protecting Marriage
The White House, February 24, 2004

For Immediate Release
Office of the Press Secretary
February 24, 2004
President Calls for Constitutional Amendment Protecting Marriage
Remarks by the President
The Roosevelt Room

10:43 A.M. EST

THE PRESIDENT: Good morning. Eight years ago, Congress passed, and President Clinton signed, the Defense of Marriage Act, which defined marriage for purposes of federal law as the legal union between one man and one woman as husband and wife.

The Act passed the House of Representatives by a vote of 342 to 67, and the Senate by a vote of 85 to 14. Those congressional votes and the passage of similar defensive marriage laws in 38 states express an overwhelming consensus in our country for protecting the institution of marriage.

In recent months, however, some activist judges and local officials have made an aggressive attempt to redefine marriage. In Massachusetts, four judges on the highest court have indicated they will order the issuance of marriage licenses to applicants of the same gender in May of this year. In San Francisco, city officials have issued thousands of marriage licenses to people of the same gender, contrary to the California family code. That code, which clearly defines marriage as the union of a man and a woman, was approved overwhelmingly by the voters of California. A county in New Mexico has also issued marriage licenses to applicants of the same gender. And unless action is taken, we can expect more arbitrary court decisions, more litigation, more defiance of the law by local officials, all of which adds to uncertainty.

After more than two centuries of American jurisprudence, and millennia of human experience, a few judges and local authorities are presuming to change the most fundamental institution of civilization. Their actions have created confusion on an issue that requires clarity.

On a matter of such importance, the voice of the people must be heard. Activist courts have left the people with one recourse. If we are to prevent the meaning of marriage from being changed forever, our nation must enact a constitutional amendment to protect marriage in America. Decisive and democratic action is needed, because attempts to redefine marriage in a single state or city could have serious consequences throughout the country.

The Constitution says that full faith and credit shall be given in each state to the public acts and records and judicial proceedings of every other state. Those who want to change the meaning of marriage will claim that this provision requires all states and cities to recognize same-sex marriages performed anywhere in America. Congress attempted to address this problem in the Defense of Marriage Act, by declaring that no state must accept another state's definition of marriage. My administration will vigorously defend this act of Congress.

Yet there is no assurance that the Defense of Marriage Act will not, itself, be struck down by activist courts. In that event, every state would be forced to recognize any relationship that judges in Boston or officials in San Francisco choose to call a marriage. Furthermore, even if the Defense of Marriage Act is upheld, the law does not protect marriage within any state or city.

For all these reasons, the Defense of Marriage requires a constitutional amendment. An amendment to the Constitution is never to be undertaken lightly. The amendment process has addressed many serious matters of national concern. And the preservation of marriage rises to this level of national importance. The union of a man and woman is the most enduring human institution, honoring—honored and encouraged in all cultures and by every religious faith. Ages of experience have taught humanity that the commitment of a husband and wife to love and to serve one another promotes the welfare of children and the stability of society.

Marriage cannot be severed from its cultural, religious and natural roots without weakening the good influence of society. Government, by recognizing and protecting marriage, serves the interests of all. Today I call upon the Congress to promptly pass, and to send to the states for ratification, an amendment to our Constitution defining and protecting marriage as a union of man and woman as husband and wife. The amendment should fully protect marriage, while leaving the state legislatures free to make their own choices in defining legal arrangements other than marriage.

America is a free society, which limits the role of government in the lives of our citizens. This commitment of freedom, however, does not require the redefinition of one of our most basic social institutions. Our government should respect every person, and protect the institution of marriage. There is no contradiction between these responsibilities. We should also conduct this difficult debate in a manner worthy of our country, without bitterness or anger.

In all that lies ahead, let us match strong convictions with kindness and goodwill and decency.

Thank you very much.

END 10:48 A.M. ES

Public Domain: accessed at http://www.whitehouse.gov/news/releases/2004/02/20040224-2.html

Chapter 2
Questions

1. Where do you think you stand on the issues of "gay marriage?" Explain your views on this issue, using information from these readings and other things you may know about this issue.

2. Many analysts of the November 2004 presidential election believe that the reelection of President George W. Bush was attributable to large numbers of conservative voters who turned out to vote against "gay marriage." Why do you think this may have happened? What other interpretations of the election would cast doubts on this explanation?

CHAPTER 3
FEDERALISM

This set of readings presents three different interpretations of the role of the Electoral College in United States presidential elections using competing testimony provided to the United States Congress. Curtis Gans, who is Director of the Committee for the Study of the American Electorate and a scholar of electoral politics, believes that the Electoral Colleges is important and can be modified to work better. A different perspective is provided by Professor Judith A. Best of the State University of New York at Cortland, who testified that the federal structure of the Electoral College produces the right person as president and argues against major changes in that presidential selection system. An argument for replacing the Electoral College with a system of direct popular vote election is presented by U.S. Representative Ray LaHood, a Republican from the 18th Congressional District of Illinois.

Electoral College Reform: Yes
Congressional Testimony of Curtis Gans, Director of the Committee for the Study of the American Electorate

House of Representatives Committee on the Judiciary Subcommittee on the Constitution

Subcommittee Hearing on "Proposals for Electoral College Reform: H.J. Res. 28 and H.J. Res. 43"

September 4, 1997
2237 Rayburn House Office Building
10:00 a.m.

Testimony of Curtis Gans
Director, Committee for the Study of the American Electorate

Mr. Chairman: I would like to thank the Chairman and this Committee for the opportunity to testify on this arcane but important issue.

My name is Curtis Gans and I helped found and have for the last 21 years directed The Committee for the Study of the American Electorate, a small non-partisan, non-profit organization whose primary mission is to explore, explain and try to correct the increasing disinclination of the American citizen to participate in our democratic processes.

There appear to me to be two questions confronting this committee:

1. Should the indirect method of electing Presidents through a state-based electoral college be replaced by direct elections in which a simple plurality or majority of voters determine the winner? and

2. If not, could the present electoral college system be improved?

The answer to the first is an unequivocal, "No." The answer to the second is a qualified, "Yes."

The arguments for direct elections seem superficially to be clear and persuasive:

Should not every citizen's vote be equal and what better way to insure that equality than direct elections?

Should the nation not protect itself from the possibility of a President elected by a minority of those voting?

Should the our laws not recognize that a demagogue, in third party guise, could throw an election, under present Constitutional rules, into the House of Representatives and thus make a mockery of the ballots cast that November?

But while these arguments are powerful, they are not compelling. Let us examine begin the examination of why with two questions:

What do William J. Clinton (twice), John F. Kennedy, Harry S. Truman, Woodrow Wilson, Abraham Lincoln, Andrew Jackson and eight other American Presidents have in common?

The answer is that each received less than a majority of the votes cast in the election which elevated him into the White House?

What does every elected President, at least since 1824, have in common?

The answer is that none received a majority of the eligible adult population living at the time they were elected and most received less than two-fifths of that possible vote.

This nation and its political system has survived and one might say prospered despite the electoral college, despite several Presidents who did not get a majority of the votes cast, despite one (Rutherford B. Hayes) who was elected while receiving fewer votes than his opposition and despite the fact that no President, at least since 1824, has received a mandate of a majority of his fellow eligible citizens.

It is not at all clear that the Republic would survive as well in a system of direct elections.

The case for keeping the indirect approach to electing Presidents represented by the electoral college is not nearly so simple and clear as the case for direct elections, but it is, I believe, more persuasive and compelling.

It rests on five concepts: manipulation, grassroots engagement, pluralism, federalism and participation. A few words about each:

1. Manipulation: The central question in the creation of any system of election is its incentive structure—what activities it encourages and what it does not. Arguably the worst thing that has happened in the modern era to the conduct of American politics is the coaxial cable and the free rein it has given political consultants to pollute our airwaves with attack ads every biennium—driving up the cost of campaigns, driving voters both from the polls and increasingly from respect either of political leadership or the political process as a whole.

While even with the electoral college, increasingly the bulk of campaign resources are poured into televised political advertising, direct elections would insure that all monetary resources would be poured into such advertising. There would be virtually no incentive to try to mobilize constituencies, organize specific interests or devote any resources to such things as voter registration and education. The result of direct elections is that campaigns would be run on the basis of polling the gross number of likely voters across America and targeting television messages to their interests and views. Our election would, in essence, not be a contest between two putative Presidents, but rather between two would-be king-makers—Squiers vs. Sipple— in a race to the bottom to see who can do the better job of turning off the other's potential voters.

What we would have is a political system that combines the worst of network television with the worst of the modern campaign. Network television, as one may note, devotes three hours every evening to pursuing precisely the same audience with precisely the same unedifying fare of sit-coms, shoot-em-ups and disaster series aimed, so they believe, at capturing the biggest share of the widest possible audience. Which may, in turn, explain the decline in civic literacy and, more recently, in the age of cable and satellite, the decline in network viewership. Couple that with the unrelentingly demagogic negative tone of the political ad campaign and we have a recipe for not, in my friend Newt Minow's words, an intellectual "wasteland," but a political wasteland of citizens permanently tuned out to politics.

2. Grassroots engagement: The same incentives that would, under a direct election system, propel all campaign resources into television advertising would virtually eliminate any resources devoted to grassroots and citizen involvement. Under the electoral college, there is a strong incentive—at least in some states—for campaigns, interests and others to organize groups on the grassroots level because some of those groups may be determinative in winning state electoral votes. It is no secret that advocacy and organization among the elderly produced a Clinton electoral victory in Florida. It is in the Republican Party's interest to organize Christian conservatives in the south to offset the Democratic Party's advantage among African-Americans in the region.

But it is unlikely that were the nation the only base of votes that any campaign would find it cost-effective to devote any resources to organization and involvement and that, in turn, would undermine the already declining base of political participation and American pluralism.

3. Pluralism: The success of American democracy has rested, in part, on achieving a balance between the will and desires of the majority of Americans and recognizing the rights and needs of various minorities. The electoral college serves to protect the latter in national politics.

To take the most obvious example, the number of farmers in the United States has dwindled so precipitously that nationally they are no longer a serious numerical factor in electoral outcomes—despite the fact that most of the food we have on our tables is due to their individual and collective effort. In a system of direct elections, their concerns could easily be ignored. But because their votes are critical to winning electoral votes in several mid-western and western states, their needs must be addressed, their views must be solicited, their allegiances must be competed for.

The needs and aspirations of America's African-American population could easily be ignored in a direct election. They comprise perhaps 12 percent of the eligible electorate. But in several Southern states, they account for nearly a majority of eligible citizens and they comprise a significant and, perhaps on occasions, pivotal minorities in several northern states. The electoral college insures, in national elections, that their views must be taken into account.

Union members, Christian fundamentalists, Latinos, rural denizens are but a few of the significant minorities whose views and needs might be ignored if campaigns were totally nationalized.

American governance—and the durability of its laws —derives its strength, not from the one-time expression of a national will, but from the coalescence of disparate interests into consensus. Direct election promotes a national will. The electoral college is one of the instruments for forging coalition and consensus.

1. Participation: The undermining of both grassroots activity and pluralism— mobilization and sub-party level engagement cannot but have a negative effect on participation. So too will the aggregation of votes solely on a national level.

In most analyses of this period when over the last 36 years we have had a nearly 25 percent decline in voting nationally and nearly 30 percent outside the south—the longest and largest sustained slide in the nation's history—one of the reasons has been the growing disbelief of citizens in the efficacy of their vote—whether that votes will make any difference, both in election outcome and policy result.

In this age of intense polling, where the movement of national numbers in the Presidential horse-race is tracked more intensively and surely more publicly than the heartbeat and blood pressure of a patient in intensive care, it will become increasingly difficult for the citizen to see how his vote will make much difference in a national electorate in which the margins of victory are usually in the millions of votes. It is much more likely that a citizen will see, in most jurisdictions (the District of Columbia excepted), that the citizen might see his or her vote making a difference in the hundreds or thousands which determine the allocation of electoral votes in individual states. In a sense the existence of an electoral college enhances both the perception and reality of electoral competition, where direct elections acts in precisely the opposite direction.

5. Federalism: There were times, particularly in the 1960's, when those who supported segregation of the races tended to use the cover of state's rights to mask their desire to keep African-Americans in their place, when the structure of American federalism—the diffusion of power between the national government and the states and localities—was called into question.

More recently, however, there is a bi- or multi-partisan consensus that perhaps the idea of states and localities might be a good one—that the administration of many programs is better handled at levels closer to the citizenry, that the states do serve as innovators and laboratories for useful, productive and, particularly in the cases of welfare reform and crime control, better public policy solutions than the national government can formulate.

In national politics, the instrumentality which forces consideration of federalism is the electoral college, mandating the gathering of votes by states, forcing the engagement of state leaders and party organizations and concern about state and local issues. We sacrifice that, I believe, to the detriment of the welfare of American democracy.

Supporters of direct elections usually cite polls to buttress their position—polls which show a majority of Americans support direct elections. But I would venture to say that none of those polls raise the consequences of direct elections in the questions that are asked. Were the public asked not only whether they desired direct elections but whether they desired direct elections even if it meant campaigns only run on television, erosion of grassroots activity and pluralism, declining voter participation and the erosion of federalism, the results might be very different.

Our founding fathers may not have had the best reasons for adopting an indirect system for the election of Presidents. They had too much fear of and too little faith in the demos. But that system, with its various modifications over the years, has served this nation well and should not be replaced.

The second question—could it be improved—deserves a qualified, "Yes," because while it could be improved, it should not be replaced and, if tampering, leads to the idea of replacement then it should not be done.

On the other hand, there are three ways in which it can be improved:

We can and should eliminate the human elector. We have had faithless electors in the past—people who were elected to cast their ballots in the electoral college on behalf of a Presidential candidate who cast their vote for someone else. These have been, over the years, protest votes which had no bearing on the outcome of the electoral college tally. But while it has never happened and may never happen, there remains the possibility of a close electoral college vote in which one or a few electors casting ballots against the wishes of the electorate can vitiate the popular result in a state and nationally and undermine public faith in American democracy. An Amendment which would eliminate the human elector in favor of the counting of state electoral votes would be desirable.

The staff of this committee raised, during preparation of this testimony, an interesting question—how does one deal with the succession question should someone be putatively elected in the November election but die before the electors cast their ballots? While this is, again, not a likely occurrence, it is something which should taken account of in law or in the amending process to the Constitution. The staff suggested that the risk of this occurrence might be mitigated by setting an earlier date certain for the electoral college votes to be counted. And while this might be helpful, we also face, in the present electoral context, some limitations to how far toward election day this vote can be held. We now have a situation in which 50 percent of the votes in certain western states are cast by absentee ballots and counted after the election. By my experience and accurate count of those ballots tends to take at least a week, and, should the tally be close in some of those states, the certification of the ballot count may take some considerable additional time.

Which is to suggest that while it might be desirable to address this statutorily, the safer method may be through amendment that establishes succession to the Vice-President-elect and down the line.

The final change can be accomplished statutorily and in the several states. It is not likely to happen soon because of its partisan implications and—in its sponsorship both in the 1960's by the late Sen. Karl Mundt and more recently by a number of Democrats—the partisan motivations of some of its sponsors. But the present method of choosing electors could be improved if every state adopted what Maine and Nebraska already have in place—a system in which the selection of electors of every state would be divided. The present electoral college allocates electors to each state on the basis of their apportioned Congressional representation. Each state has two electors for the two Senators each has and additional electors for the number of Representatives each has.

What Maine and Nebraska do is elect the two electors (or choose the electoral vote) representing the two Senators by statewide vote and elect their remaining electors by Congressional district.

This plan has several virtues:

1. It would likely, although not certainly, produce an electoral tally closer to the popular vote than the current statewide system.

2. It would certainly make the individual's vote seem more instrumental in electing the one elector which represents his or her Congressional district.

3. It would placed an additional incentive towards grassroots activity and organizational engagement in garnering the electoral vote retail—by district—rather than wholesale by state.

4. It would end the tendency of parties and campaigns to abandon states and regions when a candidacy is seen as hopelessly behind in the state or region because there would be small amounts of electoral votes to be won.

5. It would further reduce the tendency to rely solely on televised advertising as the means to communicate, mobilize and demobilize voters, because as the competitive playing field becomes smaller, the benefits of television are reduced.

6. It would have the effect of strengthening the parties, by allowing some candidates to run with (rather than against) their party's position on issues in states where those positions might be anathema on a state-wide basis.

7. It would enhance American pluralism by making the votes of significant minorities more instrumental in the overall outcome.

8. And it would have the important, if minor, additional benefit of making it virtually impossible for the television networks to continue their practice of declaring election winners while people are still voting, thus ending the practice of turning away voters in the west and, perhaps, influencing electoral outcomes in races below the level of President.

This plan will not be adopted soon because of its partisan implications. When Sen. Mundt first proposed it, it was with the intent of breaking the virtual Democratic lock on Southern electoral votes. Some Democrats are proposing it for the same reason in light of the pro-Republican realignment of that region.

But these alignments, as the recent trend shows, are not necessarily permanent, and the larger question of how we perfect a system of elections which enhances our democracy in this age—by reducing the power of television, increasing the incentives to engagement and pluralism, promoting greater active citizen participation and strengthening our political parties— is something which should be addressed.

In some small, but not unimportant way, this particular revision of the electoral college system would do just that and I would urge its consideration in this Committee's recommendations, partisan concerns notwithstanding.

Thank you again for this opportunity.

Public Domain: accessed at http://judiciary.house.gov/legacy/222316.htm

House of Representatives Committee on the Judiciary Subcommittee on the Constitution

Subcommittee Hearing on "Proposals for Electoral College Reform: H.J. Res. 28 and H.J. Res. 43"

September 4, 1997
2237 Rayburn House Office Building
10:00 a.m.

Testimony of Judith A. Best
State University of New York at Cortland

Critics of the electoral vote system believe that the principle of democratic legitimacy is numbers alone, and therefore they think the system is indefensible on the contrary, the electoral vote system is a paradigm—the very model—of the American democracy, and thus is quite easy to defend. For all practical purposes it is a direct popular federal election. (The Electors are mere ciphers, and the office of elector, but not the electoral votes, can be abolished.) The critics' principle of democratic legitimacy is inadequate because it is apolitical and anti-federal. Logically it boils down to: the majority must win and the minority must lose no matter what they lose. It is a formula for majority tyranny. But majority rule is not the principle of our Constitution. Rather it is majority rule with minority consent. The critics, however, think that because the system does not follow an arithmetical model it may produce the "wrong" winner. In fact, I contend, because it is federal it produces the right winner.

The following passage from my recent book, The Choice of the People? Debating the Electoral College explains my point.

Politics and mathematics are two very different disciplines. Mathematics seeks accuracy, politics seeks harmony. in mathematics an incorrect count loses all value once it is shown to be wrong. In politics even though some people are out-voted they still have value and must be respected in defeat. Efforts must be made to be considerate and even generous to those who lost the vote, to make then feel they are part of the community, for if they feel alienated they nay riot in the streets. Further, mathematical questions, like those in all the sciences, deal with truth and falsehood. But politics is an art, not a science. Political questions do not deal primarily with truth and falsehood, but with good and bad. We do not ask whether a political decision on war or taxation or welfare or agricultural subsidies is true. We ask, is the policy good f or the country? And, will it actually achieve its purpose?

Those who confuse politics and mathematics, the head counters, operate on an unstated assumption that the will of the people is out there like some unsurveyed land, and all we need do is send out the surveyors with accurately calibrated instruments to record what is there . They also assume that our democratic republic is a ship without a specific destination. Whatever most of the people want, most of the people must get, and the minority be damned. Mathematical accuracy being their sole criterion f or legitimacy, they make a great fuss about politically imposed devices, intermediary institutions like the electoral vote system with its federal principle and its winner-take-all rule. From their perspective, such majority building and structuring devices complicate their self-assigned task, distort the accuracy of their count and possibly produce the "wrong" result.

If their assumptions were correct they would have a point. But their assumptions are false. Ours is a ship of state bound for a port called Liberty. on such a ship majority rule doesn't suffice without the consent of the minority. Their assumption about the will of the people is particularly false in this vast and varied country, in a continental republic populated by a-people who do not share a common religion, race, or ethnic heritage, in a commercial republic populated by people with diverse and competing economic interests. In such a country the will of the people and the will of the majority can be two very different things. Therefore, the will of the people —that one thing which all can share, which is the goal of liberty for all—must be constructed and periodically reconstructed. This requires a political, not a mathematical process.

In this country, it requires a federal political process. The federal principle is one of the two fundamental structural principles of our Constitution (the other being the separation of powers). The proposals to abolish the electoral college are proposals to abolish the federal principle in presidential elections. All of our national elective offices are based on the federal principle—they are state based elections f or we are a nation of states. Thus our national motto: E Pluribus Unum.

The federal principle in presidential elections forces presidential candidates to build broad cross-national political coalitions. Thereby it produces presidents who can govern because of their broad cross-national support. In politics as well as in physics there is such a thing as a critical mass. In presidential elections numbers of votes are necessary but not sufficient. To create the critical mass necessary for a president to govern, his votes must be properly distributed. This means he must win states and win states in more than one region of the country.

Under the federal presidential election system, a successful candidate can't simply promise everything to one section of the country and neglect the others. Analogy: Why are professional football teams required to win games in order to get into the playoffs and win the Super Bowl? Why not simply select the teams that scored the most points during the regular season? Any football fan can tell you why. Such a process wouldn't produce the right winner. Teams would run up the score against their weakest opponents, and the best teams in the most competitive divisions would have the least chance to get into the playoffs. Such a system isn't the proper test of the team talent and ability. A nonfederal election is not a proper test of support for the president.

It we abandon the federal principle in presidential elections we will be abandoning a national consensus building device by allowing candidates to promise everything to the populous Eastern megalopolis, or to promise everything to white Christians, or to suburbanites who are now half of all the voters. These are formulas for inability to govern or even civil war. And a system, like direct popular election, based on raw unstructured numbers alone rather than on the structuring federal principle, would effectively reduce the influence of minorities who often are the swing votes in closely divided states—groups like farmers who are only 2 percent of national population or blacks who are only 12 percent.

We need to remember that when we change the rules, we change the game and the game strategy and the skills needed to win. Under the federal principle successful candidates must have consensus building skills. The goal of politics in this country is harmony-majority rule with minority consent. But when and why would a minority consent to majority rule? The answer is only if the minority can see that on some occasions and on some vital issues it can be part of the majority. It is irrational to consent to a game in which you can never win anything at all. To gain minority consent the Framers created many devices to allow minorities to be part of the majority, devices that give minorities more influence than their raw numbers would warrant including the state equality principle for representation in the Senate and the state distracting principle for the House of Representatives. (The majority party in the House is often "over-represented" if our - measure is raw numbers of votes nationally aggregated.) Then, of course,, there is the state equality principle in voting on constitutional amendments. And there is the three-fourths requirement for passage of amendments. Such devices are designed to give minorities an influential voice in defining the national interest. The president is a major player in defining the national interest, and therefore it is necessary that the presidency be subjected to the moderating influence of a federal election system.

An equally important outcome of a state based election system is that it serves to balance local and national interests- It is not just racial, religious, ethnic or occupational minorities that must be protected, there are local minorities whose consent must be sought; The people in small states must be protected against misuse of the phrase "the national interest" My favorite example is the problem of nuclear waste which none of us want in our backyards-not in my state. The rest of us can outvote Utah—so let's turn Utah into our national nuclear waste dump. This is majority tyranny in action. Nuclear waste is a national problem and the burden of solving it should not be placed on the people of one state without their consent. Since the president is a major player in making national policy, it is just as important that he be sensitive to balancing national and local interests, and the federal election system is designed to make it so. The right winner is a presidential candidate who recognizes the necessity and often the justice in balancing national and local interests. As Jefferson said, "the will of the majority to be rightful must be reasonable." The federal principle even and especially in presidential elections is a device for building reasonable majorities.

The opponents of the electoral vote system are head counters who confuse an election with a census. In a census our goal is mere accuracy. We want to know how many people are married or divorced, or have incomes over or under $20,000, or are Catholic or Protestant etc. In short, we want to break down the population into its multiple individual parts. In an election, especially a presidential election, we want to bring the people together. We want to build consensus, to build the support necessary and sufficient for our president to govern.

The proponents of direct national election think their system solves problems, but in fact it creates problems that are addressed or avoided by the federal election system. Presidential elections have multiple goals. Obviously we want to fill the office with someone who can govern, but we also want a swift, sure decision, and we want to reduce the premium on fraud, and most of us want to support the two party system—a major source of national stability and a consensus, coalition building system.

From this perspective, the current system has been very successful. Since 1836 with the almost universal adoption of the state unit rule, awarding all of a state's electoral votes to the winner of the popular plurality, we have had never had a contingency election. That's a proven record of 160 years. And we know the reason why: the magnifier effect of the state unit rule, a.k.a. the winner-take-all system. The victor in the popular vote contest for president will have a higher percentage of -the elect-oral vote. The Magnifier effect does not exaggerate the mandate—popular vote percentages are widely reported, not electoral vote percentages. The magnifier effect is not like a fisherman's story in which the size of the fish grows with the telling. Rather it is like the strong fishing line that serves to bring the fish, whatever its size, safely to shore. It supports the moderate two-party system, and balances national and state interests. And it makes the general election the only election.

Of course, there would be no magnifier effect under direct non-federal election, and the result is that contingency elections would become the rule. Under one proposal there would be a national run off if no candidate received 50 percent of the popular vote. This provision would turn the general election into a national primary, proliferate candidacies and weaken or destroy the two- party system. It would also increase the potential for fraud and result in contested general elections with every ballot box in the United States having to be reopened and recounted under court supervision. Even the Left-handed Vegetarians Party could bring a court challenge because 1 percent or less of the popular vote could trigger a runoff election. And there would be a reason to challenge. In a runoff election even candidates who are not in the contest can win something by making a deal with one of the remaining two in return for support in the runoff. Not only would this mean an extended period of uncertainty about who the president will be—a temptation to foreign enemies, but also little time for the orderly transfer of power.

Most proponents of direct election, recognizing that to require a majority of the popular votes would produce these problems, suggest a 40 percent instead of a 50 percent runoff rule. The fact that most supporters of direct election are willing to make this concession indicates the seriousness of the problems attending contingency elections. This is a compromise of their principle—the arithmetical majority principle. Logically, on their principle, whenever no one polls 50 percent plus one vote there should be a runoff election.

And 40 percent is not a magical figure. It could be 42 or 44% with similar result—frequent runoffs. It is true that only one president, Lincoln, (who was not on the ballot in 10 states) failed to reach-the 40 percent plurality figure. However, history under the current system cannot be used to support the 40 percent figure because when you change the rules you change the game. Under the current rules we have had 17 minority presidential terms-presidents who came to the office with less than 50 percent of the popular vote. The last two are Clinton's terms. The list includes some of our best presidents, not only Lincoln, but also Wilson (twice), Polk and Truman. Seventeen minority presidential terms out of 42 presidents! The unit rule magnified their popular pluralities into electoral vote majorities because they won states.

But under direct nonfederal election there would be no magnifier effect. Potential candidates would recognize that multiple entries would be likely to trigger a runoff wherein one losing candidate could win a veto promise, another a Supreme Court nomination and a third a special interest subsidy in return for an endorsement in the runoff. And there is no reason to believe all such deals would be struck in the open. There would be no incentive for coalition building prior to the general election. The two major national parties would lose all control over the presidential nomination process—their life blood. Factional candidates, single issue candidates, extremist candidates would serve as spoilers. As one commentator noted, on the day prior to the election, the *New York Times* would have to publish a twenty page supplement simply to identify all the candidates.

Add to this the second chance psychology that would infect voters, and you have the formula for a national ordeal. Second chance psychology arises from the recognition that a popular vote runoff is a real possibility. Many a voter, thinking he will have another chance to vote in a runoff, will use his general election vote to protest something or other—to send a message.

Recounts would be demanded not only to determine who won, but also whether any candidate actually polled the 40% minimum, and if not which two candidates would be in the runoff - Under the unit rule magnifier effect which discourages multiple candidacies, we have already had five elections in which the popular vote margin was less than one percent. In the 1880 election the margin was one tenth of one percent. If such could happen under the current system where it is unlikely to trigger a runoff, it surely will happen under a 40 percent rule with a hair trigger runoff system. Weeks or months could pass with the outcome in doubt. One candidate could claim victory and start naming his cabinet only to be told some weeks later that he would have to participate in a runoff.

Further, the electorate wearies of prolonged elections. Even in the sports world players as well as tans reach a point where they want an end to it, and so accept sudden death rules. It is so important to fill the office on a timely basis that we have even had one president, Gerald Ford, who was not confirmed by a national election. Ford succeeded to the office on the resignation of his predecessor, Richard Nixon, but unlike vice presidents who had succeeded before him, he had been nominated by Nixon and confirmed by congressional vote under the provisions for filling vice presidential vacancies in the Twenty-fifth Amendment.

No election system is perfect, but the current system has borne the test of time- It has never rejected the winner of a popular vote majority. In every case but one it gave the victory to the winner of the popular plurality. And that one case proves the rule. Cleveland, who lost in the electoral vote, won the popular vote while running a sectional campaign. He did not seek to broaden his support; he focused his message on one section of the country. Unintentionally, he thereby sent a message about the current system to all future presidential candidates: Remember 1888! Don't run a sectional campaign! Further, he won the popular vote by only eight tenths of one percent! This was an election that verged on a tie. Since a timely decision is so important, a reasonable tie breaker is the win states federal principle.

The proposed amendments would deform not reform the Constitution. it is not just the presidency that is at risk here if the federal principle is illegitimate in presidential elections, why isn't it illegitimate for Senate and House elections? Why should a state with half a million people have the same representation in the Senate as a state with twenty million people? Why should every state have at least one representative in the House? Why shouldn't states with very small populations have to share a representative with folks in another state? And why should each state regardless of its population size have an equal vote on constitutional amendments? The Framers knew the answer to these questions—the federal principle. It is true that the electoral vote system did not work out in precisely the fashion that the Framers anticipated, but it did evolve in conformity to the federal principle and the separation of powers- I have no doubt that they would recognize this if they were here today. It evolved in conformity with the federal spirit of the constitution, the "great discovery," the Framers themselves made.

For this, let us turn to Alexis de Tocqueville, who commenting on the federal principle in the Constitution, called it "a wholly novel theory, which may be considered as a great discovery in modern political science." He goes on to explain that combines the best of both worlds. He says that its advantage is to unite the benefits and avoid the weaknesses of small and large societies. He learned this not only from observation, but also from reading James Madison in Federalist 39, who said that our form of government "is, in strictness, neither a national nor a federal Constitution, but a combination of both."

Madison's word "combination" is the key. The federal principle is a "great discovery", because it is a combination like an alloy—my term not his. We create alloys because we want to combine the advantages and avoid the weakness of two different things. We fuse copper and zinc to create brass because brass is harder, more malleable and more ductile than copper. We create steel alloys for the same reason. The federal system is an alloy. It not only makes us strong as a nation, it also allows us to be diverse and flexible, to experiment. It thereby increases our freedom without destroying, our national unity. Tocqueville was right; it was a "great discovery" of modern political science. Let us preserve it.

Public Domain: accessed at http://judiciary.house.gov/legacy/222314.htm

House of Representatives Committee on the Judiciary Subcommittee on the Constitution

Subcommittee Hearing on "Proposals for Electoral College Reform: H.J. Res. 28 and H.J. Res. 43"

September 4, 1997
2237 Rayburn House Office Building
10:00 a.m.

Testimony of Representative Ray LaHood
18th District, Illinois

Thank you, Mr. Chairman, for agreeing to hold these hearings. I very much appreciate your willingness to have this forum for a discussion and a dialogue on a topic that is of profound importance to the American people and to American democratic ideals: whether there is a continued need for the Electoral College.

My answer to this question is simple: I do not believe we need the Electoral College.

I believe the Electoral College is merely a relic of times past, running counter to the democratic process.

Currently, the only offices not elected by popular vote are the President and Vice-President.

The continuance of the Electoral College tradition simply makes no sense given the fact that all other elected officials (from U.S. Senator down to those holding local offices) are elected directly by the people.

I wonder how many voting citizens really realize that a vote for the President isn't really a vote for him or her at all. In fact, when a voter steps into a polling booth during a Presidential election, they are not actually electing the President, but rather a slate of electors whose job it is to actually elect the President and Vice-President.

In an effort to correct the counter-democratic problems posed by the existence of the Electoral College, I, along with Congressman Wise, introduced H.J. Res. 28 on January 9, 1997. This resolution calls for an amendment to the Constitution of the United States to abolish the Electoral College.

The House of Representatives overwhelmingly passed legislation in 1969 that would have abolished the Electoral College, but the same legislation failed to pass in the Senate.

H.J. Res. 28 is an effort to renew this cause and return the voting power to the voters, thereby ending the Electoral College filter that has been used since the beginning of our Constitution.

Specifically, our bill proposes a direct method of electing the President and Vice President. This means that the people would directly vote for the President and Vice President, and the winner of the election would be that person who receives the most number of votes, provided they received at least 40 percent of the vote.

If no candidate receives 40 percent or more of the popular vote, then a runoff election would be held between the two candidates who received the highest number of votes.

This approach would hopefully rectify a potentially huge, looming political crisis: an election that results in a President being elected without winning the popular vote.

This situation has occurred three times in our history, resulting in the election of John Quincy Adams in 1824, Rutherford B. Hayes in 1876, and Benjamin Harrison in 1888.

I believe that it is important to act now, before this situation occurs for a fourth time. All too often, Congress is perceived as reactionary and not pro-active. Going forward with legislation aimed at dismantling the Electoral College system would help shed this perception, and help avert a potentially huge political dilemma.

While I know I am not the first Member of Congress to introduce a bill calling for the dissolution of the Electoral College, I hope, that I can be the last.

Mr. Chairman and distinguished colleagues, I hope that we can act responsibly and pro-actively by working together to end the Electoral College.

Voters deserve to know that their vote counts, not the vote of some Elector they don't even know.

Thank you, Mr. Chairman.

Public Domain: accessed at http://judiciary.house.gov/legacy/222312.htm

Chapter 3
Questions

1. In the 2000 presidential election, Democratic candidate Albert Gore won about a half million more popular votes than George W. Bush, but lost the election because Bush won a slight majority of electoral votes. What do you think—should the president be chosen directly by popular vote or indirectly by the Electoral College? Why?

2. How is the Electoral College related to federalism? How could the federal geography of the electoral vote system be adjusted to reflect popular votes more closely?

CHAPTER 4
CIVIL LIBERTIES

The readings for this chapter revolve around the topic of obscenity and free speech. The first selection presents a statement by congressman Christopher Cox, a Republican representing Orange County, California, who chairs the House Policy Committee and the Homeland Security Committee, announcing new, much higher penalties for broadcasts using words perceived as being obscene. Cox's statement is accompanied by the formal promulgation by the Federal Communications Commission of the new rules limiting freedom of expression. Following these national legislative and executive perspectives on regulating speech is a March 2004 letter sent to the House of Representatives by the American Civil Liberties Union, as an example of direct lobbying to oppose the stricter broadcast decency rules and arguing for free speech.

Obscenity Issues
SEAS Consulting, © 2004

Editors Note:

The year 2004 was one of the most intensive periods of concern about obscenity in recent memory. Singer Bono of U2 violated broadcast indecency laws when he used the "f-word" during the televised Golden Globe Awards in January 2003. Janet Jackson's "Wardrobe malfunction" that exposed her breast during a Super Bowl halftime show brought fines. The Federal Communications Commission (FCC) voted unanimously to fine each of the 20 CBS-owned television stations with the maximum indecency penalty of $27,500. The total penalty of $550,000 was the largest fine ever imposed against a television broadcaster. Most of the FCC's large fines have been against radio stations. "Shock jock" Howard Stern's antics brought fines which caused him to quit commercial radio and sign a contract with subscriber-only satellite radio, and in January of 2004 the Federal Communications Commission proposed a $755,000 fine against Clear Channel Communications for a sexually explicit radio show "Bubba the Love Sponge." On March 18, 2004 commentator Sandra Loh was fired from National Public Radio station KCRW-FM in Santa Monica, California for inadvertently allowing the "F" word to be broadcast. A technician failed to bleep an intentional use of the "F" word during a Feb. 29 radio commentary on knitting! In November 2004 many television stations refused to broadcast the award winning movie "Saving Private Ryan" because of the obscene language used by soldiers in the film and, therefore, the risk of being fined by the FCC. Many veterans were outraged at the self-censorship

Robert Peters, president of Morality in Media and a critic of the television industry, has said the FCC needs to punish networks who are guilty of "the expanding stream of gutter language and sex talk and action that pollutes network TV programming."

We thought it would be interesting for you to read Congressman Christopher Cox's statement on obscenity. After that we are reproducing the FCC statement on obscenity.

For a list of the FCC's recent enforcement actions in this area you can go to their Enforcement Bureau Web site at:
http://www.fcc.gov/eb/broadcast/opi.html

For Immediate Release
Thursday, March 11, 2004
Contact: Bailey Wood
202-225-5611

Broadcasters Face Heavy Fines For Obscenity After Bill Passes House

Cox Provision to subject networks and affiliates to same penalties

WASHINGTON (Thursday, March 11, 2004) — Rep. Christopher Cox (R-CA), Chairman of the House Policy Committee and Chairman of the Homeland Security Committee, announced today that legislation to increase penalties for television and radio broadcasters who transmit obscene, indecent, and profane language passed the House of Representatives by a vote of 391-22. Included in the legislation was a provision by Chairman Cox to subject television networks to the same penalties that local affiliates face for broadcasting indecent or obscene material. The Cox legislation was added to H.R. 3717 following a hearing before the House Energy and Commerce Committee at which Viacom Chairman Mel Karmazin, whose company owns the CBS broadcast network, told Rep. Cox that networks should be subject to penalties for supplying indecent or obscene programming. The bill increases existing penalties almost 20-fold, and adds the television networks to the list of those liable. The FCC is charged with imposing the fines against television and radio networks and/or stations that broadcast indecent, obscene, or profane material. Rep. Cox spoke today on the House floor during the debate on the broadcast indecency bill. His statement follows:

Statement of Rep. Chris Cox
Floor of the House of Representatives
March 11, 2004

Thank you, Mr. Chairman for your leadership on this issue and for crafting the bill which underscores the principle that those who have been given multi-billion-dollar assets in the form of public airwaves for free, courtesy of the taxpayers, owe in return at least some consideration of the taxpaying audience and the public interest they purport to serve.

I like free enterprise and the opportunity for every business to turn a profit. I support unlimited artistic creativity. None of these provides a reason for multi-billion-dollar spectrum subsidies for profit-making entertainment, particularly when it is indecent, obscene, and profane.

While others in telecommunications pay for their slices of the airwaves, the broadcasting industry has been given multi-billion-dollar slices of the public airwaves for free. In the 1990s, every other industry that uses the airwaves, such as wireless phone companies, paid for their pieces of the airwaves through public auctions that generated billions in revenue for taxpayers. The broadcasting industry has paid nothing to the taxpayers for their continued free use of this valuable public asset. On top of that, every TV station owner was recently given more free bandwidth to convert to digital TV, and that additional loaned spectrum has an estimated value of perhaps $100 billion. That's a payment from every man, woman, and child in America of $350. As we complete action on this bill, our attention turns naturally to the underlying question of whether taxpayers should continue the multi-billion-dollar subsidies of this obviously for-profit industry.

It's my hunch that if we were to auction the broadcast spectrum without the free ride that such programming now gets, the market and consumers would not demand 184 channels of Howard Stern. Making for-profit TV pay for its spectrum and compete with other high-tech demands for spectrum would be a far better way of dealing with the problem of indecent programming than government regulation of speech. I think this bill is welcome news. Thank you, Mr. Chairman.

Obscene, Profane & Indecent Broadcasts
FCC
Consumer Facts
http://www.fcc.gov/eb/l

It's Against the Law

It is a violation of federal law to broadcast **obscene** programming at any time. It is also a violation of federal law to broadcast **indecent** or **profane** programming during certain hours. Congress has given the Federal Communications Commission (FCC) the responsibility for administratively enforcing the law that governs these types of broadcasts. The Commission may revoke a station license, impose a monetary forfeiture, or issue a warning, for the broadcast of obscene or indecent material.

Obscene Broadcasts Are Prohibited at All Times

Obscene speech is not protected by the First Amendment and cannot be broadcast at any time. To be obscene, material must meet a three-prong test:
- An average person, applying contemporary community standards, must find that the material, as a whole, appeals to the prurient interest;
- The material must depict or describe, in a patently offensive way, sexual conduct specifically defined by applicable law; and
- The material, taken as a whole, must lack serious literary, artistic, political, or scientific value.

Indecent Broadcast Restrictions

The FCC has defined broadcast indecency as "language or material that, in context, depicts or describes, in terms patently offensive as measured by contemporary community broadcast standards for the broadcast medium, sexual or excretory organs or activities." Indecent programming contains patently offensive sexual or excretory references that do not rise to the level of obscenity. As such, the courts have held that indecent material is protected by the First Amendment and cannot be banned entirely.

It may, however, be restricted in order to avoid broadcast during times of the day when there a reasonable risk that children may be in the audience.

Consistent with a federal statute and federal court decisions interpreting the indecency statute, the Commission adopted a rule pursuant to which broadcasts — both on television and radio — that fit within the indecency definition and that are aired between 6:00 a.m. and 10:00 p.m. are subject to indecency enforcement action.

Profane Broadcast Restrictions

The FCC has defined profanity as including language that "denote[s] certain of those personally reviling epithets naturally tending to provoke violent resentment or denoting language so grossly offensive to members of the public who actually hear it as to amount to a nuisance."

Like indecency, profane speech is prohibited on broadcast radio and television between the hours of 6 a.m. to 10 p.m.

Enforcement Procedures and Filing Complaints

Enforcement actions in this area are based on documented complaints received from the public about indecent, profane, or obscene broadcasting. The FCC's staff reviews each complaint to determine whether it has sufficient information to suggest that there has been a violation of the obscenity, profanity, or indecency laws. If it appears that a violation may have occurred, the staff will start an investigation by sending a letter of inquiry to the broadcast station. Otherwise, the complaint will be dismissed or denied.

Context

In making indecency and profanity determinations, context is key! The FCC staff must analyze what was actually said during the broadcast, the meaning of what was said, and the context in which it was stated. Accordingly, the FCC asks complainants to provide the following information:

- Information regarding the details of what was actually said (or depicted) during the allegedly indecent, profane or obscene broadcast. There is flexibility on how a complainant may provide this information. The complainant may submit a significant excerpt of the program describing what was actually said (or depicted) or a full or partial recording (e.g., tape) or transcript of the material.

In whatever form the complainant decides to provide the information, it must be sufficiently detailed so the FCC can determine the words and language actually used during the broadcast and the context of those words or language. Subject matter alone is not a determining factor of whether material is obscene, profane, or indecent. For example, stating only that the broadcast station "discussed sex" or had a "disgusting discussion of sex" during a program is not sufficient. Moreover, the FCC must know the context when analyzing whether specific, isolated words are indecent or profane. The FCC does not require complainants to provide recordings or transcripts in support of their complaints. Consequently, failure to provide a recording or transcript of a broadcast, in and of itself, will not lead to automatic dismissal or denial of a complaint.

- The date and time of the broadcast. Under federal law, if the FCC assesses a monetary forfeiture against a broadcast station for violation of a rule, it must specify the date the violation occurred. Accordingly, it is important that complainants provide the date the material in question was broadcast. A broadcaster's right to air indecent or profane speech is protected between the hours of 10 p.m. and 6 a.m. Consequently, the FCC must know the time of day that the material was broadcast.

The call sign of the station involved.

Of necessity, any documentation you provide the FCC about your complaint becomes part of the FCC's records and may not be returned.

Complaints containing this information should directed to:

Federal Communications Commission
Enforcement Bureau
Investigations and Hearings Division
445 12th St., SW, Room 3-B443
Washington, DC 20554

You may also file a complaint electronically using the FCC Form 475 (complaint form) at http://www.fcc.gov/cgb/complaints.html or by e-mail at fccinfo@fcc.gov.

Reprinted with permission from © SEAS Consulting, 2004.

March 2, 2004

The Honorable Joe L. Barton
Chairman, House Energy & Commerce Committee

The Honorable John D. Dingell
Ranking Member, House Energy & Commerce Committee

Re: H.R. 3717, the Broadcast Decency Enforcement Act of 2004

Dear Chairman Barton and Ranking Member Dingell:

We are writing to express our concern about H.R. 3717, the Broadcast Decency Enforcement Act of 2004. The bill would dramatically increase fines for obscene, indecent, or profane broadcasts, sending a widening chill into the atmosphere of free expression protected by the First Amendment.

The heart of our objection to the bill is that it relies upon the FCC's definition of "indecency" which is already vague.[1] Because of the vagueness, speakers must engage in speech at their peril, guessing what the FCC will determine to be prohibited. Increasing fines merely exacerbates the problem, particularly for small broadcasters. Rather than face a potentially ruinous fine, smaller broadcasters are more likely to remain silent.

Under H.R. 3717, guessing incorrectly can have important ramifications for a broadcaster, including huge fines and possibly loss of its broadcasting license. Vague laws and interpretations create traps for broadcasters because they are unsure what conduct or speech will constitute indecency. Rather than have broadcasters act at their peril, the law prefers reasonable notice of what conduct will give rise to legal consequences, so that the speaker may act accordingly. Vagueness results in chilling of communications that may well NOT be indecent or profane, simply because the cost to the broadcaster of being wrong is too great. Vagueness encourages silence instead of robust debate. "Uncertain meanings inevitably lead citizens to 'steer far wider of the unlawful zone' . . .than if the boundaries of the forbidden areas were clearly marked.'"[2] The bottom line is that broadcasters enjoy First Amendment protection. The uncertainty inherent in the definition (or lack thereof) of "indecency" will inevitably lead broadcasters to avoid certain speech because that speech may later be deemed indecent, and the broadcaster faces tremendous liability because of the increase in the fines provided for in H.R. 3717.

FCC v. Pacifica Foundation **does not provide unlimited authority to define and punish broadcast indecency. Furthermore, subsequent developments make it questionable whether** *Pacifica* **has any continued vitality.**

In *FCC v. Pacifica Foundation*, 438 U.S. 726 (1978), the Supreme Court allowed some limited regulation of an allegedly indecent broadcast (George Carlin's "Seven Dirty Words" Monologue). Great caution, however, should be exercised in attempting to rely upon this 25-year-old case as precedent for deciding what broadcasts are indecent or the ability to impose draconian penalties.

Initially, it is important to note that, unlike obscenity, indecent speech is protected under the First Amendment. *Id.,* at 746 ("Some uses of even the most offensive words are unquestionably protected. . . .Indeed, we may assume, *arguendo*, that this monologue would be protected in other contexts.") The ability to regulate indecency in the broadcasting medium is an exception rather than the general rule. In many other contexts, the Supreme Court has invalidated efforts to restrict indecency.[3] In *Pacifica*, the Court applied a slightly different standard for broadcasting, but that decision cannot be read too broadly.

First, the decision was a fragmented one (5-4) that did not approve a particular standard for indecency, or uphold a substantive penalty against the licensee.[4] Since *Pacifica*, the Court has acknowledged that the FCC's definition of indecency was not endorsed by a majority of the Justices, and has repeatedly described the decision as an "emphatically narrow holding."[5]

Second, the rationale for the *Pacifica* decision, that "the broadcast media have established a uniquely pervasive presence in the lives of all Americans,"[6] is highly questionable twenty-five years after the decision.[7] Today we have cable television, the Internet, and satellite television, all competing with broadcast networks. Yet, the government can only impose limited content controls on the broadcast media. Paradoxically, full First Amendment protection now depends, literally, upon whether you are watching a broadcast channel or a cable channel.

Third, although technology has radically changed in the intervening years since *Pacifica*, society has also changed drastically. Gone are the days when a husband and wife could not even be shown in the same bed. This change in society has led to differing audience expectations and have contributed to different broadcast standards and practices. Whether that is seen as "good" or "bad," it is a fact, and reflects changes in the contemporary community standards for the broadcast medium.

Last, and perhaps most importantly, the law itself has evolved since 1978. In *Pacifica*, three justices who joined the plurality opinion suggested "indecent" speech was subject to diminished scrutiny because it was "low value" speech.[8] Approximately twenty-two years later, the Supreme Court rejected that notion, holding that "indecent" speech is fully protected under the First Amendment, and not subject to diminished scrutiny as "low value" speech. The Court stressed that "[t]he history of the law of free expression is one of vindication in cases involving speech that many citizens find shabby, offensive, or even ugly," and that the government cannot assume that it has greater latitude to regulate because of its belief that "the speech is not very important."[9] Additionally, the Court since *Pacifica* has invalidated government-imposed indecency restrictions on cable television, despite its "pervasiveness." While *Pacifica* noted the pervasiveness of broadcast television as part of its rationale, the Court in striking such regulation in the cable television context found specifically that "[c]able television broadcasting, including access channel broadcasting, is as 'accessible to children' as over-the-air broadcasting, if not more so."[10] Thus, the rationale in *Pacifica* is undercut by the Court's later decision. And, finally, and most importantly, in *Reno v. ACLU*, the Court for the first time subjected the indecency definition (in the Internet context) to rigorous scrutiny, and found it to be seriously deficient.[11] All of these later decisions undercut *Pacifica's* rationale and raise serious questions about its vitality.

The Committee should not further compound the vagueness problem by attempting to regulate "violence."

We understand there may be an amendment proposed to allow the FCC to regulate "violence" or "gratuitous violence" in the media. We urge you to reject any such amendment, as any definition of violence will undoubtedly be too vague to provide any guidance to broadcasters.

Parents are justifiably concerned that their children learn their values. Parents are, of course, the ones most suitable to make the determination of what is and is not in their children's best interest. The government may assist parents and children in learning about various aspects of the media—for example, funding media literacy courses that teach parents and children how to evaluate and analyze what they see. When, however, the heavy hand of government steps in to "assist" those parents in regulating media violence, constitutional problems abound. Moral and esthetic judgments are "for the individual to make, not for the Government to decree, **even with the mandate or approval of a majority**."[12]

"Material limited to forms of violence is given the highest degree of First Amendment protection."[13] In *Winters v. New York*, 333 U.S. 507 (1948), the Supreme Court invalidated a law that prohibited the distribution to minors of any publication "principally made up of . . .accounts of criminal deeds, or pictures, or stories of deeds of bloodshed, lust or crime."[14] Even though the Court saw "nothing of any possible value to society in these magazines," the justices held that the material was "as much entitled to the protection of free speech as the best of literature."[15]

Shielding children from violence ignores reality and ill-prepares them for participation in a world that embraces violence: "Violence has always been and remains a central interest of humankind and a recurrent, even obsessive theme of culture both high and low. It engages the interest of children from an early age, as anyone familiar with the classic fairy tales collected by Grimm, Andersen, and Perrault is aware. To shield children right up to the age of 18 from exposure to violent descriptions and images would not only be quixotic, but deforming; it would leave them unequipped to cope with the world as we know it."[16]

If not all violence is bad, then any regulation must accomplish the gargantuan task of distinguishing between what is "good" violence from "bad" or "gratuitous" violence. The task is even more difficult, because, as the Federal Trade Commission noted in September, 2000, those who research the effects of media violence inconsistently define "violence."[17] If the researchers cannot concur on an objective definition, then how will any regulation provide truly objective definitions that please all parents?

It is simply impossible to constitutionally distinguish between "good violence" and "bad violence." As the Supreme Court has stated, "What is one man's amusement, teaches another's doctrine."[18] Americans do not want the government to serve as their "taste police."

Conclusion

The indecency standard already suffers from vagueness, making it difficult for broadcasters to know what will result in sanctions. That uncertainty is heightened when the FCC itself has difficulty applying the standard. H.R. 3717, far from avoiding constitutional inquiry, exacerbates an already serious problem. The effect of the bill is to turn down the thermostat in an already chilly atmosphere, deterring speech that is constitutionally protected.

Adding "violence" to the definition of indecency, or otherwise regulating violence, raises a host of constitutional problems as well.

While we do not endorse H.R. 3717, it is nonetheless is a better alternative than H.R. 3687. H.R. 3717 may make a bad situation worse, but it at least does not suffer from creating even more constitutional problems.

Sincerely,

Laura W. Murphy
Director

Marvin J. Johnson
Legislative Counsel

Cc: Members of the House Energy & Commerce Committee

[1] *Reno v. ACLU*, 521 U.S. 844 (1997) was the first Supreme Court case to undertake a rigorous examination of the definition of "indecency" in the Communications Decency Act. By a 9-0 decision, the Court invalidated that portion of the statute, finding the definition to be vague and overbroad. The Communications Decency Act definition was essentially the same as that used by the FCC.

[2] *Grayned v. City of Rockford*, 408 U.S. 104, 109 (1972).

[3] Print medium: *Butler v. Michigan*, 352 U.S. 380, 383 (1957); *See also Hamling v. United States*, 418 U.S. 87, 113-114 (1974) (statutory prohibition on "indecent" or "obscene" speech may be constitutionally enforced only against obscenity); Film: *United States v. 12 200-ft. Reels of Film,*, 413 U.S. 123, 130 n.7 (1973); In the mails: *Bolger v. Youngs Drug Products Corp.* 463 U.S. 60 (1983); In the public forum: *Erzoznik v. City of Jacksonville*, 422 U.S. 205 (1975); Cable Television: *United States v. Playboy Entertainment Group, Inc.*, 529 U.S. 803 (2000); the Internet: *Reno v. ACLU*, 521 U.S. 844 (1997).

[4] *See Pacifica,* 438 U.S. at 743 (plurality op.) and at 755-56 (Powell, J., concurring) ("[t]he Court today reviews only the Commission's holding that Carlin's monologue was indecent 'as broadcast' at two o'clock in the afternoon, and not the broad sweep of the Commission's opinion"). *See also Carlin Communications, Inc. v. FCC,* 837 F.2d 546, 559 (2d Cir. 1988) ("[t]he *Pacifica* Court declined to endorse the Commission definition of what was indecent"); *ACLU v. Reno,* No. Civ. A. 96-963, 1996 WL 65464 at *3 (E.D.Pa. Feb. 15, 1996) (Buckwalter, J.) ("it simply is not clear, contrary to what the government suggests, that the word 'indecent' has ever been defined by the Supreme Court").

[5] *Reno,* 521 U.S. at 866-867, 870; *Sable,* 492 U.S. at 127; *Bolger,* 463 U.S. at 74.

[6] *Paifica,* 438 U.S. at 748.

[7] Chairman Powell has criticized as a "willful denial of reality" the Commission's failure to reexamine the "demonstrably faulty premises for broadcast regulation," including the claim "that broadcasting is uniquely intrusive as a basis for restricting speech." Regarding this rationale for regulating the broadcasting medium, he has said "[t]he TV set attached to rabbit ears is no more an intruder into the home than cable, DBS, or newspapers for that matter. Most Americans are willing to bring TVs into their living rooms with no illusion as to what they will get when they turn them on." Remarks by Commissioner Michael K. Powell, *Willful Denial and First Amendment Jurisprudence,* Media Institute, (Washington, D.C., April 22, 1998). The Chairman has explained that "[t]echnology has evaporated any meaningful distinctions among distribution [media], making it unsustainable for the courts to segregate broadcasting from other [media] for First Amendment purposes. It is just fantastic to maintain that the First Amendment changes as you click through the channels on your television set." Remarks by Commissioner Michael K. Powell, *The Public Interest Standard: A New Regulator's Search for Enlightenment,* American Bar Association 17th Annual Legal Forum on Communications Law (Las Vegas, Nevada, April 5, 1998).

[8] Only Justices Stevens, Rehnquist, and Chief Justice Burger joined in that part of the opinion asserting that indecent speech lies "at the periphery of First Amendment concern." *Pacifica,* 438 U.S. at 743.

[9] *Playboy Entertainment Group,* 529 U.S. at 826.

[10] *Denver Area Educ. Telecomms. Consortium v. FCC,* 518 U.S. 717, 744 (1996).

[11] 521 U.S. at 871-881. In the context of obscenity which is not protected under the First Amendment, the work must be reviewed as a whole, the effect of the material is judged based on the average person, and material that has literary, artistic, political or scientific value cannot be restricted. None of these findings are required in determinations of indecency, although indecent speech is protected under the First Amendment. If the Supreme Court requires such findings before speech can be deemed obscene, it makes little sense to apply a lesser standard to speech that is, in fact, protected.

[12] United States v. Playboy Entertainment Group, Inc., 529 U.S. 803, 818 (2000)[Emphasis

added.]

[13] *Sovereign News Co. v. Falke*, 448 F. Supp.306, 394 (N.D. Ohio 1977), *remanded on other grounds*, 610 F.2d 428 (6th Cir. 1979), *cert. denied*, 447 U.S. 923 (1980).

[14] *Winters*, at 508.

[15] *Id.* at 510.

[16] American Amusement Machine Ass'n v. Kendrick, 244 F.3d 572, 578 (7th Cir. 2001).

[17] Federal Trade Commission, "Marketing Violent Entertainment to Children: A Review of Self-Regulation and Industry Practices in the Motion Picture, Music Recording & Electronic Game Industries," September, 2000, Appendix A

[18] *Winters*, 333 U.S. at 510.

Public Domain.

Chapter 4
Questions

1. During the 2004 Super Bowl halftime show, Janet Jackson suffered a case of "wardrobe failure," in which one of her breasts was revealed briefly. This caused a major furor and added to the push for more "moral" broadcasting. What is the relationship between the Super Bowl event and these readings on morality on broadcasting? How do you think episodes like Janet Jackson's wardrobe failure and those discussed in these readings should be addressed?

2. What do you believe makes something "obscene?" What role, if any, do you think national, state, or local government should play in regulating "obscenity?" Why?

CHAPTER 5
CIVIL RIGHTS: EQUAL PROTECTION

The readings for Chapter 5 deal with different interpretations of equality and equal opportunity. President George W. Bush's 2002 executive order establishing equal protection for faith-based organizations reflects his strong political support among the Religious Right and represents a major departure from past government efforts to maintain separation between church and state. Statements by Congressman Rubén Hinojosa and Ciro D. Rodriguez show how different the policy objectives of the Congressional Hispanic Caucus are from what they see as the agenda of the Bush administration and its supporters. The House of Representative speech by member Barbara Lee, a Texas Democrat, provides an African-American perspective on the importance of the 1954 *Brown v. Board of Education* Supreme Court decision desegregating the nation's public schools and discusses the meaning for today of the civil rights movement that led to and resulted from the *Brown* decision.

The Caucus Corner: Hispanic Heritage Month - A Proud History, A Bright Future
by 108th Congress Congressman Ciro D. Rodriguez, Chair, Congressional Hispanic Caucus, September 17, 2004

Over five hundred years ago Christopher Columbus, under the auspices of the Spanish crown, landed in the Americas triggering the beginning of Hispanic influence in the western hemisphere. Since then, Hispanics have had cultural, social, and familial ties with the people and nations of this continent.

There is no better testament to Hispanic influence than the story of Hispanics in the United States. St. Augustine, Florida is the oldest European city in the United States. Juan Menendez de Aviles established the settlement forty-two years before the English colony at Jamestown, Virginia, and fifty-five years before the Pilgrims landed on Plymouth Rock in Massachusetts.

And now, annually, we celebrate Hispanic Heritage Month from September 15th to October 15th to pay tribute to a people who have contributed to the development of the Americas.

Throughout our history and today, Hispanics have died bravely for our country, served with pride, and defended our great nation with valor. Almost 10,000 Mexican Americans served during the Civil War, some 200,000 Hispanics were mobilized for World War I, about 50,000 Hispanics served during World War II, 148,000 Hispanics served in the Korean War, 80,000 Hispanics served in Vietnam, and 20,000 Hispanics served in the first gulf war.

Currently, there are more than 100,000 Hispanics enlisted in active duty. More than 122 Hispanic solders have died in Iraq. The first casualty in Operation Iraqi Freedom was Lance Corporal Jose Gutierrez. He came to the United States at the age of fourteen from Guatemala in search of the American dream. At the age of eighteen, he decided that despite the fact that he was not a citizen, he would enlist in the military in order to serve his new home country.

Hispanic influence can also be seen all across the United States. From the old missions and churches in the Southwest to contemporary Mexican and Cuban restaurants nationwide. From Jennifer Lopez on the big screen to George Lopez on television. Prominent Hispanic government officials, doctors, lawyers and other professionals abound. We also have a proud workforce that farms our lands, tends to our hospitality needs and takes care of our children.

Today, at forty million, Hispanics are the largest and fastest growing minority community. The Census Bureau projects that Hispanics will constitute twenty four percent of the nation's total population in the year 2050. That translates to more than one hundred million Hispanics.

With this emergence comes the serious responsibility of our community to begin taking a more active role in our society. Now more than ever, it will fall upon us to lead this nation into a prosperous future and to address the needs of our community.

The Congressional Hispanic Caucus was established twenty-eight years ago as a congressional organization composed of members of Congress of Hispanic descent to fill this leadership role in Washington D.C. The Caucus is dedicated to voicing and advancing, through the legislative process, issues affecting Hispanic Americans in the United States and the insular areas.

In the area of health, the Caucus has worked on eliminating health disparities, covering the uninsured, increasing Hispanics in health professions and strengthening Medicare and Medicaid. On the education front, the CHC has fought to preserve our nation's Head Start system. We have expressed our deep concern over funding the "No Child Left Behind" initiative. These issues, as well as many others, have been at the forefront of the CHC and our community's agenda.

For over half a millennium, we have contributed to every facet of our nation's society. We are a vibrant and exciting community and we are up to the challenges that await us. As we celebrate Hispanic Heritage Month and with an eye towards our nation's future, we begin yet again on another journey full of hope.

Public Domain.

Commemorating 50th Anniversary of *Brown v. Board of Education*
Speech of Hon. Barbara Lee of California in the House of Representatives,
May 18, 2004

Mr. Speaker, this is an enormously important day in the lives of African Americans and in the history of this country.

Brown vs. Board of Education, almost without question, is the most important Supreme Court case of the twentieth century. With Brown, the Court threw out decades of doctrine and centuries of racist practice in this country in their conclusion that "Separate educational facilities are inherently unequal." By making this just assertion, they forced this nation to begin to live up to its own promises and its own ideals. In the words of Dr. Martin Luther King, Jr., Brown represented a "joyous daybreak to end the long night of enforced segregation."

Brown was a transforming moment in the life of this country. Sadly, it was not immediately transformative, nor is the metamorphosis complete, even today. It took years—even decades in many cities and states—for the mandate of the Court to be carried out. In many places, it was met with fervent political opposition and violent resistance.

In Virginia, for instance, the Governor closed the public school system rather than allow it to be integrated. And in 1957, National Guard troops had to be sent in to guard school children in Little Rock, Arkansas when they tried to begin their studies at Central High School.

In the years after Brown, many, heroic people risked and sometimes lost their lives in the fight to desegregate schools, universities, stores and lunch counters, the workplace. And they risked their well-being in the fight to ensure that they enjoyed that fundamental American right of being able to vote.

But in the end, the forces of racism did not prevail because of the Thurgood Marshalls of the world, the Medger Evers, the Rosa Parks, the Fannie Lou Hamers, the Martin Luther King Jrs, and the Malcolm X's. They ensured that this nation would live up to its own promises, the guarantees that were laid out in Brown.

The Civil Rights Act of 1964, for instance, came about because brave men and women demanded it through bus boycotts and sit-ins and marches on Washington and a thousand other battles.

The Voting Rights Act of 1965 came about because people like Fannie Lou Hamer dared to fight to register to vote, dared to form the Mississippi Freedom Democratic Party, dared to take on the Democratic Party and the establishment, and dared to win.

The Civil Rights Act of 1968, which established the principles of fair access to housing, came about because African Americans demanded the full rights of citizenship and because they knew that housing is a human right. Unfortunately, there are some people in Washington today who still need to recognize that fact.

Thanks to their efforts, Brown became the reality of the nation, not just the law of the land.

Today, on this 50th anniversary, Brown is still the law of the land, but it is no longer a national reality. Legal walls of segregation have been replaced in many areas by de facto separation by neighborhood and community. Our schools are becoming less integrated by the year, and in too many cases, integration has vanished entirely from some schools.

Across the country, efforts have been made—some of which have been successful, unfortunately—to undo the affirmative action programs, whose goal has been to create the fully diverse and integrated justice that the Supreme Court envisioned.

In my home state of California, an African American, Ward Connerly, led the Proposition 209 initiative in 1996, which eliminated affirmative action programs for women and people of color run by state or local governments in the areas of public employment, contracting, and education.

As chair of the California Black Legislature at the time, I fought against it, as did many, many Californians of all races.

In what was a giant setback for Brown and racial equality, Proposition 209 passed, and in one fell swoop, it wiped out a very significant program that was intended to level an extremely uneven playing field. The results have been devastating. African American and Latino enrollments at far too many of our state's universities are in serious decline.

As a recent story in the San Francisco Chronicle indicated, African American admissions at UC–Berkeley, which is in my district, are down 29 percent this year. In this year's freshman class, fewer than two and a half percent of the students accepted were African American. Two and a half percent. And compounding this serious injustice, Governor Schwarzenegger is cutting the budget for the outreach efforts of our universities.

These numbers are an embarrassment. They are an embarrassment for our students, ourselves, and for the promise of Brown. These shameful statistics have profound economic, political, and cultural meaning.

Do these bleak numbers that I have cited mean that Brown v Board of Education failed? No, but it means that our revolution is not over yet. It means that our revolution is still incomplete.

On this 50th anniversary of this enormous Supreme Court victory, we must rededicate ourselves to carry out that opinion whose words rang out clear as a bell when Earl Warren, the former California governor and Oakland resident, read them, ''Separate educational facilities are inherently unequal.''

We can not—we will not—let the victories that were won so hard 50 years ago by Thurgood Marshall, Linda Brown, and so many others be reversed.

Tonight we celebrate that moment, and we rededicate ourselves to ensuring that justice thrives in this country.

Public Domain.

Chapter 5
Questions

1. Of the views presented in these readings, which seem closest to your own? Why?

2. If you had to devise a structure for government that would provide the greatest equality for everyone, what would that government look like? How similar or different from today's national government in the U.S. do you think this would be?

CHAPTER 6
CIVIL RIGHTS: BEYOND EQUAL PROTECTION

Extending the concept of equality into new areas takes many different routes. "Don't laugh at me" programs discussed in the excerpts from the April 2003 congressional colloquy reproduced here are part of the national effort against bullying in schools. Whether those who are convicted of having committed capital offenses when they were children should be executed is another issue involved in extending equality, discussed here in congressional remarks by Wisconsin Democratic Senator Russ Feingold.

Recognizing the Achievements of Operation Respect, the "Don't Laugh at Me" Programs, and Peter Yarrow, House of Representatives, April 29, 2003

Mr. PORTER. Madam Speaker, I move to suspend the rules and agree to the resolution (H. Res. 161) recognizing the achievements of Operation Respect, the "Don't Laugh At Me" programs, and Peter Yarrow, as amended.

The Clerk read as follows:

H. RES. 161

Whereas Operation Respect is a nonprofit organization engaged in a national effort to transform participating schools, after-school programs, and children's summer camps into more compassionate and respectful environments through its "Don't Laugh At Me" program materials that address the issues of emotional and physical violence among children;

Whereas Operation Respect has conducted 230 workshops, reaching over 18,000 educators in 27 States and distributing 50,000 copies of its professionally developed curriculum;

Whereas representatives of this organization have appeared before over 240 educational organizations in 36 States on behalf of Operation Respect, as well as before the Republican conference and Democratic caucus of the United States House of Representatives;

Whereas the "Don't Laugh At Me" program increases mutual respect and fellowship among hundreds of thousands of elementary school children, creating an environment for students that improves focus on academic achievement and encourages an atmosphere of respect and responsibility;

Whereas the "Don't Laugh At Me" camp programs have made the environment at summer camps safer and more secure for children by creating a greater sense of responsibility, justice and fairness;

Whereas the "Don't Laugh At Me" programs have made a significant impact on schools and camps through a curriculum of character education and social and emotional learning;

Whereas the overwhelming majority of students participating in a recent survey concluded that the "Don't Laugh At Me" program was a valuable and beneficial experience and resulted in a diminution of negative behaviors such as bullying, and increased openness and trust;

Whereas counselors and campers alike who participated in the "Don't Laugh At Me" programs agreed that the programs were effective, enjoyable, and positively influenced the academic and character education of the children;

Whereas the success of Operation Respect and the "Don't Laugh At Me" programs has been recognized by the National Conference of State Legislatures and various educational associations, including the National Association of Elementary School Principals, the National Association of Secondary School Principals, the American Association of School Administrators, the Council of Great City Colleges of Education, the National Education Association, the Council of Great City Schools, the American School Counselors Association, the National School Boards Association, the National Middle School Association, and the American Federation of Teachers; and

Whereas the National Conference of State Legislatures passed a resolution on August 12, 2001, encouraging funding and other support from States for professional development of educators in this arena and recognizing the contributions of Operation Respect in advancing State legislative initiatives to expand social and emotional learning and character education programs: Now, therefore, be it

Resolved, That Operation Respect and the "Don't Laugh At Me" program are commended for their major contributions to the sound academic focus, character development, and improved physical safety of children throughout the United States.

The SPEAKER pro tempore. Pursuant to the rule, the gentleman from Nevada (Mr. PORTER) and the gentleman from California (Mr. GEORGE MILLER) each will control 20 minutes.

The Chair recognizes the gentleman from Nevada (Mr. PORTER).

GENERAL LEAVE

Mr. PORTER. Madam Speaker, I ask unanimous consent that all Members may have 5 legislative days within which to revise and extend their remarks on H. Res. 161.

The SPEAKER pro tempore. Is there objection to the request of the gentleman from Nevada?

There was no objection.

Mr. PORTER. Madam Speaker, I yield myself such time as I may consume.

I rise today in support of H. Res. 161, which commends Operation Respect, the ''Don't Laugh At Me'' programs' efforts to provide character education.

I would like to take this opportunity to commend the gentleman from California (Mr. GEORGE MILLER) and the gentleman from California (Mr. CUNNINGHAM) for their efforts to draw attention to the importance of character education programs in our schools.

In 2001, Congress recognized the importance of character education programs like Operation Respect when we passed the No Child Left Behind Act. This landmark legislation contains the partnerships in character education program that provide grants for character education programs that emphasize academic achievement and focuses on elements such as citizenship, respect, responsibility, and trustworthiness.

As some may know, Operation Respect is a nonprofit organization that assists schools, after-school programs, and summer camps in their efforts to create safe and respectful environments for students and teachers. Specifically, Operation Respect utilizes music and video, along with a conflict-resolution curriculum, to help address the problems of bullying and teasing among elementary and middle school youth.

Operation Respect also recognizes the importance of professional development by offering workshops designed to provide educators with the tools that they need to effectively implement character education programs. In fact, over 18,000 teachers have participated in 230 ''Don't Laugh At Me'' workshops in 27 States throughout the United States.

I would also like to commend Operation Respect for their efforts to leverage the private sector support for their programs. Through the cooperative efforts of community-based organizations, schools, and the private sector, students are better able to understand the importance of acting responsibly and treating one another with respect.

Again, I am pleased to recognize the achievements of Operation Respect and the ''Don't Laugh At Me'' programs, and I urge that Members support this resolution.

Madam Speaker, I reserve the balance of my time.

Mr. GEORGE MILLER of California. Madam Speaker, I yield myself such time as I may consume.

Madam Speaker, I am very pleased that the House of Representatives today is considering my resolution to honor the outstanding program that is working with school districts, camps, teachers, and students across America to promote the healthy social and emotional development of children.

I want to thank the gentleman from California (Mr. CUNNINGHAM) for his cosponsorship of this legislation and for his own strong support of Operation Respect. The gentleman from California (Mr. CUNNINGHAM) was responsible for arranging for Peter Yarrow to visit the Republican Conference last year to talk about this program and to sing some of the songs, an achievement that deserves recognition in the House as well.

I also want to thank my cosponsors for their support of this resolution, particularly the gentleman from Wisconsin (Mr. OBEY), who is a strong supporter of character education programs in the Labor-HHS appropriations bill in recent years.

Lastly, I thank the gentleman from Ohio (Mr. BOEHNER) and his staff for their assistance in having this resolution placed before the House expeditiously.

Most of us here are familiar with the ''Don't Laugh At Me'' program. Last year, its founder and tireless advocate, Peter Yarrow of the legendary trio Peter, Paul and Mary, spoke to both the Republican Conference and the Democratic Caucus about the necessity for, and the success of, this program. Many of us have seen him as he has appeared before dozens of school boards, teacher organizations, parents groups throughout this Nation promoting sound emotional development and tolerance among our children.

We are all painfully aware of the images, language and experiences of children that assault their self-esteem, their attitudes toward others and their sense of compassion and tolerance. From bullying in the schoolyards to the lyrics of many popular songs, to the violence in film and news broadcasts, young children in our society, and adults too, are assaulted by messages and images of intolerance, brutality, victimization, and bias. Any reasonable person must be concerned about the impact of those values on these young children, now and throughout their lives. And we were concerned that they be taught alternative values that help us build closer personal relationships and stronger communities.

These concerns have great immediacy. Just last week, there was yet another example of terrible school violence. A study of school violence in California recently concluded that ''alienated and disaffected young people are escaping the attention of families, friends and teachers until they explode.'' Meanwhile, programs like boot camps, may enjoy public approval but consume huge amounts of money and do not have a record of success.

Fortunately, there are efforts and institutions that are effectively promoting positive values and respect, tolerance and understanding and compassion. Our churches and synagogues play that role. Programs like Head Start and after-school programs and sports and cultural experiences heavily influence children as well. The character education programs that this Congress has been funding in recent years have similarly made great contributions.

One of the innovations enjoying great popularity and success and which we honor today by the passage of this resolution is Operation Respect. Through the diligent efforts of Peter

Yarrow and many educators, psychologists and advocates that work with him, Operation Respect has conducted over 230 workshops throughout the Nation reaching over 18,000 educators in 27 States. Tens of thousands of copies of its professionally developed curriculum have been distributed to teachers in after-school programs and camp operators and others who are similarly committed to making a difference in the lives of these children. Teachers love this program and have given it their strong endorsement. And today we should add the United States House of Representatives to that list saluting this great effort on behalf of America's children and America's best values.

As H. Res. 161 states, the "Don't Laugh At Me" program "increases mutual respect and fellowship among hundreds of thousands of elementary school children, creating an environment for students that improves focus on their schoolwork and encourages social and emotional growth." Evaluations of the program have found overwhelming support for its message among teachers, parents and students alike, as well as increased tolerance and a reduction in such negative behaviors such as bullying.

Among professional educators and others, Operation Respect has enjoyed similar popularity. Operation Respect and the "Don't Laugh At Me" program has been recognized by the National Conference of State Legislatures, the National Association of Elementary School Principals, the National Association of Secondary School Principals, the American Association of School Administrators, the Council of Great City Colleges and Education, the National Education Association, the Council of Great City Schools, the American School Counselors Association, the National School Boards Association, the National Middle School Association, and the American Federation of Teachers.

Teachers love this program; here's a representative comments from a teacher in southwestern Virginia:

Over the years I have used many approaches and programs, all of which have good points. "Don't Laugh At Me" encompasses all those strong points into one easy to use program. I've seen a difference in my class even though we have only used it for a few months. One of the biggest benefits is the dialog that comes from using the program. The kids love the CD and found the video to be very powerful. Now that I have had a chance to use "Don't Laugh At Me" and see its benefits, I will be doing a presentation to our staff about it. I guess I sound like a commercial, but I honestly loves this program!

Today, we should add the United States House of Representatives to that list saluting this great effort on behalf of America's children and America's best values.

Lastly, I would like to note that Steve Seskin, the composer of the song "Don't Laugh At Me," which has inspired Mr. Yarrow's efforts, is a resident of my congressional district. Mr. Seskin is a very highly respected composer and recording artist as well in the folk and country venues; and in this case his music has helped to inspire a movement that is having dramatic and beneficial effects on millions of young Americans. And I appreciate the support of all Members of this House on the resolution.

I appreciate the support of all Members for this Resolution today.

Madam Speaker, I reserve the balance of my time.

Mr. PORTER. Madam Speaker, I yield 5 minutes to the gentleman from California (Mr. CUNNINGHAM), a prior member of our committee.

Mr. CUNNINGHAM. Madam Speaker, the gentleman from California (Mr. GEORGE MILLER) and I quite often get in a rhubarb right here on the House floor on issues. This is one we agree on. And I am a hawk. I am a conservative. Well, maybe not a hawk, maybe a well-armed dove; but I was asked to go to an event and hear a man speak. And I said, Who is speaking? And they said, Peter Yarrow. And I said, Who is Peter Yarrow? And they said, You know, Peter, Paul and Mary. And I said, I am not going to go listen to that anti-war, left-wing guy. And I went. And I want to tell Members something. Coming from a conservative and a hawk, he is one of the nicest guys I have ever met in my life.

His heart is true. His politics are terrible. I would say extremely wrong. And I disagree with my colleague on tax rates, as well as with Peter Yarrow. But I want to say this: Peter Yarrow is doing this not for money but for the profound belief that there is a better way to reach out to children.

Maybe music does bring people together because I have another ''left wing'' friend in Steven Stills, as a matter of fact, I think he was one of the heads of the DNC and yet we are still good friends. Aviation brought us together and music brought us together as well.

Madam Speaker, I want to read something. This is the song ''Don't Laugh at Me,'' and I would like every single Member, and Madam Speaker, you too, to listen to this.

''I'm a little boy with glasses, the one they call a geek.'' Remember that in school? I do. ''A little girl who never smiles cuz I got braces on my teeth and I know how it feels to cry myself to sleep. I am that kid on every playground, who's always chosen last.'' That was me. ''A single teenage mother trying to overcome her past. You don't have to be my friend if it's too much to ask. Don't laugh at me, don't call me names, don't get your pleasure from my pain. In God's eyes, we're all the same. Some day we'll all have perfect wings. Don't laugh at me.

''I'm a cripple on a corner, you pass me on the street. I wouldn't be out here begging if I had enough to eat. And don't think I don't notice that our eyes never meet. I lost my wife and little boy when someone crossed that yellow line. The day we laid 'em in the ground was the day I lost my mind.''

And the song goes on and on, Madam Speaker. Peter Yarrow's idea is that maybe in Columbine, where one of the worst things we did was we took the young men that knew about the young man that went in and killed a bunch of students was arrested, and they drove him out further, but Peter Yarrow's idea is that we are all the same yet we are all different.

I look at Gary Condit on this House floor. Many of us tried to befriend Gary Condit. Think about how he must have felt. I think we need to think about those kinds of things as individuals when we see people that are outside. In our major military institutions, the Naval Academy, the Air Force Academy, we will find each year that someone takes a dive off the top of a building. They have found that in most cases the individual has isolated themselves away from the rest of his group.

Maybe in Columbine, instead of the young men that had been ostracized from their group, maybe if they had been brought back into the group, the suicides and things like Columbine maybe would not have happened.

Madam Speaker, this is endorsed by every major school institution we take a look at. When I went through POW training in Eglin Air Force Base, one of the things they showed us was that if someone was going over to the other side, the enemy side, instead of chastising that person, you reach out to bring them in, to bring them into your group, to make them feel whole. That is what this program does.

I want to thank my friend, the gentleman from California (Mr. GEORGE MILLER), and my Republican colleague for supporting this, as well as the gentleman from Wisconsin (Mr. OBEY), who is a good friend who knows Peter Yarrow very well, and I ask my colleagues, Madam Speaker, to support this.

This is about a program that I believe in and that is going to help not only children, but adults all over the United States.

Mr. GEORGE MILLER of California. Madam Speaker, I yield myself such time as I may consume to thank the gentleman for his remarks. The fact that he and I are working together on this, when we disagree on so many other issues, is in the spirit of this program. And as our great former Speaker, Tip O'Neill, used to say, you have to be able to disagree around here and not be disagreeable. I am working on that talent, but I have not achieved it yet. But this is in that spirit.

Madam Speaker, I yield such time as he may consume to the gentleman from Texas (Mr. FROST).

(Mr. FROST asked and was given permission to revise and extend his remarks.)

Mr. FROST. Madam Speaker, I thank the gentleman for yielding me this time, and I am here today to express my support for House Resolution 161 honoring Peter Yarrow's Operation Respect and ''Don't Laugh at Me'' programs. These important programs are designed to promote compassion and tolerance among children in after-school programs and summer camps.

I first met Peter Yarrow some years ago and became better acquainted with him when I served as co-chair of the Bipartisan Task Force on Youth Violence. And during the last Congress, when I was Chair of the Democratic Caucus, I arranged for Peter to appear before our caucus and make a presentation about his program, and it was an extraordinary presentation.

One of the things our task force heard from youth violence experts was the extremely harmful effect of bullying and ridiculing among young people. The goals of these important programs are aimed at making sure the tragedies of Columbine never occur again. They seek to build an environment of respect so that our children will grow to be kind to others and foster positive social relationships throughout their lives.

Several years ago, I witnessed firsthand the positive impact this program can have. Peter Yarrow held a concert as a part of the ''Don't Laugh at Me'' summer program, a program that served more than 2 million campers that summer. As part of the event, children came up on the stage to call for greater compassion and respect and to declare their commitment to ending bullying and ridiculing. It was a powerful display, and I am so glad this resolution is on the floor today.

I commend the ''Don't Laugh at Me'' and Operation Respect programs. They are truly unique, and they make a difference by encouraging greater tolerance among classmates while making the classroom environment more conducive to learning and improving academic performance. That is why I urge my colleagues to vote in favor of this resolution.

Let us honor a truly great program and the men and women who work so hard to make a positive impact on our children's lives.

Mr. GEORGE MILLER of California. Madam Speaker, I yield such time as she may consume to the gentlewoman from Illinois (Ms. SCHAKOWSKY).

Ms. SCHAKOWSKY. Madam Speaker, I thank both the gentleman from Nevada and my colleague from California for offering this resolution in support of Operation Respect and the ''Don't Laugh at Me'' program. I feel so privileged to have not only heard the presentation, the incredible voice, and the power of Peter Yarrow, as the gentleman from California (Mr. CUNNINGHAM) said, part of Peter, Paul and Mary group, sing this, but the way that it resonates in one's heart when you hear it, and I am sure in the minds of school children who welcome the words of tolerance and respect that are in this song written by Steve Seskin.

The program is to create the sound emotional development, the personal growth, the physical safety of our children, to promote antibullying and compassion and tolerance among children. The gentleman from California (Mr. CUNNINGHAM) began to read some of the lyrics that are in this song, and we can just picture that wonderful voice of Peter Yarrow, so let me once again add a few more words in this song.

''Don't laugh at me, don't call me names, don't get your pleasure from my pain. In God's eyes we're all the same. Some day we'll all have perfect wings. Don't laugh at me. I'm fat, I'm thin, I'm short, I'm tall, I'm deaf, I'm blind. Hey aren't we all. Don't laugh at me. Don't call me names. Don't get your pleasure from my pain. In God's eyes we're all the same. Some day we'll all have perfect wings. Don't laugh at me.''

In 2002, Operation Respect began shifting its strategy from making presentations to a lot of these educational organizations to fostering systemic and sustainable implementation of its own programs as well as long-term comprehensive character education and social and emotional learning by opening State affiliates around the country. Now there are affiliates in California, Colorado, Connecticut, Georgia, Illinois, where I am from, and Ohio.

In Illinois, it is headed up by this wonderful woman, Flora LeZar, who was Executive Director of Operation Respect. She is helping, and I am working with them, to set up this program in Illinois identifying supporters in and around Chicago. And we are now in discussions with Columbia College's Office of Community Arts Partnerships, as well as an Evanston-based, that is my hometown, arts and education foundation, the Shanti Foundation, to partner in the implementation of ''Don't Laugh at Me'' in several Chicago public schools.

I am looking forward to one of the schools in my district, an elementary school called Boone School, we are hoping that that school will have the benefit of the don't laugh at me program.

Finally, let me just say this. Our world today is so marked by mistrust, where there is so much intolerance around the globe and here at home as well; a failure to really understand each other's cultures. In a country like the United States of America, which is so wonderful because of its diversity, because we have so many people and children with different values that come to our public schools, that is our strength. But we need to help develop an appreciation of that in our children. It prepares them to be adults and leaders in a world that embraces diversity, that understands the differences among people and then can work to bring us all together for a world of peace and harmony.

So this is more than just a little program or one song, this is a philosophy of education and really a philosophy about the way that all of us should live our lives. So I congratulate Peter Yarrow and Operation Respect and the ''Don't Laugh at Me'' program. I am just happy to be able to support this resolution and to be part of advancing this effort.

Mr. GEORGE MILLER of California. Madam Speaker, I yield myself such time as I may consume to thank the gentlewoman for her remarks, and to thank again the gentleman from Ohio (Mr. BOEHNER) for his help in getting this legislation to the floor; to the gentleman from California (Mr. CUNNINGHAM) for his cosponsorship and his support for this program; to our speakers this afternoon in support of this resolution; and the gentleman from Nevada for taking time out to bring this to the floor this afternoon under suspensions.

Finally, I want to thank my very long-time dear friend, Peter Yarrow, for all the time and the effort that he has taken on behalf of the children of this Nation to promote their healthy development and their emotional stability. He has reached out to so many people across this country and made them aware of this effort, of this need on behalf of our children. It is a wonderful gift that he has given to the children of this Nation, to the educators of this Nation, to caregivers in all different settings for our children, and I just really want to thank him for that effort. I am honored to sponsor this legislation, and I want to thank the House for giving us time to bring it to their attention and I ask my colleagues to support it.

Madam Speaker, I yield back the balance of my time.

Mr. PORTER. Madam Speaker, I have no further requests for time, and I yield back the balance of my time.

The SPEAKER pro tempore (Mrs. BIGGERT). The question is on the motion offered by the gentleman from Nevada (Mr. PORTER) that the House suspend the rules and agree to the resolution, House Resolution 161, as amended.

The question was taken; and (two-thirds having voted in favor thereof) the rules were suspended and the resolution, as amended, was agreed to.

The title of the resolution was amended so as to read: ''Resolution recognizing the achievements of Operation Respect and the 'Don't Laugh At Me' programs.''.

A motion to reconsider was laid on the table.

Public Domain.

The Supreme Court's Review of the Execution of Child Offenders, Senate, March 2, 2004

Mr. FEINGOLD. Mr. President I want to speak today on the Supreme Court's recent decision to review whether the execution of child offenders—those under 18 at the time the crime was committed—is constitutional. The Court will soon hear the case of Christopher Simmons, a Missouri man who was sentenced to die for a crime he committed at the age of 17. The case is called Roper v. Simmons.

In the past few years, our Nation has taken important strides toward fairness and justice in the administration of the death penalty. In 2000, former Illinois Gov. George Ryan took the courageous step of halting executions in his State pending a top-to-bottom study of the use of capital punishment in Illinois. Following an exhaustive review of his State's system, Gov. Ryan commuted the death sentences of all death row inmates in Illinois in December 2002. Former Maryland Gov. Parris Glendening suspended executions in his State in the face of glaring racial and geographic disparities in the Maryland death penalty system. Current Maryland Gov. Robert Ehrlich has since lifted the State's moratorium, but an execution has not taken place in Maryland since 1998.

A number of State legislatures have inched closer and closer to abolishing the death penalty or instituting moratoria in their jurisdictions. And in 2002, in a significant turning point for our Nation, the Supreme Court ruled unconstitutional the execution of the mentally retarded.

That decision, in the case of Atkins v. Virginia, confirmed that our Nation's standards of decency concerning the ultimate punishment are indeed evolving and maturing.

While these events are steps toward fairness and indications of progress, they also serve as reminders that our system is seriously flawed. The statistics and stories of innocent people wrongly convicted are shocking. In the modern death penalty era, 113 individuals in 25 different States have been exonerated after being convicted and put on death row. The most recent exoneration occurred just last week in a case from North Carolina. This should be disturbing to all Americans who believe in the founding principles of our Nation, liberty and justice for all.

As Supreme Court Justice John Paul Stevens wrote in a 2002 dissent, after the Court refused to consider another case involving child offenders, the practice of executing child offenders is "inconsistent with evolving standards of decency in a civilized society." In my view, Justice Stevens is right. Executions of child offenders have occurred in only eight countries since 1990: China, the Democratic Republic of the Congo, Iran, Nigeria, Pakistan, Saudia Arabia, Yemen, and the United States of America. Most of these countries, however, have since banned executions of child offenders, leaving the United States as the only country that acknowledges its use of capital punishment for child offenders.

According to Amnesty International, there have been 34 executions of child offenders since 1990—19 of them in the United States. And there are currently America who are scheduled to be executed this year. In fact, incredibly, Texas has scheduled the execution of four child offenders between March and June of this year, despite the Supreme Court's announcement that it will consider the constitutionality of such executions in the Simmons case this term. Currently, 38 States authorize the use of the death penalty. Nineteen of those States have decided that they will only execute defendants who were 18 or older at the time of the crime. But 5 States use 17 as the minimum age, and the other 16 States permit the execution of defendants who were as young as 16 when they committed the crime.

The State Department has said: "Because the promotion of human rights is an important national interest, the United States seeks to hold governments accountable to their obligations under universal human rights norms and international human rights instruments." But we can only call ourselves protectors of human rights if we practice what we preach. Here at home, we continue to apply capital punishment to those who were convicted of crimes committed before legally becoming adults. Spreading decency and humanity must begin here at home. As long as America executes child offenders, our reputation as a shining example of respect for human rights is tarnished.

At the beginning of the 108th Congress, I introduced the National Death Penalty Moratorium Act, which would suspend Federal executions while we conduct a thorough study of the administration of the Federal death penalty at the State and Federal levels. My bill would specifically require a commission to review all aspects of the system, including the practice of sentencing child offenders to death. I urge my colleagues to cosponsor and support the National Death Penalty Moratorium Act, and I look forward to the Supreme Court's review of this important issue. I am hopeful that the Court will build upon the progress it made two years ago when it ended the execution of the mentally retarded. Banning the execution of child offenders is the right thing to do. Congress should act if the Court doesn't.

Chapter 6
Questions

1. How should the system of government and politics in the United States adapt to new demands for equality? Should some demands be ignored? Why, or why not?

2. Would limits on bullying do much to improve the education system, or to produce better citizens? Why, or why not? Base your conclusion on the issues raised in these readings.

The role of public opinion in the 2004 U.S. elections is the subject of these essays. Ilya Somin's "Political Ignorance" argues that the continued ignorance about politics by most American voters and their lack of interest in many political matters make it difficult to achieve democratic government. The article on the University of Iowa's Electronic Market shows one way to make highly accurate forecasts of election outcomes using a political equivalent of the stock market in which students invest real money by trading "shares in political candidates or parties.

Political Ignorance
by Ilya Somin

Although the 2004 election was unusually close and hard-fought, the majority of Americans remained ignorant about many of the issues at stake. This reflects a lack of interest in politics that may be, in many cases, entirely rational. But at a time of war and economic uncertainty, it seriously impairs democratic self-government.

How could citizens assess the Bush Administration's handling of the War on Terror if they are unaware of many of its most important antiterrorism policies? How could they vote to protect their economic interests if they are largely ignorant about relevant policies in that field?

The answer, in both cases, is that they often can't. But the solution to the problem of political ignorance in America does not depend primarily on the willingness of average people to take a crash course in civics. Instead, it partly depends on reducing the scope and complexity of the federal government so that voters can more easily understand what is going on.

The severity of voter ignorance is well-documented. Polls show that 70 percent of American adults, for instance, don't know Congress recently passed a prescription drug benefit for seniors, even though the new law—projected to cost some $500 billion over the next 10 years—is probably the most significant domestic legislation passed during the Bush administration.

More than 60 percent do not know that President Bush's term has seen a massive 25 percent rise in domestic spending that has led to a major increase in the national debt. And despite extensive media attention focused on employment numbers, almost two-thirds of the public don't know that there has been a net increase in jobs this year.

Public knowledge of the war on terrorism is not much better. 58 percent admit they have heard little or nothing about the USA Patriot Act and 52 percent of Americans admit they do not know enough about the highly publicized report of the 9/11 Commission to have an opinion about it. Since research shows that many people are reluctant to admit ignorance on surveys, the true proportion of citizens with little or no knowledge of the Patriot Act and the 9/11 Commission report is likely to be even greater than the poll numbers suggest.

However sad those results may be, they are not surprising. Decades of research show that most citizens know very little about politics and public policy. Even more alarming is that most citizens lack basic background knowledge about political leaders, parties and the structure of government.

For example, about 85 percent of Americans don't know the name of their congressman, and most do not know which branches or levels of government are responsible for which issues. Most do not understand the basic differences between liberalism and conservatism. Immediately after the 2002 congressional elections, only 32 percent knew that Republicans had controlled the U.S. House of Representatives prior to the balloting.

Voters do not have to be policy wonks to make an informed decision. Sometimes they can get by through the use of what scholars call "information shortcuts," relying on small bits of telling information as a substitute for deeper knowledge of issues. For example, even if a voter knows nothing about Candidate X as an individual, a lot of useful information about X's stances can be derived simply from knowing what party he belongs to.

But the lack of basic knowledge is difficult to overcome through shortcuts. Knowing that a candidate is a Democrat is only useful information to a voter if he or she has some idea of what positions the Democrats stand for, how they differ from the Republicans and how those positions and differences are likely to have an impact on issues.

It is tempting to conclude that voters must be lazy or stupid. But even a smart and hardworking person can rationally decide not to pay much attention to political information. No matter how well-informed a citizen is, one vote has only a tiny chance of affecting the outcome of an election; about one chance in 100 million in the case of a presidential race. As a result, even a citizen who cares greatly about the outcome of elections has almost no incentive to acquire sufficient knowledge to make an informed choice. Becoming a more informed voter is, in most situations, simply irrational. Unfortunately, the rational decisions of individuals create a dysfunctional collective outcome in which the majority of the electorate is dangerously ill-informed.

People who can influence politics in ways beyond casting a vote and those who simply find politics interesting might learn about it for perfectly rational reasons. Certainly, political professionals such as lobbyists and interest group leaders have strong incentives to become informed. But few of us are influential activists, or otherwise have political clout that goes beyond the power of the vote. And most Americans find politics far less interesting than other forms of entertainment. Polls show that many more people know the names of the judges on "The People's Court" than those on the Supreme Court. Indeed, the rise of modern high-tech entertainment may have reduced interest in politics by presenting us with a wide range of appealing alternative interests. The average person apparently prefers watching reality TV or a football game to following politics closely.

If political ignorance is rational, of course, there are limits to our ability to reduce it by reforming the education system or by improving media coverage of politics. Studies show that knowledge levels have remained roughly constant for over 50 years, despite massive increases in education levels and greatly increased availability of information. With the rise of the Internet and 24-hour news channels, political knowledge is readily available to those willing to take the time and effort to find it. The problem is not that the truth isn't out there, but that most don't bother to seek it.

Even if the majority of voters were willing to pay more attention to politics than they do, that still might not be enough to cope with the complexities of modern government. The federal government alone spends over 20 percent of our national gross domestic product and adopts thousands of regulations that touch on almost every aspect of our lives. Even attentive voters are unlikely to be aware of more than a small fraction of this activity.

Thus, many important aspects of government power are likely to escape public scrutiny, and thereby also escape public accountability and democratic control. To take just one of many examples, every year the federal government spends tens of billions of dollars on counterproductive subsidies to industrial and agricultural interests that economists across the political spectrum condemn. Yet such porkbarrel spending persists because most voters are largely unaware of its existence, while the small, well-organized interest groups that benefit are not only aware, but prepared to punish politicians who refuse to satisfy their desires.

If government had fewer functions, it might be easier for voters to keep track of them, and thereby combat interest group machinations. It would also be easier for voters to ensure that government is properly fulfilling its most essential purposes, such as that of national defense. In time of war, effective democratic accountability is even more important than usual.

Reducing the size and scope of government is a difficult proposition. Obviously, political ignorance is far from the only problem that must be considered when we try to determine how large a role the state should play in our society. Trying to decide exactly how much government we should have and how we should get to that point is a large and complex question that cannot be fully answered here. But it is essential to understand that decisions about the size of government involve not only policy questions about specific issues, but also the overall viability of democratic control of government. A smaller state might be both more democratic and more effective, since stronger public accountability might increase political leaders' incentives to carry out their functions properly and avoid inefficient porkbarreling and waste. In any discussion of the size and scope of government, the problem of political ignorance should play a much more important role than has so far been the case.

The problem of political ignorance is not going to be solved anytime soon. But it may be possible to ensure that more people possess at least basic political knowledge. At the same time, we should consider the possibility that a government with fewer functions might be easier for voters to understand and control.

Ilya Somin is Assistant Professor of Law at George Mason University. He is the author of the new Cato Institute study "When Ignorance Isn't Bliss: How Political Ignorance Threatens Democracy," and the forthcoming book Democracy and the Problem of Political Ignorance.

This piece is a revised version of an article in the Newark Star Ledger edited for this book by the author.

Public Opinion: Predicting Elections by Putting Real Money Where Your Political Opinions Are?

Editors Introductory Note: Although polls are the most common and popular form of measuring political preference and predicting likely outcomes of pending elections, the Iowa Electronic Market has been a remarkably accurate tool. In the 2004 election it predicted the final outcome more accurately than any of the polls quoted by the news media. The following information explains what this is and how it works.

What is The Iowa Electronic Market?

"The faculty at the University of Iowa developed the IEM to be an Internet-based teaching and research tool. It allows students to invest real money ($5.00-$500.00) and to trade in a variety of contracts. You may be familiar with the best-known part of the IEM, the political markets. Here students can trade "shares" of political candidates or parties (the payoff depends on the election results). Students also have the opportunity to trade in contracts whose eventual payoff depends on a future event such as an economic indicator, a company's quarterly earnings, a corporation's stock price returns or a movie's box office receipts."

Who Uses the IEM?

According to the University "since its inception in 1988, over 100 universities throughout the world have enrolled in the IEM (mainly large research-oriented institutions such as Harvard, MIT, Michigan, and Northwestern). Faculty members use the IEM in accounting, finance, macroeconomics, microeconomics, and political science courses across the country. The IEM is used to teach business, economics, and technology concepts in a hands-on interactive environment."

As a teaching/learning instrument, this "marketplace" has two "common elements" that help students increase their economic literacy, according to the program.

- "First, the IEM is a forecasting tool. In each class, students can forecast the outcome of future events like an election outcome, an economic indicator or a movie's box office receipts. To make such a forecast, students have to learn about the economic and business relationships that determine the outcome. In a political science class for example, students must think about how economic and business factors (among others) can affect the mood of the electorate and how this, in turn, affects each candidate's election chances."

- "Second, the IEM is an incentive mechanism. Because they earn a real monetary reward by trading, students are more willing to learn, which helps them make better forecasts and more profitable trades. Instructors using the IEM have reported that its use leads to students actively following elections, reading about the campaign and business events of the day, and coming to class eager to engage their teachers and classmates in discussions about the elections and current events."

The program is "… eager to have students use the IEM to learn about financial markets, politics, business and technology. We believe this program will increase the awareness of students who use it and it will help them make more informed decisions about the above issues."

Editor Steffen Schmidt's note: I had the opportunity to spend four days at CNN headquarters in Atlanta, Georgia at the invitation of CNN en Español, the Spanish language television channel. Since I have closely followed the IEM I brought it up on the CNN computer network and shared the results with some of the anchors and producers for whom I was doing analysis. Even though this market has a very good track record in accurately reflecting elections, I found a great deal of hesitation to use these figures. Instead, the much less accurate public opinion polls with which Americans (and TV producers) are more familiar, were more widely used.

Editors Note: The following is a press release from the University of Iowa that explains in simple terms how this market operates.

NEWS AND INFORMATION: Press Releases
Release: July 01, 2004

Iowa Electronic Markets Trade in Presidential Futures

Who will be elected president in November? Traders in the Iowa Electronic Markets (IEM) can make their predictions with dollars invested in this real-money, web-based futures market known for its accurate predictions of election outcomes.

The IEM has opened its "winner-takes-all" market where contracts for candidate with the largest share of the popular vote pay $1, while contracts for the losing candidate pay nothing.

Operated as research and teaching tool by six professors at the University of Iowa's Henry B. Tippie College of Business, the IEM political markets are open to the public. For an investment of as little as $5 or as much as $500, anyone can buy futures contracts based the outcome of the 2004 presidential election.

For a prospectus and current prices, see www.biz.uiowa.edu/iem/markets/Pres04_WTA.html.

The IEM "winner-takes-all" market shows a fairly close race based on early trading. As of June 28, George W. Bush has a slight lead over John Kerry, with Bush contracts at about 53 cents, compared to Kerry contracts at 47 cents. IEM prices reflect the probability of each candidate's winning the election. Current IEM prices can be viewed at the IEM website.

Since its beginning in the 1988 U.S. presidential election, the IEM has established a reputation for forecasting election results with great accuracy, predicting the outcome of the popular vote with an average election eve prediction error of 1.37 percent.

"Because traders have a financial stake in the outcome, they make their choices based on who they think has the best chance of winning, not necessarily on who they want to win," said Joyce Berg, an IEM co-director and UI professor of accounting. "We've found this market-based approach to be a very informative way to predict outcomes of elections and other events."

The IEM has also opened a vote share market for the 2004 presidential election to determine how the nominees would fare against George W. Bush). Payoffs in this vote-share market are based on the percentage of the popular vote that Bush and Kerry will receive in the 2004 election.

Prices in this market show that Bush would get about 54 percent of the popular vote, compared to Kerry at 46 percent. "This is a major difference between the IEM and most opinion polls. We've shown Kerry consistently trailing Bush whereas the polls have shown Kerry ahead or the two candidates switching positions," said Berg.

For more information, contact the IEM office at (319) 335-0881, or iem@uiowa.edu.

Source: UI News Service
Writer: George McCrory
Contact: George McCrory
         UI News Service
         319-384-0012

On October 10, 2004 reporter John Tierney had a piece in the *New York Times* on the Iowa Political market titled "Speculators Still Bullish on Bush."

Tierney wrote, "The instant polls gave Senator John Kerry the edge in Friday night's debate. [November 9, 2004] The punditocracy generally called it a draw. But the online speculators betting real money on the election—the ones who probably have the best track record at instant analysis—seemed more impressed by President Bush at the end of the debate."

The Iowa Political market has in fact been an effective and accurate political seismograph, measuring the ups and downs better than most polls. Tierney noted that the investors in the market "… had turned bearish on Mr. Bush in the first debate, and they remained so early in Friday's debate, when he was shouting and waving his arm while Mr. Kerry remained steely. During that first half-hour, the price of a Bush futures contract in the Iowa Electronic

Markets dropped a point, to 51 cents, meaning that investors gave him a 51-percent chance of a victory on Nov. 2, his lowest level since the start of the Republican convention."

This is an interesting point. This political market, like the real stock market not only measures overall investor "confidence" in the candidates but since it trades constantly it also is a very sensitive and accurate indicator of how people feel about specific moments (and candidate performance) in the debates.

Continuing his observations Tierney notes that "… by the end of the debate, the Bush price was back up to 55 cents. Perhaps some investors were swayed by the substance of the debate, although there wasn't a lot new in the way of policy except for Mr. Kerry's pledge directly into the camera never to raise taxes on the middle class, and that's not likely to hurt him on Nov. 2. (Of course, he could have trouble afterwards, as Mr. Bush's father discovered after his 1988 pledge, "Read my lips, no new taxes.")"

Speculating on the causes of the ups and downs Tierney wrote, "So what did the investors like about Mr. Bush's performance? Maybe they were reassured simply to see that by the end of the debate he and Mr. Kerry were back in character: the amiable (if occasionally belligerent) cowboy versus the solemn Brahmin, the cheerful mangler of syntax against the hyper-articulate debater, the guy who could joke about himself against the guy who couldn't tell a joke."

Farhad Manjoo wrote in the Sept. 29, 2004 online issue of Salon.com, "As I've written, I'm supporting Kerry for the White House, but on the Iowa Electronic Markets, I've been betting on Bush. This is not meant as a slight against Kerry—it's just that I have doubts about his ability as a campaigner, and more important, I think that the Bushies are extremely good, not to mention that historically, incumbents running during a time of economic growth tend to win reelection. So far, alas, my bet is panning out, as measured not just by Kerry's shortfall in the polls but also by the performance of Kerry shares on the market. As of Monday, traders on the IEM give Bush about a 70 percent chance of winning in November. To look at the graph of the IEM is to despair over the prospect of four more years—a confident red line aims straight for the stratosphere, while a morose blue line nosedives."

This is a very interesting comment and gives validity (credibility really) to this market-driven tool for measuring public opinion. If you Google the Iowa Political Electronic market you will find a large number of postings and many people tracking this indicator.

Perhaps Jumpcity.com had the best comments on this electronic market:

On the assumption that people will lie to pollsters without batting eye, but always tell the truth when they put their own money down, the University of Iowa College of Business Administration has created this real-money futures market. Here you can buy and sell futures based on your feelings about a political candidate, or just see how the runners stack up against each other. The flaw in using this as an opinion poll is that it doesn't reflect how people will vote. Rather, it is based on how traders think people will vote. Regardless, it's a fascinating site to browse. Each market, including the Presidential election, the party conventions, and others, includes a prospectus, current quotes and

histories of price movements. There also are links to relevant Web sites, so you can do your own research before making a "buy."
http://www.jumpcity.com/cgi-bin/go?review:2655:

To see the final results of the Iowa Presidential Political market for the 2004 election you can visit the web site
www.biz.uiowa.edu/iem/markets/Pres04_VS.html.

Public Domain.

Chapter 7
Questions

1. Here's an old joke. "Question: What's the difference between ignorance and apathy? Answer: I don't know, and I don't care." Using information from these readings and from Chapter 7 in the textbook, would you say this is a reasonable characterization of the state of American politics, or not?

2. Why do you think the Iowa Electronic Market produces such good forecasts of U.S. presidential election outcomes? What other ways can you think of to determine how a presidential election is going to come out?

CHAPTER 8
INTEREST GROUPS

The first two articles in this chapter address the political impact of two large—and rapidly growing—parts of the electorate. In "S. Florida Voters Over 65 Could Swing the Vote with Diverse Concerns," William E. Gibson shows how the political clout of older voters turns on their perceptions of their political role. Andres Oppenheimer's "Hispanic Vote Should Increase Focus Southward" demonstrates how the votes of Hispanic voters can affect both domestic and international politics. The remaining two articles show how the pre-college teaching of science can become embroiled in the politics of interest group activity. Evan Ratliff's article, "The Crusade Against Evolution," explores the issues surrounding the debate between science educators and conservative interest groups pressing to have "creation science" and "intelligent design" taught in Ohio classrooms and elsewhere in the country as an alternative approach to Darwinian evolution. A counterpoint is provided by Scott Rank's op-ed commentary, which notes what its opponents regard as the hidden agenda of the creation science argument—to use public education to spread Christian religious ideology.

S. Florida Voters Over 65 Could Swing the Vote with Diverse Concerns
by William E. Gibson

BOCA RATON · Thousands of Democrats in the retirement communities of Palm Beach County were full of dismay four years ago when they realized they had mistakenly cast their ballots and effectively handed the presidential election to George W. Bush.

Their dismay turned into a fierce determination to oust the incumbent Republican president. And yet, even in this corner of the land of the hanging chad, many older Democrats who once were fighting mad now are uncertain, or downright defeatist, about this year's election.

So much has happened since 2000 to change the political landscape, leaving senior citizens throughout Florida and nationwide just about evenly divided between Bush and Democratic challenger John Kerry.

National security has replaced health care or education as the top issue, despite controversies over Medicare and education reform laws that Bush pushed through Congress. And the passing of the World War II generation, dying at the rate of a thousand Americans a day, has depleted the ranks of loyal Democrats.

Nevertheless, compared with other age groups, older voters appear slightly more likely to support the Democratic ticket, and polls consistently show senior citizens generally are less inclined to support President Bush's war policy in Iraq. As domestic policy re-emerges in the last few weeks of the campaign, late-deciding senior citizens, particularly older women, offer Kerry his best chance of winning the election.

So far, he has sparked little enthusiasm.

"He is the best that we can do. He is the answer right now," said David Garelick, 83, who used a walker to make his way through the cavernous clubhouse at Century Village, a retirement enclave in Boca Raton with about 6,000 registered Democrats.

"The Republicans probably will win," he said. "I hope not."

DEMOCRATIC ROOTS

Senior citizens, too numerous and varied to be a distinct voting bloc, long have tended to reflect the entire electorate and side with the winner. Along the margins, however, they have leaned toward Democrats in recent elections, especially in South Florida.

In 2000, for example, nationwide exit polls showed that voters 65 and older supported Democrat Al Gore over Bush by 51 percent to 47 percent. Among all age groups, Gore gathered 48.38 percent of the votes nationwide, while Bush got 47.87 percent of the popular vote.

Bush won the electoral vote after prevailing in Florida by a margin of 537 votes. But if senior citizens alone had decided the election, Gore would have gone to the White House.

This Democratic tilt goes back to Franklin Roosevelt's New Deal, when today's oldest generation formed its political identity. Americans of that era created huge government institutions to help them survive hard times, win World War II and withstand the Cold War. And they formed a liberal Democratic establishment that dominated American politics for a half-century.

"Older voters have a tendency not to view government as the enemy," said Steffen Schmidt, professor of political science at Iowa State University and host of a political talk show in Iowa, a swing state this year with an especially large elderly population. "That is clearly the reason you see lots of older people at Democratic Party activities. People who work hardest for Kerry are in their 70s. Unfortunately, some of them are gone. The generation that puts its trust in government is passing away."

2004 INFLUENCE

Senior citizens, who now include some who grew up after the Depression, still exert great influence. Voters 65 and older cast 20 percent of the ballots nationwide in the last election, and 28 percent in Florida.

"The older generation is increasingly looking like the entire population, as the hard-core Democratic FDR generation goes on to glory," said Susan MacManus, political scientist at the

University of South Florida and author of the book Targeting Senior Voters. "The senior vote is maybe leaning a bit to Kerry, but not by much.

"The Kerry leaners are heavily women," MacManus said. "Among that oldest generation, these are women who didn't work, didn't have a pension and economic security is their big issue."

Poll results are somewhat mixed, though offer some encouragement to Kerry.

A Gallup Poll on Oct. 1-3 included a small sample of 207 senior citizens, who favored Kerry over Bush by 52 percent to 43 percent. A Pew Research Center poll during the same period said senior voters slightly favored Bush over Kerry by 43 percent to 41 percent, a smaller Bush advantage than among younger age groups.

At Century Village, several voters said they strongly oppose Bush yet are pessimistic about Kerry's prospects.

"I don't really think that Bush is for the common man. It's all business. And I think future generations will suffer from it," said Frances Block, 87.

But when asked about Kerry, she said, "I don't think the Democrats have a real strong candidate. I thought this whole thing about his war record [in Vietnam] was stupid to start with. I don't think that's important at all. I think he's sunk."

REPUBLICAN OUTREACH

Bush tells senior citizens at rallies around the country that he fulfilled his promise to them by signing a Medicare reform bill that includes a new benefit to help pay for prescription drugs. Republican supporters say this action will reassure at least some senior citizens and show that Bush is responsive to their needs.

"During the [Bill] Clinton years, we didn't do anything about helping people with the cost of medicine," said Peter Lebowitz, who has organized a Republican outreach effort in another corner of Boca Raton, a gated community called Boca Pointe. "The fact that Bush did do something in the area of prescription drugs takes something away from the issue. It has convinced many people to give [the new law] a chance."

He and many other Republicans say the president will get a higher percentage of senior votes in this election, enough to keep Florida in his column.

The drug bill remains controversial, however, and many senior citizens say the vastly expensive drug benefit will boost the federal deficit yet provide little help to the great majority of Medicare patients. Kerry and other critics say the law does nothing to restrain runaway drug prices because it does not allow importation of cheaper drugs and forbids Medicare from negotiating with pharmaceutical companies to rein in costs.

"For some older people — if they are really on the fence — health care could tip them one way or another," said Jeffery Love, who supervises voter surveys for AARP. "But Iraq and terrorism are really the issues on the table. They aren't the only issues, but they do sort of trump everything. Both campaigns have made it so."

FOUR-YEAR GRUDGE

The conflicting trends that have roiled the older population leave a huge group of well-informed voters who turn out at the polls in high numbers, carefully watch the presidential debates, have a big stake in federal policies, tend to look suspiciously at Bush's Iraq policy but have the same security concerns as younger Americans.

If Kerry can motivate these voters in the last days of the campaign, he could prevail in Florida and nationwide. If not, the incumbent commander in chief has the advantage.

One change since 2000: voters in Palm Beach County, at least, are sure to carefully cast their ballots. Four years ago, befuddled by the notorious butterfly ballot, many trooped to the polls intending to vote for the Democratic ticket but mistakenly picked conservative Reform Party candidate Patrick Buchanan.

As a result, Buchanan got 3,407 votes in this Democratic stronghold, far more than in any other Florida county. The diversion apparently cost Gore the election, a wound that has festered for four years.

"The 2000 election was one time that seniors really made the difference, because of all those who mistakenly voted for Buchanan," said Robert H. Binstock, professor of aging, health and society at Case Western Reserve University.

This time, he predicts, seniors will distribute their votes about the same as the rest of the electorate, making a limited impact on the final result.

October 16, 2004.

William E. Gibson, Washington Bureau Chief, can be reached at wgibson@sun-sentinel.com or 202-824-8256 in Washington.

Despite predictions of worsening relations between a second Bush administration and Latin America, I'm not sure that will happen. Bush will be forced to pay greater attention to the region because of the emergence of a more powerful than expected Hispanic voters' bloc in Tuesday's election.

Exit polls show that, for the first time, the nation's estimated 9 million Hispanic voters became a truly bipartisan voting bloc in Tuesday's election, leaving behind their past overwhelming support for the Democratic party and becoming a key factor in Bush's nationwide victory.

A record 44 percent of Hispanics nationwide voted for Bush, compared to 54 percent for Democratic candidate Sen. John Kerry, according to a joint exit poll by CNN and other major U.S. networks. In 2000, Bush got only 35 percent of the Hispanic vote, and former Democratic candidate Al Gore received 62 percent, exit polls showed four years ago.

Tuesday's election results show that the Hispanic vote will be up for grabs in the 2008 elections and will thus be worth courting by the next U.S. presidential candidates.

In addition, Hispanic voters elected their first two senators, Mel Martinez in Florida and Ken Salazar of Colorado, and increased their participation from 7 percent to 8 percent of the overall U.S. electorate.

"This election puts the Hispanic community with one foot in each major political party and gives it a huge political advantage," says Steffen Schmidt, a professor of political science at Iowa State University. ``Future elections in the United States will be win-win for Hispanics."

WILL AFFECT TIES

All of this will definitely impact U.S. relations with Latin America, regardless of whether U.S. presidents care about the region or not. A pre-election Herald-Zogby International poll showed that more than 70 percent of Hispanic voters believe that U.S. policy toward Latin America is an issue they consider very or somewhat important when making their decision to vote.

Granted, there was no big fiesta in Latin America following Bush's victory. The news was received in most countries with resignation, occasional sadness, and many predictions of worsening U.S.-Latin American ties.

In Argentina, the country with some of the highest levels of anti-American sentiment in the region, the pro-government leftist daily *Pagina 12* ran a picture of Bush across its front page with the banner headline, "La Misma Piedra," or ``(Stuck with) The same Stone."

In Brazil, the left-of-center daily *Folha de Sao Paulo* led its entire election coverage under the banner, "The empire votes." It was hard to find any trace of pro-Bush emotion in any headline in the region.

But it's an open secret that President Bush is not popular in most of Latin America and that an overwhelming majority in the region rooted for Kerry. Except in Colombia and Central American countries, the positive image of the United States in the region has dropped sharply.

CLOUDED IMAGE

According to the Latinobarómetro poll, a survey of more than 18,000 people in 18 Latin American countries, the region's overall positive image of the United States has fallen from 71 percent in 2002 to 64 percent this year.

In Mexico, Brazil and Argentina, the drop has been steeper than average. Mexicans' positive opinion about the United States has dropped from 72 percent in 2000 to a low of 41 percent this year. In Brazil, it has dropped to a 50 percent low, and in Argentina to a 32 percent low over the same period.

MUST BUILD BRIDGES

On Wednesday, I asked Latinobarómetro director Marta Lagos in Santiago, Chile, whether Bush's victory would bring about a pragmatic accommodation or greater criticism from Latin American critics. She didn't have to think very hard.

"We will see a further consolidation of the idea that Latin America has been abandoned by the United States," Lagos said.

"The feeling in Latin America, especially in South America, is that the United States will be entirely focused on Iraq."

Maybe so. But, regardless of what Latin Americans think, Bush — and his successors — will have no option but to spend more time trying to build bridges with the region. It will be a matter of votes — the one thing politicians pay attention to.

Thu, Nov. 04, 2004
The Miami Herald

Andres Oppenheimer
The Oppenheimer Report

Reprinted with permission from Miami Herald, The Herald Print and Pub. Co.

The Crusade Against Evolution
by Evan Ratliff

On a spring day two years ago, in a downtown Columbus auditorium, the Ohio State Board of Education took up the question of how to teach the theory of evolution in public schools. A panel of four experts - two who believe in evolution, two who question it - debated whether an antievolution theory known as intelligent design should be allowed into the classroom.

This is an issue, of course, that was supposed to have been settled long ago. But 140 years after Darwin published On the Origin of Species, 75 years after John Scopes taught natural selection to a biology class in Tennessee, and 15 years after the US Supreme Court ruled against a Louisiana law mandating equal time for creationism, the question of how to teach the theory of evolution was being reopened here in Ohio. The two-hour forum drew chanting protesters and a police escort for the school board members. Two scientists, biologist Ken Miller from Brown University and physicist Lawrence Krauss from Case Western Reserve University two hours north in Cleveland, defended evolution. On the other side of the dais were two representatives from the Discovery Institute in Seattle, the main sponsor and promoter of intelligent design: Stephen Meyer, a professor at Palm Beach Atlantic University's School of Ministry and director of the Discovery Institute's Center for Science and Culture, and Jonathan Wells, a biologist, Discovery fellow, and author of Icons of Evolution, a 2000 book castigating textbook treatments of evolution. Krauss and Miller methodically presented their case against ID. "By no definition of any modern scientist is intelligent design science," Krauss concluded, "and it's a waste of our students' time to subject them to it."

Meyer and Wells took the typical intelligent design line: Biological life contains elements so complex - the mammalian blood-clotting mechanism, the bacterial flagellum - that they cannot be explained by natural selection. And so, the theory goes, we must be products of an intelligent designer. Creationists call that creator God, but proponents of intelligent design studiously avoid the G-word - and never point to the Bible for answers. Instead, ID believers speak the language of science to argue that Darwinian evolution is crumbling.

The debate's two-on-two format, with its appearance of equal sides, played right into the ID strategy - create the impression that this very complicated issue could be seen from two entirely rational yet opposing views. "This is a controversial subject," Meyer told the audience. "When two groups of experts disagree about a controversial subject that intersects with the public-school science curriculum, the students should be permitted to learn about both perspectives. We call this the 'teach the controversy' approach."

Since the debate, "teach the controversy" has become the rallying cry of the national intelligent-design movement, and Ohio has become the leading battleground. Several months after the debate, the Ohio school board voted to change state science standards, mandating that biology teachers "critically analyze" evolutionary theory. This fall, teachers will adjust their lesson plans and begin doing just that. In some cases, that means introducing the basic tenets of intelligent design. One of the state's sample lessons looks as though it were lifted from an ID textbook. It's the biggest victory so far for the Discovery Institute. "Our opponents would say that these are a bunch of know-nothing people on a state board," says Meyer. "We think it shows that our Darwinist colleagues have a real problem now."

But scientists aren't buying it. What Meyer calls "biology for the information age," they call creationism in a lab coat. ID's core scientific principles - laid out in the mid-1990s by a biochemist and a mathematician - have been thoroughly dismissed on the grounds that Darwin's theories can account for complexity, that ID relies on misunderstandings of evolution and flimsy probability calculations, and that it proposes no testable explanations.

As the Ohio debate revealed, however, the Discovery Institute doesn't need the favor of the scientific establishment to prevail in the public arena. Over the past decade, Discovery has gained ground in schools, op-ed pages, talk radio, and congressional resolutions as a "legitimate" alternative to evolution. ID is playing a central role in biology curricula and textbook controversies around the country. The institute and its supporters have taken the "teach the controversy" message to Alabama, Arizona, Minnesota, Missouri, Montana, New Mexico, and Texas.

The ID movement's rhetorical strategy - better to appear scientific than holy - has turned the evolution debate upside down. ID proponents quote Darwin, cite the Scopes monkey trial, talk of "scientific objectivity," then in the same breath declare that extraterrestrials might have designed life on Earth. It may seem counterintuitive, but the strategy is meticulously premeditated, and it's working as planned. The debate over Darwin is back, and coming to a 10th-grade biology class near you.

At its heart, intelligent design is a revival of an argument made by British philosopher William Paley in 1802. In Natural Theology, the Anglican archdeacon suggested that the complexity of biological structures defied any explanation but a designer: God. Paley imagined finding a stone and a watch in a field. The watch, unlike the stone, appears to have been purposely assembled and wouldn't function without its precise combination of parts. "The inference," he wrote, "is inevitable, that the watch must have a maker." The same logic, he concluded, applied to biological structures like the vertebrate eye. Its complexity implied design.

Fifty years later, Darwin directly answered Paley's "argument to complexity." Evolution by natural selection, he argued in Origin of Species, could create the appearance of design. Darwin - and 100-plus years of evolutionary science after him - seemed to knock Paley into the dustbin of history.

In the American public arena, Paley's design argument has long been supplanted by biblical creationism. In the 1970s and 1980s, that movement recast the Bible version in the language of scientific inquiry - as "creation science" - and won legislative victories requiring "equal time" in some states. That is, until 1987, when the Supreme Court struck down Louisiana's law. Because creation science relies on biblical texts, the court reasoned, it "lacked a clear secular purpose" and violated the First Amendment clause prohibiting the establishment of religion. Since then, evolution has been the law of the land in US schools - if not always the local choice.

Paley re-emerged in the mid-1990s, however, when a pair of scientists reconstituted his ideas in an area beyond Darwin's ken: molecular biology. In his 1996 book Darwin's Black Box, Lehigh University biochemist Michael Behe contended that natural selection can't explain the "irreducible complexity" of molecular mechanisms like the bacterial flagellum, because its integrated parts offer no selective advantages on their own. Two years later, in The Design Inference, William Dembski, a philosopher and mathematician at Baylor University, proposed that any biological system exhibiting "information" that is both "complex" (highly improbable) and "specified" (serving a particular function) cannot be a product of chance or natural law. The only remaining option is an intelligent designer - whether God or an alien life force. These ideas became the cornerstones of ID, and Behe proclaimed the evidence for design to be "one of the greatest achievements in the history of science."

The scientific rationale behind intelligent design was being developed just as antievolution sentiment seemed to be bubbling up. In 1991, UC Berkeley law professor Phillip Johnson published Darwin On Trial, an influential antievolution book that dispensed with biblical creation accounts while uniting antievolutionists under a single, secular-sounding banner: intelligent design. In subsequent books, Johnson presents not just antievolution arguments but a broader opposition to the "philosophy of scientific materialism" - the assumption (known to scientists as "methodological materialism") that all events have material, rather than supernatural, explanations. To defeat it, he offers a strategy that would be familiar in the divisive world of politics, called "the wedge." Like a wedge inserted into a tree trunk, cracks in Darwinian theory can be used to "split the trunk," eventually overturning scientific materialism itself.

That's where Discovery comes in. The institute was founded as a conservative think tank in 1990 by longtime friends and former Harvard roommates Bruce Chapman - director of the census bureau during the Reagan administration - and technofuturist author George Gilder. "The institute is futurist and rebellious, and it's prophetic," says Gilder. "It has a science and technology orientation in a contrarian spirit."... In 1994, Discovery added ID to its list of contrarian causes, which included everything from transportation to bioethics. Chapman hired Meyer, who studied origin-of-life issues at Cambridge University, and the institute signed Johnson - whom Chapman calls "the real godfather of the intelligent design movement" - as an adviser and adopted the wedge.

For Discovery, the "thin end" of the wedge - according to a fundraising document leaked on the Web in 1999 - is the scientific work of Johnson, Behe, Dembski, and others. The next step involves "publicity and opinion-making." The final goals: "a direct confrontation with the advocates of material science" and "possible legal assistance in response to integration of design theory into public school science curricula."

Step one has made almost no headway with evolutionists - the near-universal majority of scientists with an opinion on the matter. But that, say Discovery's critics, is not the goal.

"Ultimately, they have an evangelical Christian message that they want to push," says Michael Ruse, a philosopher of science at Florida State. "Intelligent design is the hook."

It's a lot easier to skip straight to steps two and three, and sound scientific in a public forum, than to deal with the rigor of the scientific community. "It starts with education," Johnson told me, referring to high school curricula. "That's where the public can have a voice. The universities and the scientific world do not recognize freedom of expression on this issue." Meanwhile, like any champion of a heretical scientific idea, ID's supporters see themselves as renegades, storming the gates of orthodoxy. "We all have a deep sense of indignation," says Meyer, "that the wool is being pulled over the public's eyes."

The buzz phrase most often heard in the institute's offices is *academic freedom*. "My hackles go up on the academic freedom issue," Chapman says. "You should be allowed in the sciences to ask questions and posit alternative theories."

None of this impresses the majority of the science world. "They have not been able to convince even a tiny amount of the scientific community," says Ken Miller. "They have not been able to win the marketplace of ideas."

And yet, the Discovery Institute's appeals to academic freedom create a kind of catch-22. If scientists ignore the ID movement, their silence is offered as further evidence of a conspiracy. If they join in, they risk reinforcing the perception of a battle between equal sides. Most scientists choose to remain silent. "Where the scientific community has been at fault," says Krauss, "is in assuming that these people are harmless, like flat-earthers. They don't realize that they are well organized, and that they have a political agenda."

Taped to the wall of Eugenie Scott's windowless office at the National Center for Science Education on the outskirts of Oakland, California, is a chart titled "Current Flare-Ups." It's a list of places where the teaching of evolution is under attack, from California to Georgia to Rio de Janeiro. As director of the center, which defends evolution in teaching controversies around the country, Scott has watched creationism up close for 30 years. ID, in her view, is the most highly evolved form of creationism to date. "They've been enormously effective compared to the more traditional creationists, who have greater numbers and much larger budgets," she says.

Scott credits the blueprint laid out by Johnson, who realized that to win in the court of public opinion, ID needed only to cast reasonable doubt on evolution. "He said, 'Don't get involved in details, don't get involved in fact claims,'" says Scott. "'Forget about the age of Earth, forget about the flood, don't mention the Bible.'" The goal, she says, is "to focus on the big idea that evolution is inadequate. Intelligent design doesn't really explain anything. It says that evolution can't explain things. Everything else is hand-waving."

The movement's first test of Johnson's strategies began in 1999, when the Kansas Board of Education voted to remove evolution from the state's science standards. The decision, backed by traditional creationists, touched off a fiery debate, and the board eventually reversed itself after several antievolution members lost reelection bids. ID proponents used the melee as cover to launch their own initiative. A Kansas group called IDNet nearly pushed through its own textbook in a local school district.

Two years later, the Discovery Institute earned its first major political victory when US senator Rick Santorum (R-Pennsylvania) inserted language written by Johnson into the federal No Child Left Behind Act. The clause, eventually cut from the bill and placed in a nonbinding report, called for school curricula to "help students understand the full range of scientific views" on topics "that may generate controversy (such as biological evolution)."

As the institute was demonstrating its Beltway clout, a pro-ID group called Science Excellence for All Ohioans fueled a brewing local controversy. SEAO - consisting of a few part-time activists, a Web site, and a mailing list - began agitating to have ID inserted into Ohio's 10th-grade-biology standards. In the process, they attracted the attention of a few receptive school board members.

When the board proposed the two-on-two debate and invited Discovery, Meyer and company jumped at the opportunity. Meyer, whom Gilder calls the institute's resident "polymath," came armed with the Santorum amendment, which he read aloud for the school board. He was bringing a message from Washington: Teach the controversy. "We framed the issue quite differently than our supporters," says Meyer. The approach put pro-ID Ohioans on firmer rhetorical ground: Evolution should of course be taught, but "objectively." Hearing Meyer's suggestion, says Doug Rudy, a software engineer and SEAO's director, "we all sat back and said, Yeah, that's the way to go."

Back in Seattle, around the corner from the Discovery Institute, Meyer offers some peer-reviewed evidence that there truly is a controversy that must be taught. "The Darwinists are bluffing," he says over a plate of oysters at a downtown seafood restaurant. "They have the science of the steam engine era, and it's not keeping up with the biology of the information age."

Meyer hands me a recent issue of *Microbiology* and *Molecular Biology Reviews* with an article by Carl Woese, an eminent microbiologist at the University of Illinois. In it, Woese decries the failure of reductionist biology - the tendency to look at systems as merely the sum of their parts - to keep up with the developments of molecular biology. Meyer says the conclusion of Woese's argument is that the Darwinian emperor has no clothes.

It's a page out of the antievolution playbook: using evolutionary biology's own literature against it, selectively quoting from the likes of Stephen Jay Gould to illustrate natural selection's downfalls. The institute marshals journal articles discussing evolution to provide policymakers with evidence of the raging controversy surrounding the issue.

Woese scoffs at Meyer's claim when I call to ask him about the paper. "To say that my criticism of Darwinists says that evolutionists have no clothes," Woese says, "is like saying that Einstein is criticizing Newton, therefore Newtonian physics is wrong." Debates about evolution's mechanisms, he continues, don't amount to challenges to the theory. And intelligent design "is not science. It makes no predictions and doesn't offer any explanation whatsoever, except for 'God did it.'"

Of course Meyer happily acknowledges that Woese is an ardent evolutionist. The institute doesn't need to impress Woese or his peers; it can simply co-opt the vocabulary of science - "academic freedom," "scientific objectivity," "teach the controversy" - and redirect it to a public trying to reconcile what appear to be two contradictory scientific views. By appealing to a sense of fairness, ID finds a place at the political table, and by merely entering the debate it can claim victory. "We don't need to win every argument to be a success," Meyer says. "We're trying to validate a discussion that's been long suppressed."

This is precisely what happened in Ohio. "I'm not a PhD in biology," says board member Michael Cochran. "But when I have X number of PhD experts telling me this, and X number telling me the opposite, the answer is probably somewhere between the two."

An exasperated Krauss claims that a truly representative debate would have had 10,000 pro-evolution scientists against two Discovery executives. "What these people want is for there to *be* a debate," says Krauss. "People in the audience say, Hey, these people sound reasonable. They argue, 'People have different opinions, we should present those opinions in school.' That is nonsense. Some people have opinions that the Holocaust never happened, but we don't teach that in history."

Eventually, the Ohio board approved a standard mandating that students learn to "describe how scientists continue to investigate and critically analyze aspects of evolutionary theory." Proclaiming victory, Johnson barnstormed Ohio churches soon after notifying congregations of a new, ID-friendly standard. In response, anxious board members added a clause stating that the standard "does not mandate the teaching or testing of intelligent design." Both sides claimed victory. A press release from IDNet trumpeted the mere inclusion of the phrase *intelligent design*, saying that "the implication of the statement is that the 'teaching or testing of intelligent design' is permitted." Some pro-evolution scientists, meanwhile, say there's nothing wrong with teaching students how to scrutinize theory. "I don't have a problem with that," says Patricia Princehouse, a professor at Case Western Reserve and an outspoken opponent of ID. "Critical analysis is exactly what scientists do."

The good feelings didn't last long. Early this year, a board-appointed committee unveiled sample lessons that laid out the kind of evolution questions students should debate. The models appeared to lift their examples from Wells' book *Icons of Evolution*. "When I first saw it, I was speechless," says Princehouse.

With a PhD in molecular and cell biology from UC Berkeley, Wells has the kind of cred that intelligent design proponents love to cite. But, as ID opponents enjoy pointing out, he's also a follower of Sun Myung Moon and once declared that Moon's prayers "convinced me that I should devote my life to destroying Darwinism." *Icons* attempts to discredit commonly used examples of evolution, like Darwin's finches and peppered moths. Writing in *Nature*, evolutionary biologist Jerry Coyne called *Icons* stealth creationism that "strives to debunk Darwinism using the familiar rhetoric of biblical creationists, including scientific quotations out of context, incomplete summaries of research, and muddled arguments."

After months of uproar, the most obvious Icons-inspired lessons were removed. But scientists remain furious. "The ones they left in are still arguments for special creation - but you'd have to know the literature to understand what they are saying. They've used so much technical jargon that anybody who doesn't know a whole lot of evolutionary biology looks at it and says 'It sounds scientific to me, what's the matter with it?'" says Princehouse. "As a friend of mine said, it takes a half a second for a baby to throw up all over your sweater. It takes hours to get it clean."

As Ohio teachers prepare their lessons for the coming year, the question must be asked: Why the fuss over an optional lesson plan or two? After all, both sides agree that the new biology standards - in which 10 evolution lessons replace standards that failed to mention evolution at all - are a vast improvement. The answer: In an era when the government is pouring billions into biology, and when stem cells and genetically modified food are front-page news, spending even a small part of the curriculum on bogus criticisms of evolution is arguably more detrimental now than any time in history. Ironically, says Ohio State University biology professor Steve Rissing, the education debate coincides with Ohio's efforts to lure biotech companies. "How can we do that when our high school biology is failing us?" he says. "Our cornfields are gleaming with GMO corn. There's a fundamental disconnect there."

Intelligent design advocates say that teaching students to "critically analyze" evolution will help give them the skills to "see both sides" of all scientific issues. And if the Discovery Institute execs have their way, those skills will be used to reconsider the philosophy of modern science itself - which they blame for everything from divorce to abortion to the insanity defense. "Our culture has been deeply influenced by materialist thought," says Meyer. "We think it's deeply destructive, and we think it's false. And we mean to overturn it."

It's mid-July, and the Ohio school board is about to hold its final meeting before classes start this year. There's nothing about intelligent design on the agenda. The debate was settled months ago. And yet, Princehouse, Rissing, and two other scientists rise to speak during the "non-agenda" public testimony portion.

One by one, the scientists recite their litany of objections: The model lesson plan is still based on concepts from ID literature; the ACLU is considering to sue to stop it; the National Academy of Sciences opposes it as unscientific. "This is my last time," says Rissing, "as someone who has studied science and the process of evolution for 25 years, to say I perceive that my children and I are suffering injuries based on a flawed lesson plan that this board has passed."

During a heated question-and-answer session, one board member accuses the scientists of posturing for me, the only reporter in the audience. Michael Cochran challenges the scientists to cite any testimony that the board hadn't already heard "ad infinitum." Another board member, Deborah Owens-Fink, declares the issue already closed. "We've listened to experts on both sides of this for three years," she says. "Ultimately, the question of what students should learn "is decided in a democracy, not by any one group of experts."

The notion is noble enough: In a democracy, every idea gets heard. But in science, not all theories are equal. Those that survive decades - centuries - of scientific scrutiny end up in classrooms, and those that don't are discarded. The intelligent design movement is using scientific rhetoric to bypass scientific scrutiny. And when science education is decided by charm and stage presence, the Discovery Institute wins.

Originally published in WIRED, Issue 12.10, October 2004.

Is Intelligent Design Science or Creationism 2.0?
by Scott Rank

Hold on to your copies of "On the Origin of Species," Iowa State. Whether you know it or not, the battle for the future of how to teach evolution in public schools is happening right here at our university.

This battle is also happening all across the nation, and it's embodied in a new scientific theory that is gaining steam among scientists and laymen.

It's called intelligent design (ID), the argument that life shows signs of having been designed by an intelligent agent.

To critics, this "intelligent agent" sounds suspiciously like the Christian Triune God, but ID is a secular theory, and there are many ID researchers who are Jewish, Eastern Orthodox and Agnostic. The goal of the ID movement is not to kick evolution out of schools, but to allow students to question certain parts of Darwinian materialism.

But mainstream scientists don't acknowledge ID as science. Prominent researchers are scrambling to write articles against it, universities are firing staff members who publicly advocate it and Wired magazine even devoted a cover article to it, affectionately titled "The Crusade Against Evolution."

This battle isn't just national—it's also taking place right here at Iowa State. Some of the most cutting-edge research in this controversial field is coming from Guillermo Gonzalez, an ISU physics professor who wrote a groundbreaking book called "The Privileged Planet."

The books premises that the same unlikely circumstances that allow life to exist on earth are also the best circumstances for scientific discovery. Gonzalez states that with all these fantastic circumstances running around, it must have been in the cards for Earth to be in the place in the universe that it is.

However, Darwinists won't have it. They paint this type of ID research as "creationism in a lab coat," an attempt to smuggle the Genesis account of creation into a 10th-grade biology class. They think that ID should be thrown in to history's dustbin, along with alchemy and bloodletting.

Some ISU professors have jumped on the bandwagon to bash ID. Last week, two ISU professors—Hector Avalos and John Patterson—presented a forum on the flaws in ID and specifically attacked "The Privileged Planet."

Avalos, Iowa State's most beloved atheist, argued against ID science from a philosophical point of view, which was odd, since Avalos is neither a scientist nor a philosopher. But most ISU students know that Avalos will throw mud at theism whenever possible (if the ISU dietetic program hosted a Christian cooking conference, Avalos would show up with a batch of homemade atheist cookies).

Patterson, a retired ISU professor who gained national recognition as an outspoken critic of creation science, said that "scientific" explanations, like ID, are worse than no explanations at all because they are absurdly wrong.

There are few things Patterson doesn't understand. First of all, modern science wouldn't exist without a belief in a designer. The entire bedrock of Western science is founded on being open-minded to natural things that transcend nature, an idea that started with Aristotle.

Second, Patterson, along with all other neo-Darwinists, is a victim to several bad presuppositions. Darwin didn't derive his theory from nature, but superimposed his naturalistic worldview on nature and spent his life trying to attach scientific facts to his philosophy to make it meritable.

Today, some of Darwin's ideas look as cartoonish as "The Far Side." He believed that undirected processes, principally natural selection, is enough to create biological complexity.

But Darwin's own research contradicted this. In "On the Origin of the Species," Darwin said, "Can we believe that natural selection could produce… an organ so wonderful as the eye? How could organisms that need it survive without it while it was evolving over thousands of millions of years?"

If his type of inconsistency is taught as gospel in the classroom, then I'm baffled why most scientists are so threatened by having minor criticisms of Darwin taught as well. But it doesn't really matter what mainstream science thinks. ID is slowly gaining acceptance, and it's not going away anytime soon.

Originally published in the Iowa State Daily, October 18, 2004.

Chapter 8
Questions

1. Why do you think conservative interest groups are pressing so hard to teach "intelligent design" in the science classroom? Does teaching "creation science" violate the separation of church and state that is part of the First Amendment to the U.S. Constitution? Why, or why not?

2. If Hispanic and older voters have such a big impact on American politics, why don't younger people (like college students) have a bigger role in elections and public policy? Given what you see here about how Hispanic and older voters play a large political role, what two or three top things would you do to increase the impact that younger people have in American politics?

CHAPTER 9
POLITICAL PARTIES

Political party orientations develop for a lot of different reasons and in many ways. In "I'm a Democrat Now," Marty Jezer argues forcefully for a Democratic candidate who appeals to leftist values. In contrast, "Why I am a Republican," by Steven M. Warshawsky, presents the case for being a Republican. Beyond the two major parties, Daryl A. Northrop argues that supporting the Green Party would produce a better government. Finally, to end on a lighter note, David Burge presents a humorous take on partisanship that demonstrates the often fleeting nature of partisan values.

I am a Democrat Now
by Marty Jezer

When this presidential campaign started, I thought John Kerry would be a shoe-in. He had everything going for him: a Vietnam combat hero and then an articulate and courageous leader of the anti-war veterans' movement. He had a strong liberal record on the environment, on social issues, on labor. He was an early supporter of the clean money bill for publicly financed elections; he understood the corrosive effect that big money and special interests have on American politics. During the Iran Contra hearings, he exposed the folly of American foreign policy. His vote to support the Iraqi war was, as I saw it, an act of commonplace political cowardice, but in explaining his position, he ably articulated the flaws in the Bush administration's bully-boy foreign policy. I was ready to support him for President.

Building on his mistaken stance on Iraq, Kerry proceeded to run a textbook campaign on how to alienate his supporters. He was petty, arrogant, and seemingly more opposed to Howard Dean than he was to the Bush administration.

As a Vermonter, I was astonished by Dean's rise to frontrunner status. But Howard Dean, the governor, was a different politician than Howard Dean the candidate. History will be kind to our former governor, even if his support dwindles in the on-going primary season.

Whereas Kerry and the other Democrats tried to forge politically safe positions, Dean galvanized and articulated the disgust that most Democrats have toward the Bush administration. His boldness gave the other candidates the courage to go after the president. Dean took the heat from the media for standing up to Bush (something that the media itself, with a few notable exceptions, lacked the courage to do). And he also took heat from the other Democratic candidates. This made them seem petty and threatened to destroy the party. When, after Saddam Hussein was captured, Dean said that his capture would not make the war go better or the American people safer, he was right, as the evidence has shown. Shame on the press for attacking Dean for telling the truth! Shame on the other candidates for echoing the shallow and cowardly conventional wisdom!

Many Vermonters have suspected all along that Howard Dean lacks the temperament and gravitons to be a viable candidate. Let's give up our small state fantasy and admit that truth. But three big cheers for out ex-Gov. He gave the campaign its focus and excitement. He gave substance to Paul Wellstone's wonderful line, "I stand for the Democratic wing of the Democratic party". Now it's up to the other Democrats to represent that wing.

Forget how they voted on Iraq. The fact is, when Bush made his case to Congress, he lied. I wish John Kerry had seen through that lie, as Dean did, and as most rank-and-file Democrats did. It bothers me that he was so easily conned. I wish also that John Kerry would advertise his courageous anti-Vietnam activism as much as he advertises his combat heroism. But he's good on every issue, including now, Iraq.

Once again it's Kerry's nomination to lose. If the party deadlocks, Wesley Clark, the General on the white horse, takes the prize. He is thoughtful and decent, a General who helped to administrate a racially and gender integrated military. I honor him for wanting to intervene to stop the genocide in Rwanda. Obviously he isn't a pacifist, but he is committed to international structures and humanitarian goals. If Clark doesn't become president, he is my first choice for Secretary of State.

John Edwards has shown himself to be an authentic populist with humane social values. He'd make a great Attorney General. Dick Gephardt for secretary of Labor, or, given his congressional experience, Vice President. Carole Mosely Braun is a smart and articulate woman. She belongs in the cabinet or back in the Senate. Dennis Kucinich, if he wants to move up, has also earned a place in the cabinet. Doctor Dean, a proven administrator can run Health, Education, and Welfare, or serve us all as an outspoken Surgeon General.

All Democratic candidates except Dick Gephardt are free traders. Globalization represents a technological revolution. There is no turning back. I believe all the Democrats can be moved to a more labor and environmentally friendly position on fair trade. Utopianism isn't on the table. In this election I'll settle for common sense.

A word to the Deaniacs: you pushed the Democrats into the 21st century. You served an historical purpose. You inspired young people to get into politics. Don't go away!

As my friends and readers know, I'm a Vermont progressive, left of center. I've never been a card carrying Democrat. But this year, until election day is past, I am a Democrat. To be a Democrat is not to hold one's nose in the voting booth or complain about the lesser of two evils. It's to do the right thing. It's to answer history's call, with enthusiasm and pride.

The day after election day, we can all go back into opposition. A basic fact of American politics is that Democrats have to heed the voters on their left. Right wing Republicans, by contrast, gain strength by bashing the left. Give us a candidate who will stand up to the Bush administration and we will do what has to be done to get out the vote and make sure that the ballots are counted right—each and every one.

Marty Jezer is a columnist for the Brattleboro (VT) Reformer. His books include *Abbie Hoffman: American Rebel* and *The Dark Ages: Life in the U.S. 1945-1960.*

Originally published on Friday, January 23, 2004 by CommonDreams.org

---

Why I am a Republican
by Steven M. Warshawsky

As the 2004 presidential election draws near, when the citizens of this country will be faced with a clear choice between Republican and Democratic candidates, I find myself moved to offer these reflections on why I believe the Republican Party is the best party for America and why I will be voting for George W. Bush this November. The purpose of this essay is not to compare the candidates' positions on specific policy issues, but to clarify the underlying principles that shape and inform each party's approach to governance. Because I believe that the principles espoused by the Republican Party, which have their origins in the founding of our nation and were reinvigorated in our lifetime by Ronald Reagan, offer the only basis upon which to build a free and prosperous society, I am a Republican.

I have not always been a Republican. I grew up in a liberal Democratic family, and from my earliest years I espoused the government-based "do-goodism" that joins together liberals, socialists, radicals, and assorted other "reformers." My do-goodism was of the typical naïve, sentimental variety that believes the solution to all human problems can be found in utopian fantasies, government programs, and the redistribution of wealth. Like other do-gooders, I professed to care deeply about "equality" and "justice"—but failed to recognize that without freedom there is nothing, only tyranny.

The education I received in high school and college merely reflected and reinforced my do-goodism. As has been chronicled extensively in recent years, liberal dogma permeates, indeed suffocates, education in this country. Other than some passing references to the Founding Fathers (derided, of course, as racists and elitists, unworthy of our current age), I was not exposed to any of the wellsprings of conservative thought and scholarship. On the other hand, I became quite familiar with the theories of Karl Marx, and of his modern day followers who perceive invidious "inequalities" of race, class, gender, and sexual orientation in all aspects of American life, from its earliest beginnings to the present day.

Fortunately, my youthful do-goodism was rooted in patriotism, in my fervent, heartfelt belief that the United States of America is the greatest country in the world, and the greatest country the world has ever known. As I grew older, I began to understand precisely what it is that makes America great—her freedom. It is the unique American commitment to freedom that has produced the richest, strongest, most influential civilization in all of human history. It is America's commitment to freedom that produced the Revolution of 1776, ended slavery, won two world wars, and defeated the communist menace.

For more than two centuries, America has served as a beacon of hope to the people of the world. Yet beginning with the counterculture movement of the 1960s, America has been under attack, first by radical and now by liberal elements within our own society. I finally turned away from the Democratic Party when I realized that the people who make up that party, and the ideas and policies they support, are at their core anti-American. Democrats are ashamed of our history, distrustful of our freedoms, and opposed to our values and traditions. Rather than providing an example to the world of a society built on freedom, Democrats seek to re-make America in the image of European and Third World socialism. To accomplish this goal, they actively work to weaken America's political, economic, and military might, and—even more devastatingly—to undermine the country's belief in itself as "a shining city upon a hill." Because I believe in the American dream—and believe that dream is worth fostering and defending—I became a Republican.

Individualism. I am a Republican because I believe first and foremost in the individual as the foundation stone of society. Not groups, or classes, or even "humanity" itself, but flesh-and-blood human beings. The genius of America has been to unleash each individual's energies, interests, ambitions, and desires in a system of free market capitalism that has produced an unparalleled record of growth, productivity, innovation, and wealth. Starting as a small English outpost in a hostile and undeveloped land, America became, within 100 years of the Revolution of 1776, the world's leading agricultural, industrial, and scientific nation, and remains so to this day. Americans, rich and poor alike, enjoy a standard of living superior to that of any other country on earth. Even "poor" Americans have higher rates of home and automobile ownership, consume more food and energy, and enjoy more modern amenities than "middle class" people of other developed countries. And unlike the centrally-planned economies of Europe, the American economy remains vibrant and strong, promising to bring us even greater wealth and opportunity in the future.

Inextricably bound to America's system of free enterprise, is our system of constitutional democracy—the only political system known to man in which the individual's rights and interests are protected, not suppressed, by the government. Indeed, the very purpose of government is to protect those rights that inhere in every individual, regardless of race, gender, creed, or station in life. Our Founding Fathers taught the world this lesson many years go: "We hold these truths to be self-evident, that all men are created equal, that they are endowed by their Creator with certain unalienable rights, that among these are Life, Liberty, and the Pursuit of Happiness. That to secure these rights, Governments are instituted among men, deriving their just powers from the consent of the governed."

The American political and economic tradition thus is rooted in individual rights, including freedom of speech, freedom of association, private property, and freedom of contract. The Republican Party supports and defends these rights. The Democratic Party does not. The Republican Party recognizes that rights are not granted to citizens by government, but inhere in each of us as individual human beings. That each of us has the right to speak our minds, to join together with others of our own choosing, and to pursue our own self-interest. Democrats vehemently disagree. Their prevailing philosophy is premised upon group rights, not individual rights. Instead of a society populated by unique individuals of all different types, Democrats see only "women" or "minorities" or—through rather differently colored glasses—"white males." Whether in the form of speech codes, affirmative action programs, tax-and-spend policies, or government regulations, Democrats consistently seek to limit the freedom of individuals to benefit the groups they favor. The inevitable results of this misguided philosophy are stagnation, mediocrity, and injustice.

Limited Government. I am a Republican because I subscribe to the maxim (famously endorsed by Henry David Thoreau), "That government is best which governs least." The Republican Party believes that the proper role of government—especially the federal government—is a limited one. These limits are prescribed by the Constitution itself, which delegates specific, enumerated powers to the federal government and reserves the rest to the people and the states. Among the powers properly exercised by the federal government are establishing a republican political system, ensuring the national defense, maintaining the free flow of commerce, guaranteeing the equal protection of the laws, and promoting the general welfare (for example, through pure food and drug laws). While it is impossible to identify in advance the entire universe of legitimate federal power, one thing is clear: The Framers of the Constitution intended to create a political, economic, and legal framework that maximized individual freedom, so that individuals—not government—decide how best to pursue their own happiness.

As Thomas Jefferson warned: "The course of history shows that as a government grows, liberty decreases." After a century scarred by the twin totalitarian nightmares of communism and nazism, Jefferson's warning is as relevant today as it was two hundred years ago. The Republican Party recognizes that we must be ever vigilant to confine government to its proper sphere, so that the benefits of freedom can be enjoyed by all. This includes not only limiting the size and scope of the federal government, but reining in an activist federal judiciary and returning power to state and local governments that are closer to the people. In sharp contrast, the Democratic Party is wedded to a statist vision, proposing failed socialist solutions to every "problem" (real or imagined) in the country. Recall Hillary Clinton's health care debacle. Ironically, while Democrats seek to move America towards greater and greater socialism, socialist countries across the globe are moving in the opposite direction—towards individual freedom, private property, and free market capitalism. The Republican position.

Personal Responsibility. I am a Republican because I believe that the onus of responsibility for success or failure in life rests with the individual, not with government or "society." With very few exceptions, each of us is capable of living a decent, productive, satisfying life. This does not mean, of course, that we all can be rich or famous. But it does mean—as millions of immigrants attest—that there is an abundance of opportunity in our society for anyone who desires it, who is willing to work hard and "play by the rules." The policies of the Republican Party fundamentally are aimed at fostering this kind of effort and success—the very effort and success that built this country into what it is today—by promoting free enterprise, lowering taxes, and reducing the amount of burdensome and unnecessary government regulation.

Republicans seek to encourage and reward individual initiative and achievement because history proves that is the only way to grow the economy, increase wealth and opportunity, and raise the standard of living for everyone. As the saying goes, "a rising tide lifts all boats." The Democratic Party does not share this vision. Instead of growth and progress, they see limits and "crises" (of poverty, energy, health care, and so on, ad infinitum); instead of merit, they see "discrimination." In short, Democrats do not believe in the essential fairness and efficiency of the free market. As a result, the entire Democratic project for the past 35 years has served one overarching goal: the forced redistribution of wealth through confiscatory taxation on the most productive members of our society. Indeed, if elected President, John Kerry promises to increase taxes on "the wealthiest Americans"—despite the fact that the top 10% of taxpayers already pay 50% of all federal taxes!

The choice between the Republican Party and the Democratic Party is often described as the choice between equality of opportunity and equality of results, between "leveling up" and "leveling down." Regardless of the issue—jobs, education, health care, welfare, etc.—Democrats propose to take from some citizens and give to others. In this, they are no different from totalitarians the world over ("From each according to his ability, to each according to his need . . ."). Although Republicans are sensitive to the basic needs of the poorest and least capable members of our society, they nevertheless reject this zero-sum approach to governance. They recognize that we all are made better off by living in a dynamic, competitive society that promotes effort and achievement based on merit, rather than one that uses government coercion to allocate "opportunities" and redistribute wealth.

Teddy Roosevelt summed it up best in his famous speech to the Sorbonne in 1910: "There should, so far as possible, be equality of opportunity to render service; but just so long as there is inequality of service, there should and must be inequality of reward. . . . To say that the thriftless, the lazy, the vicious, the incapable, ought to have the reward given to those who are far-sighted, capable, and upright, is to say what is not true and can not be true. Let us try to level up, but let us beware of the evil of leveling down. If a man stumbles, it is a good thing to help him to his feet. Every one of us needs a helping hand now and then. But if a man lies down, it is a waste of time to try to carry him; and it is a very bad thing for every one, if we make men feel that the same reward will come to those who shirk their work and to those who do it."

Strong National Defense. I am a Republican because I believe in the vital importance of a strong national defense. As the leader of the free world, the United States must always have the strongest, most advanced ground, sea, air, and nuclear forces. The atrophy that occurred in the 1970s and 1990s, as defense spending was cannibalized to fund social programs, cannot be allowed to happen again. Social programs did not defeat the nazis and communists; they will not defeat the Islamofacists. Republicans understand that national defense and military preparedness must be the federal government's top priority.

The dangers we face today are as deadly as ever, and call for a swift, resolute, and powerful response. President Bush and the Republican leadership are up to the task. The same cannot be said of the Democrats. Under the guise of a false and dangerous "internationalism," Democrats would abdicate American leadership and subordinate American sovereignty to the

United Nations, a corrupt and ineffectual organization dominated by Third World dictatorships. Worse, they would let the people of France and Germany—well-known for their disdain of American society—exercise a veto over American foreign policy. Why? Because Democrats distrust their own country, and seek assurances through phony international "consensus" that America is doing the right thing. As if the support of Great Britain, Australia, Japan, Italy, the former Soviet-bloc nations of Eastern Europe, and numerous other countries, means nothing. Republicans know that Americans do not need the approval of the French or Germans (let alone the Russians or Chinese) to do what is in our—and the free world's—best interest. Unlike Democrats, Republicans have confidence in American leadership and believe the world is better off because of it.

Civic Virtue. I am a Republican because I agree with our Founding Fathers that "morality is a necessary spring of popular government" (George Washington) and "only a virtuous people are capable of freedom" (Benjamin Franklin). The Republican Party takes seriously the moral conditions necessary for a free and prosperous society, what the Founding Fathers called "civic virtue." Among the values that make up civic virtue are hard work, thrift, temperance, honesty, and respect for others. Republicans understand that without these values, individuals and communities become mired in poverty, disorder, and crime. So that each of us can enjoy the benefits of freedom, the Republican Party supports policies aimed at promoting and strengthening these values in all Americans.

The difference between the two parties on this point could not be clearer. Where the Republican Party believes in right and wrong, the Democratic Party advocates moral relativism, which it dresses up in the rhetoric of "compassion" and "choice." The results of this philosophy—the terrible effects of which can be seen in many parts of our country today—are profligacy and dependency, promiscuity and illegitimacy, vandalism and violence, failure and lack of hope. All subsidized, of course, by the vast majority of hard-working, law-abiding citizens whose values—the very values that bring success in life (even for liberals!)—Democrats reject as outmoded and "oppressive." But Democrats do not merely oppose these values, they actively work to destroy the institutions that sustain them (for example, the Boy Scouts). The Republican Party stands opposed to these efforts. Republicans understand that America is the great country she is today because of her traditional moral values—and only by preserving these values can we ensure America's greatness tomorrow.

Patriotism. Ultimately, as I stated at the beginning of this essay, I am a Republican because I love my country and believe, to quote Teddy Roosevelt one more time, that "no people on earth have more cause to be thankful than ours." There has never been a freer or happier or more successful people in all of history. From being the first nation to reject monarchy, to being the first to put a man on the moon, the story of the United States of America is one of freedom, prosperity, and progress. My heart swells with gratitude each time I reflect that I too am part of this story, a beneficiary of this great legacy. As Ronald Reagan reminded us in one of his last public addresses: "For two hundred years, we have been set apart by our faith in the ideals of democracy, of free men and free markets, and of the extraordinary possibilities that lie within seemingly ordinary men and women." I believe in these ideals. This is why I am a Republican. This is why I will be voting for George W. Bush this November.

Originally published in AmericanDaily.com on 8/31/04.
You can email your comments to Steven M. Warshawsky at the following email address:
smwarshawsky@hotmail.com.

Steven M. Warshawsky is an attorney in New York City

Green Party Pushes Good Governance
by Daryl A. Northrop

As the election draws near, Iowans are asking themselves: Which candidate do I trust? Which political party do I believe in? Who will stand up for me?

There is a real choice at the polls: the Green Party. Across the United States, citizens are joining and forming Green Parties that stand for grassroots democracy, social justice, sound ecology and nonviolence.

I am running for the U.S. Senate as a Green in Iowa. It is high time Iowans have someone in Congress to represent our voices, our needs and our aspirations. It is my sincere belief that political campaigns should be contests of big ideas, not big fund-raising contests. In the common parlance, there is a word for large sums of money that are given to public officials: bribes.

Some say that casting a vote for a Green Party candidate is a waste. I disagree. Your vote is only wasted when you end up casting it for a candidate you do not like or for a candidate who is incapable of representing citizens.

A vote for a Green Party candidate is an investment in democracy, not only for the election on Nov. 2, but for the future. Greens are building a progressive, people's party that is free from the influence of special interests. To grow that party, and to give a voice to the people of this state and this nation, we will continue to participate in, and win, elections.

Democrats and Republicans label this "spoiling." What they call spoiling, we call participating. Every citizen has the right to run for public office, and if this somehow is a problem, then the solution is not to block people or parties from participating, but to improve our voting system. Greens support instant-runoff voting, a majoritarian system that allows voters to rank-order the candidates by preference. After all the first-choice preferences are counted, if an individual candidate gets 50 percent plus one vote or more, they win. If no candidates receive a majority of the vote, the "instant runoff" occurs. The candidate who received the lowest amount of votes is eliminated, and those votes transfer to the second preference candidate whom each individual voter specified. The votes are counted again to determine the winner. This system solves the spoiler problem on the left and right of the political spectrum.

How is the Green Party different from the Republicans or Democrats?

Foremost, we only represent people. We refuse all special-interest money. This ensures that our party and candidates are not bought and paid for by corporate interests that put profit over citizens' needs. When our elected representatives accept millions of dollars each year from special interests, they end up forsaking citizens like you and me.

Second, we base all policies and actions on Ten Key Values: diversity, social justice, grassroots democracy, gender equity, community, decentralization, environmentalism, nonviolence, responsibility and future focus.

In the United States, Greens stand for policies that benefit all Americans: single-payer universal health care, sustainable agriculture, energy independence, peaceful foreign policy and an educational system that invests in our children and pays teachers like the professionals they are.

The Green Party has grown dramatically in eight years. In 1996, 10 states had organized Green Parties and 87 Greens holding elected office. Now, 44 states have organized parties with 207 Greens holding office, from the mayor of New Paltz, N.Y., to the Emmetsburg, Ia., city council, to the president of the board of supervisors in San Francisco, Calif. Worldwide, Greens are active in 90 countries across six continents. The Green Party represents a people's movement toward good governance.

DARYL A. NORTHROP of Des Moines is the Iowa Green Party candidate for U.S. Senate. His Web site is www.NorthropForSenate.org.

Originally published in the Des Moines Register, October 15, 2004.

Why I am a Democrat
by David Burge

I sometimes hear the question, "Why are you a Democrat?" and frankly, I have to laugh. Laugh and laugh, because perhaps this person may tire of my laughing, and he will eventually wander off. Sometimes I ponder seriously when I hear this question, because I'll look around and around and there's nobody there asking the question. Why am I a Democrat?

I am a Democrat because I believe everyone deserves a chance. And if necessary, a second chance. And if, by the eighth or ninth chance, this guy needs another chance, I mean, *come on*. This guy is *due*.

I am a Democrat because I believe in helping those in need. All of us, you and I, have an obligation to those less fortunate. You go first, okay? I'm a little short this week.

I am a Democrat because I believe in the equality of all people, regardless of their race. That is why I think we should give free medical degrees to minorities because, well, duh. Like any of *those* types are going to make it through medical school.

I am a Democrat because I fervently believe in tolerance. Tolerance is critical in our diverse society, and if you have a problem with that, mister, then I will inform the authorities and I bet that after a few hours in their "special room" you too will agree that tolerance is critical.

I am a Democrat because I believe that we should take our noses out of other people's bedrooms. I say we move the noses to their banks and storage sheds and scout troops, and so forth.

I am a Democrat because I hold sacred freedom of the press, as well as freedom of the TV and freedom of the movie. Where I draw the line is freedom of the talk radio, and don't even get me started about that damn Internet business.

I am a Democrat because I recognize that education is important. Very, very, extremely very important. We must increase spending on education and enact important education reforms, such as eliminating standardized tests. Because we can never hope to measure this beautiful, elusive, important thing we call education.

I am a Democrat because I believe in the separation of church and state. We must stop the religious extremists who want school-sanctioned prayers. Now, you tell me - with all that chanting and praying and incense-burning going on, how can our kids concentrate on the big condom-and-banana midterm?

I am a Democrat because I believe in the rights of women, be they lawyers or housewives or skanky interns. For too long women have been the victims of discrimination, and we must target programs to help these women, and also the various people who have descended from women.

I am a Democrat because I believe in women's right to choose. I mean, not a church school or a tax shelter, or something like that, obviously. Let's be reasonable.

I am a Democrat because I believe in the rule of law. Or, at least, lawyers. Because hey, according to my attorney, I *could* have been on the Number 7 bus when it crashed yesterday. As far as you know.

I am a Democrat because I believe a healthy economy depends on good jobs at good wages. So fork 'em over, you fat bastard boss man.

I am a Democrat because I believe the government should step in to create good jobs when that fat bastard boss man moves my good job to Mexico. Hey, I know! Maybe we can take all the money that boss man spends on non-job-creating stuff, like solid gold yachts and mink spats, and use *that* money to create jobs.

I am a Democrat because I fear the power of giant unrestrained monopolies, such as Microsoft, Nike, Parker Brothers, Univac and the Erie Canal Company. The government must wage an unrelenting, all-out war to crush these scary monopolies to a pulp before they get too powerful.

I am a Democrat because I believe in a strong military. Strong, yes, but caring and thoughtful too, and ready to face new challenges. A military that enjoys long strolls on the beach, cuddling in front of a warm fire, unafraid to show its vulnerable side. Must be NS/DDF.

I am a Democrat because I believe there is too much violence in society, especially in our schools. To avoid another Columbine tragedy, we should have mellow "rap" sessions with at-risk teens, such as the Goths. The violence will only end after the teen Goths see that we adults really care, and are "hip" to their groovy teen Goth scene.

I am a Democrat because I believe in campaign finance reform. Sadly, our politics are dominated by advertisements, paid for by the contributions of giant corporations. All too often, these drown out legitimate grassroots opinions, like the kind heard on TimeWarner-AOL-CNN, TimesCorp, or Disney-ABC.

I am a Democrat because I believe in public support of the arts. By "the arts," I of course mean those things made by, or excreted by, an artist of some sort. It is especially important that art be provocative and take controversial stances, like opposing Jesse Helms, and so on.

I am a Democrat because I believe in the environment and conservation. For instance, we must raise the price of gasoline, like they do in Europe, to increase conservation. If we don't, there will soon be a big gas shortage, and this will mean higher gasoline prices for you and me.

I am a Democrat because I detest greed. Especially the sickening greed of those who struck it rich in the 1980s, and greedily refuse to give me any of their stuff.

I am a Democrat because I... hey look! A new episode of Survivor! Geez, I hope they don't vote off Jenna, she's my favorite.

http://iowahawk.typepad.com/iowahawk/2003/12/why_i_am_a_demo.html

Chapter 9
Questions

1. What political persuasion do you have now, or how would you define yourself in political terms if you had to choose? Why?

2. Have you ever changed your political orientations or can you imagine every doing so? Why, or why not?

CHAPTER 10
CAMPAIGNS, CANDIDATES, AND ELECTIONS

Dueling speeches by Arizona Senator John McCain at the 2004 Republican National Convention and by former President Bill Clinton at the 2004 Democratic National Convention show major differences in the kind of messages that the two major parties want to convey to you and others whom they want to attract. As you read these selections, look carefully for hidden messages that are designed to advertise for each party's position.

Speech by Arizona Senator John McCain at the Republican National Convention, New York, NY, August 30, 2004

Thank you, Lindsey [Graham], and, thank you, my fellow Republicans.

I'm truly grateful for the privilege of addressing you. This week, millions of Americans, not all Republicans, weigh our claim on their support for the two men who have led our country in these challenging times with moral courage and firm resolve.

So I begin with the words of a great American from the other party, given at his party's convention in the year I was born.

My purpose is not imitation, for I can't match his eloquence, but respect for the relevance in our time of his rousing summons to greatness of an earlier generation of Americans.

In a time of deep distress at home, as tyranny strangled the aspirations to liberty of millions, and as war clouds gathered in the West and East, Franklin Delano Roosevelt accepted his party's nomination by observing: "There is a mysterious cycle in human events. To some generations much is given. Of other generations much is expected. This generation of Americans has a rendezvous with destiny."

The awful events of September 11, 2001 declared a war we were vaguely aware of, but hadn't really comprehended how near the threat was, and how terrible were the plans of our enemies.

It's a big thing, this war.

It's a fight between a just regard for human dignity and a malevolent force that defiles an honorable religion by disputing God's love for every soul on earth. It's a fight between right and wrong, good and evil.

And should our enemies acquire for their arsenal the chemical, biological and nuclear weapons they seek, this war will become a much bigger thing.

So it is, whether we wished it or not, that we have come to the test of our generation, to our rendezvous with destiny.

And much is expected of us.

We are engaged in a hard struggle against a cruel and determined adversary.

Our enemies have made clear the danger they pose to our security and to the very essence of our culture...liberty. Only the most deluded of us could doubt the necessity of this war.

Like all wars, this one will have its ups and downs. But we must fight. We must.

The sacrifices borne in our defense are not shared equally by all Americans.

But all Americans must share a resolve to see this war through to a just end.

We must not be complacent at moments of success, and we must not despair over setbacks.

We must learn from our mistakes, improve on our successes, and vanquish this unpardonable enemy.

If we do less, we will fail the one mission no American generation has ever failed...to provide to our children a stronger, better country than the one we were blessed to inherit.

Remember how we felt when the serenity of a bright September morning was destroyed by a savage atrocity so hostile to all human virtue we could scarcely imagine any human being capable of it.

We were united.

First, in sorrow and anger.

Then in recognition we were attacked not for a wrong we had done, but for who we are - a people united in a kinship of ideals, committed to the notion that the people are sovereign, not governments, not armies, not a pitiless, inhumane theocracy, not kings, mullahs or tyrants, but the people.

In that moment, we were not different races. We were not poor or rich. We were not Democrat or Republican, liberal or conservative. We were not two countries.

We were Americans.

All of us, despite the differences that enliven our politics, are united in the one big idea that freedom is our birthright and its defense is always our first responsibility.

All other responsibilities come second.

We must not lose sight of that as we debate who among us should bear the greatest responsibility for keeping us safe and free.

We must, whatever our disagreements, stick together in this great challenge of our time.

My friends in the Democratic Party—and I'm fortunate to call many of them my friends—assure us they share the conviction that winning the war against terrorism is our government's most important obligation.

I don't doubt their sincerity.

They emphasize that military action alone won't protect us, that this war has many fronts: in courts, financial institutions, in the shadowy world of intelligence, and in diplomacy.

They stress that America needs the help of her friends to combat an evil that threatens us all, that our alliances are as important to victory as are our armies.

We agree.

And, as we've been a good friend to other countries in moments of shared perils, so we have good reason to expect their solidarity with us in this struggle.

That is what the President believes.

And, thanks to his efforts we have received valuable assistance from many good friends around the globe, even if we have, at times, been disappointed with the reactions of some.

I don't doubt the sincerity of my Democratic friends. And they should not doubt ours.

Our President will work with all nations willing to help us defeat this scourge that afflicts us all. War is an awful business. The lives of a nation's finest patriots are sacrificed. Innocent people suffer. Commerce is disrupted, economies are damaged.

Strategic interests shielded by years of statecraft are endangered as the demands of war and diplomacy conflict.

However just the cause, we should shed a tear for all that is lost when war claims its wages from us. But there is no avoiding this war. We tried that, and our reluctance cost us dearly. And while this war has many components, we can't make victory on the battlefield harder to achieve so that our diplomacy is easier to conduct.

That is not just an expression of our strength.

It's a measure of our wisdom.

That's why I commend to my country the re-election of President Bush, and the steady, experienced, public-spirited man who serves as our Vice-President, Dick Cheney. Four years ago, in Philadelphia, I spoke of my confidence that President Bush would accept the responsibilities that come with America's distinction as the world's only superpower.

I promised he would not let America "retreat behind empty threats, false promises and uncertain diplomacy;" that he would "confidently defend our interests and values wherever they are threatened."

I knew my confidence was well placed when I watched him stand on the rubble of the World Trade Center, with his arm around a hero of September 11th, and in our moment of mourning and anger, strengthen our unity and summon our resolve by promising to right this terrible wrong, and to stand up and fight for the values we hold dear.

He promised our enemies would soon hear from us. And so they did.

So they did.

He ordered American forces to Afghanistan and took the fight to our enemies, and away from our shores, seriously injuring al Qaeda and destroying the regime that gave them safe haven.

He worked effectively to secure the cooperation of Pakistan, a relationship that's critical to our success against al Qaeda.

He encouraged other friends to recognize the peril that terrorism posed for them, and won their help in apprehending many of those who would attack us again, and in helping to freeze the assets they used to fund their bloody work.

After years of failed diplomacy and limited military pressure to restrain Saddam Hussein, President Bush made the difficult decision to liberate Iraq. Those who criticize that decision would have us believe that the choice was between a status quo that was well enough left alone and war. But there was no status quo to be left alone.

The years of keeping Saddam in a box were coming to a close. The international consensus that he be kept isolated and unarmed had eroded to the point that many critics of military action had decided the time had come again to do business with Saddam, despite his near daily attacks on our pilots, and his refusal, until his last day in power, to allow the unrestricted inspection of his arsenal. Our choice wasn't between a benign status quo and the bloodshed of war.

It was between war and a graver threat. Don't let anyone tell you otherwise. Not our critics abroad. Not our political opponents.

And certainly not a disingenuous film maker who would have us believe that Saddam's Iraq was an oasis of peace when in fact it was a place of indescribable cruelty, torture chambers, mass graves and prisons that destroyed the lives of the small children held inside their walls.

Whether or not Saddam possessed the terrible weapons he once had and used, freed from international pressure and the threat of military action, he would have acquired them again.

The central security concern of our time is to keep such devastating weapons beyond the reach of terrorists who can't be dissuaded from using them by the threat of mutual destruction.

We couldn't afford the risk posed by an unconstrained Saddam in these dangerous times.

By destroying his regime we gave hope to people long oppressed that if they have the courage to fight for it, they may live in peace and freedom.

Most importantly, our efforts may encourage the people of a region that has never known peace or freedom or lasting stability that they may someday possess these rights.

I believe as strongly today as ever, the mission was necessary, achievable and noble.

For his determination to undertake it, and for his unflagging resolve to see it through to a just end, President Bush deserves not only our support, but our admiration.

As the President rightly reminds us, we are safer than we were on September 11th, but we're not yet safe. We are still closer to the beginning than the end of this fight. We need a leader with the experience to make the tough decisions and the resolve to stick with them; a leader who will keep us moving forward even if it is easier to rest. And this President will not rest until America is stronger and safer still, and this hateful iniquity is vanquished. He has been tested and has risen to the most important challenge of our time, and I salute him.

I salute his determination to make this world a better, safer, freer place.

He has not wavered. He has not flinched from the hard choices. He will not yield.

And neither will we.

I said earlier that the sacrifices in this war will not be shared equally by all Americans. The President is the first to observe, most of the sacrifices fall, as they have before, to the brave men and women of our Armed Forces. We may be good citizens, but make no mistake, they are the very best of us.

It's an honor to live in a country that is so well and so bravely defended by such patriots.

May God bless them, the living and the fallen, as He has blessed us with their service.

For their families, for their friends, for America, for mankind they sacrifice to affirm that right makes might; that good triumphs over evil; that freedom is stronger than tyranny; that love is greater than hate.

It is left to us to keep their generous benefaction alive, and our blessed, beautiful country worthy of their courage.

We should be thankful—for the privilege.

Our country's security doesn't depend on the heroism of every citizen. But we have to be worthy of the sacrifices made on our behalf.

We have to love our freedom, not just for the material benefits it provides, not just for the autonomy it guarantees us, but for the goodness it makes possible.

We have to love it as much, if not as heroically, as the brave Americans who defend us at the risk, and often the cost of their lives.

No American alive today will ever forget what happened on the morning of September 11th.

That day was the moment when the pendulum of history swung toward a new era.

The opening chapter was tinged with great sadness and uncertainty.

It shook us from our complacency in the belief that the Cold War's end had ushered in a time of global tranquility. But an absence of complacency should not provoke an absence of confidence. What our enemies have sought to destroy is beyond their reach. It cannot be taken from us. It can only be surrendered.

My friends, we are again met on the field of political competition with our fellow countrymen.

It is more than appropriate, it is necessary that even in times of crisis we have these contests, and engage in spirited disagreement over the shape and course of our government.

We have nothing to fear from each other.

We are arguing over the means to better secure our freedom, and promote the general welfare.

But it should remain an argument among friends who share an unshaken belief in our great cause, and in the goodness of each other.

We are Americans first, Americans last, Americans always.

Let us argue our differences.

But remember we are not enemies, but comrades in a war against a real enemy, and take courage from the knowledge that our military superiority is matched only by the superiority of our ideals, and our unconquerable love for them.

Our adversaries are weaker than us in arms and men, but weaker still in causes. They fight to express a hatred for all that is good in humanity.

We fight for love of freedom and justice, a love that is invincible. Keep that faith. Keep your courage. Stick together. Stay strong.

Do not yield. Do not flinch. Stand up. Stand up with our President and fight.

We're Americans.

We're Americans, and we'll never surrender.

They will.

Public Domain: accessed at http://www.gopconvention.com/

Speech by President Bill Clinton at the Democratic National Convention, Boston, MA, July 26, 2004

Thank you. I am honored to share the podium with my Senator, though I think I should be introducing her. I'm proud of her and so grateful to the people of New York that the best public servant in our family is still on the job and grateful to all of you, especially my friends from Arkansas, for the chance you gave us to serve our country in the White House.

I am also honored to share this night with President Carter, who has inspired the world with his work for peace, democracy, and human rights. And with Al Gore, my friend and partner for eight years, who played such a large role in building the prosperity and progress that brought America into the 21st century, who showed incredible grace and patriotism under pressure, and who is the living embodiment that every vote counts—and must be counted in every state in America.

Tonight I speak as a citizen, returning to the role I have played for most of my life as a foot soldier in the fight for our future, as we nominate a true New England patriot for president. The state that gave us John Adams and John Kennedy has now given us John Kerry, a good man, a great senator, a visionary leader. We are constantly told America is deeply divided. But all Americans value freedom, faith, and family. We all honor the service and sacrifice of our men and women in uniform in Iraq, Afghanistan and around the world.

We all want good jobs, good schools, health care, safe streets, a clean environment. We all want our children to grow up in a secure America leading the world toward a peaceful future. Our differences are in how we can best achieve these things, in a time of unprecedented change. Therefore, we Democrats will bring the American people a positive campaign, arguing not who's good and who's bad, but what is the best way to build the safe, prosperous world our children deserve.

The 21st century is marked by serious security threats, serious economic challenges, and serious problems like global warming and the AIDS epidemic. But it is also full of enormous opportunities—to create millions of high paying jobs in clean energy, and biotechnology; to restore the manufacturing base and reap the benefits of the global economy through our diversity and our commitment to decent labor and environmental standards everywhere; and to create a world where we can celebrate our religious and racial differences, because our common humanity matters more.

To build that kind of world we must make the right choices; and we must have a president who will lead the way. Democrats and Republicans have very different and honestly held ideas on that choices we should make, rooted in fundamentally different views of how we should meet our common challenges at home and how we should play our role in the world. Democrats want to build an America of shared responsibilities and shared opportunities and more global cooperation, acting alone only when we must.

We think the role of government is to give people the tools and conditions to make the most of their lives. Republicans believe in an America run by the right people, their people, in a world in which we act unilaterally when we can, and cooperate when we have to.

They think the role of government is to concentrate wealth and power in the hands of those who embrace their political, economic, and social views, leaving ordinary citizens to fend for themselves on matters like health care and retirement security. Since most Americans are not that far to the right, they have to portray us Democrats as unacceptable, lacking in strength and values. In other words, they need a divided America. But Americans long to be united. After 9/11, we all wanted to be one nation, strong in the fight against terror. The president had a great opportunity to bring us together under his slogan of compassionate conservatism and to unite the world in common cause against terror.

Instead, he and his congressional allies made a very different choice: to use the moment of unity to push America too far to the right and to walk away from our allies, not only in attacking Iraq before the weapons inspectors finished their jobs, but in withdrawing American support for the Climate Change Treaty, the International Court for war criminals, the ABM treaty, and even the Comprehensive Nuclear Test Ban Treaty.

Now they are working to develop two new nuclear weapons which they say we might use first. At home, the President and the Republican Congress have made equally fateful choices indeed. For the first time ever when America was on a war footing, there were two huge tax cuts, nearly half of which went to the top one percent. I'm in that group now for the first time in my life.

When I was in office, the Republicans were pretty mean to me. When I left and made money, I became part of the most important group in the world to them. At first I thought I should send them a thank you note—until I realized they were sending you the bill.

They protected my tax cuts while:
- Withholding promised funding for the Leave No Child Behind Act, leaving over 2 million children behind
- Cutting 140,000 unemployed workers out of job training
- 100,000 working families out of child care assistance
- 300,000 poor children out of after school programs
- Raising out of pocket healthcare costs to veterans
- Weakening or reversing important environmental advances for clean air and the preservation of our forests.

Everyone had to sacrifice except the wealthiest Americans, who wanted to do their part but were asked only to expend the energy necessary to open the envelopes containing our tax cuts. If you agree with these choices, you should vote to return them to the White House and Congress. If not, take a look at John Kerry, John Edwards and the Democrats.

In this year's budget, the White House wants to cut off federal funding for 88,000 uniformed police, including more than 700 on the New York City police force who put their lives on the line on 9/11. As gang violence is rising and we look for terrorists in our midst, Congress and the President are also about to allow the ten-year-old ban on assault weapons to expire. Our crime policy was to put more police on the streets and take assault weapons off the streets. It brought eight years of declining crime and violence. Their policy is the reverse, they're taking police off the streets and putting assault weapons back on the streets. If you agree with their choices, vote to continue them. If not, join John Kerry, John Edwards and the Democrats in making America safer, smarter, and stronger.

On Homeland Security, Democrats tried to double the number of containers at ports and airports checked for Weapons of Mass Destruction. The one billion dollar cost would have been paid for by reducing the tax cut of 200,000 millionaires by five thousand dollars each. Almost all 200,000 of us would have been glad to pay 5,000 dollars to make the nearly 300 million Americans safer—but the measure failed because the White House and the Republican leadership in the House decided my tax cut was more important- If you agree with that choice, re-elect them. If not, give John Kerry and John Edwards a chance.

These policies have turned the projected 5.8 trillion dollar surplus we left—enough to pay for the baby boomers retirement—into a projected debt of nearly 5 trillion dollars, with a 400 plus billion dollar deficit this year and for years to come. How do they pay for it? First by taking the monthly surplus in Social Security payments and endorsing the checks of working people over to me to cover my tax cut. But it's not enough. They are borrowing the rest from foreign governments, mostly Japan and China. Sure, they're competing with us for good jobs but how can we enforce our trade laws against our bankers? If you think it's good policy to pay for my tax cut with the Social Security checks of working men and women, and borrowed money from China, vote for them. If not, John Kerry's your man.

We Americans must choose for President one of two strong men who both love our country, but who have very different worldviews: Democrats favor shared responsibility, shared opportunity, and more global cooperation. Republicans favor concentrated wealth and power, leaving people to fend for themselves and more unilateral action. I think we're right for two reasons: First, America works better when all people have a chance to live their dreams. Second, we live in an interdependent world in which we can't kill, jail, or occupy all our potential adversaries, so we have to both fight terror and build a world with more partners and fewer terrorists. We tried it their way for twelve years, our way for eight, and then their way for four more.

By the only test that matters, whether people were better off when we finished than when we started, our way works better—it produced over 22 million good jobs, rising incomes, and 100 times as many people moving out of poverty into the middle class. It produced more health care, the largest increase in college aid in 50 years, record home ownership, a cleaner environment, three surpluses in a row, a modernized defense force, strong efforts against terror, and an America respected as a world leader for peace, security and prosperity.

More importantly, we have great new champions in John Kerry and John Edwards. Two good men with wonderful wives—Teresa a generous and wise woman who understands the world we are trying to shape. And Elizabeth, a lawyer and mother who understands the lives we are all trying to lift. Here is what I know about John Kerry. During the Vietnam War, many young men—including the current president, the vice president and me—could have gone to Vietnam but didn't. John Kerry came from a privileged background and could have avoided it too. Instead he said, send me.

When they sent those swift-boats up the river in Vietnam, and told them their job was to draw hostile fire—to show the American flag and bait the enemy to come out and fight—John Kerry said, send me. When it was time to heal the wounds of war and normalize relations with Vietnam—and to demand an accounting of the POWs and MIAs we lost there—John Kerry said, send me.

When we needed someone to push the cause of inner-city kids struggling to avoid a life of crime, or to bring the benefits of high technology to ordinary Americans, or to clean the environment in a way that creates jobs, or to give small businesses a better chance to make it, John Kerry said send me.

Tonight my friends, I ask you to join me for the next 100 days in telling John Kerry's story and promoting his plans. Let every person in this hall and all across America say to him what he has always said to America: Send Me. The bravery that the men who fought by his side saw in battle I've seen in the political arena. When I was President, John Kerry showed courage and conviction on crime, on welfare reform, on balancing the budget at a time when those priorities were not exactly a way to win a popularity contest in our party.

He took tough positions on tough problems. John Kerry knows who he is and where he's going. He has the experience, the character, the ideas and the values to be a great President. In a time of change he has two other important qualities: his insatiable curiosity to understand the forces shaping our lives, and a willingness to hear the views even of those who disagree with him. Therefore his choices will be full of both conviction and common sense.

He proved that when he picked a tremendous partner in John Edwards. Everybody talks about John Edwards' energy, intellect, and charisma. The important thing is how he has used his talents to improve the lives of people who—like John himself—had to work hard for all they've got. He has always championed the cause of people too often left out or left behind. And that's what he'll do as our Vice President.

Their opponents will tell you to be afraid of John Kerry and John Edwards, because they won't stand up to the terrorists—don't you believe it. Strength and wisdom are not conflicting values—they go hand in hand. John Kerry has both. His first priority will be keeping America safe. Remember the scripture: Be Not Afraid.

John Kerry and John Edwards, have good ideas:
- To make this economy work again for middle-class Americans;
- To restore fiscal responsibility;
- To save Social Security; to make healthcare more affordable and college more available;
- To free us from dependence on foreign oil and create new jobs in clean energy;
- To rally the world to win the war on terror and to make more friends and fewer terrorists.

At every turning point in our history we the people have chosen unity over division, heeding our founders' call to America's eternal mission: to form a more perfect union, to widen the circle of opportunity, deepen the reach of freedom, and strengthen the bonds of community.

It happened because we made the right choices. In the early days of the republic, America was at a crossroads much like it is today, deeply divided over whether or not to build a real nation with a national economy, and a national legal system. We chose a more perfect union.

In the Civil War, America was at a crossroads, divided over whether to save the union and end slavery—we chose a more perfect union. In the 1960s, America was at a crossroads, divided again over civil rights and women's rights. Again, we chose a more perfect union. As I said in 1992, we're all in this together; we have an obligation both to work hard and to help our fellow citizens, both to fight terror and to build a world with more cooperation and less terror. Now again, it is time to choose.

Since we're all in the same boat, let us chose as the captain of our ship a brave good man who knows how to steer a vessel though troubled waters to the calm seas and clear skies of our more perfect union. We know our mission. Let us join as one and say in a loud, clear voice: Send John Kerry.

Public Domain: accessed at http://www.dems2004.org/

Chapter 10
Questions

1. Of these two statements, which do you find to be more convincing? Why?

2. If you were being paid to give advice to a major political party about how to advertise to attract the "youth vote" from people like yourself, what would you advise them to do? How should they go about doing it? What would you advise them not to do, and why?

CHAPTER 11
THE MEDIA

The readings for this chapter are directed to how the legislative and executive branches of American national government deal with contemporary policy issues about communications. The congressional speeches on the "Global Internet Freedom Act" show how the House of Representatives and Senate use the joint resolution as a way to make policy statements about who should control the World Wide Web, electronic mail, and other aspects of modern electronic communications. The "About the FCC" selection shows you what the leaders of the Federal Communications Commission, which is part of the executive branch, officially want you to know about it.

Statements on Introduced Bills and Joint Resolutions, Senate, October 10, 2002

By Mr. WYDEN (for himself and Mr. Kyl):

S. 3093. A bill to develop and deploy technologies to defeat Internet jamming and censorship; to the Committee on Commerce, Science, and Transportation.

Mr. WYDEN. Mr. President, over the past seven years, Congressman Chris Cox and I have teamed up several times on legislation affecting the Internet. The Global Internet Freedom Act that I will introduce today could be called "Cox-Wyden V," because this is our fifth collaboration. I am pleased to be joined by Senator Kyl in introducing this bill in the Senate.

This legislation aims to foster the development and deployment of technologies to defeat state-sponsored Internet jamming and censorship, and in turn, to help unleash the potential of the Internet to promote the causes of freedom and democracy worldwide.

This is a time when Americans are acutely focused on security threats emanating from sources beyond U.S. borders. The terrorist attacks of September 11 made plain that ignorance, extremism, and hate abroad can have terrible consequences not just in other countries, but right here at home. And the daily drumbeat of debate over Iraq emphasizes that oppressive foreign regimes can pose serious hazards. The world is truly getting smaller.

In the field of information technology, Americans have rightly responded with a renewed emphasis on cybersecurity. The interlinked computer networks that make up the Internet, and on which American's critical infrastructure increasingly relies, must be secured against would-be cyberterrorists. This is a matter of top importance, and I have sponsored legislation, as Chairman of the Science and Technology Subcommittee, to promote research and innovation in this area. It is my hope that the Cybersecurity Research and Development Act will be signed by the President in the coming weeks.

But it is important to remember that the international nature of the Internet does not just create new threats. It also presents tremendous new opportunities.

Openness, transparency, and the unfettered flow of information have always been the allies of freedom and democracy. Over time, nothing erodes oppression and intolerance like the widespread dissemination of knowledge and ideas. And technology has often played a key role in this process. From the printing press to radio, technological advances have revolutionized the spread information and ideas and opened up new horizons for people everywhere. Not surprisingly, the foes of freedom, understanding the threat these technologies pose, have often responded with such steps as censoring the press, jamming radio broadcasts, and putting media outlets under state control.

The Internet promises to revolutionize the spread of information yet again. Unlike its predecessor technologies, it offers a truly worldwide network that makes geographic distance irrelevant. It enables any person connected to it to exchange ideas quickly and easily with people and organizations on the other side of the globe. The quantity and variety of information it permits access to are virtually unlimited.

So once again, governments that fear freedom are trying to rein in the technology's potential. They block access to websites. They censor websites and email. They interrupt Internet search engines when users try explore the "wrong" topics. They closely monitor citizens' Internet usage and make it known that those who visit the "wrong" websites will be punished. Or they prevent Internet access altogether, by prohibiting ownership of personal computers.

For a confirmed example of this, I would simply call attention to the inaugural report of the Congressional-Executive Commission on China, issued just last week, October 2. This report, the product of a bipartisan commission with members from the Senate, the House of Representatives, and the Administration, finds that "over the last 18 months, the Chinese government has issued an extensive and still growing series of regulations restricting Internet content and placing monitoring requirements on industry." It goes on to cite accounts of the Chinese government using high-tech software and hardware to "block, filter, and hack websites and e-mail." Offshore dissident websites, foreign news websites, search engines, and Voice of America's weekly e-mail to China are all subject to being blocked. Internet users attempting to access foreign web-sites often find themselves redirected to Chinese government-approved websites.

Other countries, from Cuba to Burma to Tunisia to Vietnam, engage in similar activity.

There are technologies that can help defeat the firewalls and filters that these governments choose to erect. Proxy servers, intermediaries, "mirrors," and encryption may all have useful applications in this regard. But the U.S. Government has done little to promote technological approaches. This country devotes considerable resources to combat the jamming of

Voice of America broadcasting abroad. But to date, it has budgeted only about $1 million for technologies to counter Internet jamming and censorship.

This country can and should do better. The Internet is too important a communications medium, and its potential as a force for freedom and democracy is too great, to make a second-rate effort in this area.

That is why Senator Kyl and I are introducing the Global Internet Freedom Act today. It is time for the U.S. Government to make a serious commitment to support technology that can help keep the Internet open, available, and free of political censorship for people all over the world.

This legislation would establish an Office of Global Internet Freedom, with the express mission of promoting technology to combat state-sponsored Internet jamming. The office would be based in the Department of Commerce's National Telecommunications and Information Administration, NTIA, to take advantage of NTIA's extensive expertise in international telecommunications and Internet issues. Location within the Department of Commerce will also help ensure close ties with American technology companies, whose active involvement will be essential for any technology-based effort to succeed. Cooperation with the International Broadcasting Bureau will be indispensable as well, and is required in the legislation.

Funding for the new office would be authorized at $30 million for each of the next two fiscal years. The office would make an annual report to Congress on its activities, and on the extent of state-sponsored Internet blocking in different countries around the world.

Finally, the bill would express the sense of Congress that the United States should denounce the practice of state-sponsored blocking of access to the Internet, should submit a resolution on the topic to the United Nations Human Rights Convention, and should deploy technologies to address the problem as soon as practicable.

As I mentioned at the outset, Representatives Chris Cox and Tom Lantos have already introduced companion legislation in the House, and I strongly applaud them for taking the lead on this issue. Here in the Senate, I urge my colleagues to join Senator Kyl and myself in this important, bipartisan effort.

I ask unanimous consent that the text of the bill be printed in the Record.

There being no objection, the bill was ordered to be printed in the Record, as follows:

S. 3093

Be it enacted by the Senate and House of Representatives of the United States of America in Congress assembled,

SECTION 1. SHORT TITLE.

This Act may be cited as the "Global Internet Freedom Act".

SEC. 2 FINDINGS.

The Congress makes the following findings:

(1) Freedom of speech, freedom of the press, and freedom of association are fundamental characteristics of a free society. The first amendment to the Constitution of the United States guarantees that "Congress shall make no law . . . abridging the freedom of speech, or of the press; or the right of the people peaceably to assemble." These constitutional provisions guarantee the rights of Americans to communicate and associate with one another without restriction, including unfettered communication and association via the Internet. Article 19 of the United Nation's Universal Declaration of Human Rights explicitly guarantees the freedom to "receive and impart information and ideas through any media and regardless of frontiers".

(2) All people have the right to communicate freely with others, and to have unrestricted access to news and information, on the Internet.

(3) With nearly 10 percent of the world's population now online, and more gaining access each day, the Internet stands to become the most powerful engine for democratization and the free exchange of ideas ever invented.

(4) Unrestricted access to news and information on the Internet is a check on repressive rule by authoritarian regimes around the world.

(5) The governments of Burma, Cuba, Laos, North Korea, the People's Republic of China, Saudi Arabia, Syria, and Vietnam, among others, are taking active measures to keep their citizens from freely accessing the Internet and obtaining international political, religious, and economic news and information.

(6) Intergovernmental, nongovernmental, and media organizations have reported the widespread and increasing pattern by authoritarian governments to block, jam, and monitor Internet access and content, using technologies such as firewalls, filters, and "black boxes". Such jamming and monitoring of individual activity on the Internet includes surveillance of e-mail messages, message boards, and the use of particular words; "stealth blocking" individuals from visiting websites; the development of "black lists" of users that seek to visit these websites; and the denial of access to the Internet.

(7) The Voice of America and Radio Free Asia, as well as hundreds of news sources with an Internet presence, are routinely being jammed by repressive governments.

(8) Since the 1940s, the United States has deployed anti-jamming technologies to make Voice of America and other United States Government sponsored broadcasting available to people in nations with governments that seek to block news and information.

(9) The United States Government has thus far commenced only modest steps to fund and deploy technologies to defeat Internet censorship. To date, the Voice of America and Radio Free Asia have committed a total of $1,000,000 for technology to counter Internet jamming by the People's Republic of China. This technology, which has been successful in attracting 100,000 electronic hits per day from the People's Republic of China, has been relied upon by Voice of America and Radio Free Asia to ensure access to their programming by citizens of the People's Republic of China, but United States Government financial support for the technology has lapsed. In most other countries there is no meaningful United States support for Internet freedom.

(10) The success of United States policy in support of freedom of speech, press, and association requires new initiatives and technologies to defeat totalitarian and authoritarian controls on news and information over the Internet.

SEC. 3. PURPOSES.

The purposes of this Act are—
> (1) to adopt an effective and robust global Internet freedom policy;
> (2) to establish an office within the National Telecommunications and Information Administration with the sole mission of promoting technological means of countering Internet jamming and blocking by repressive regimes;
> (3) to expedite the development and deployment of technology to protect Internet freedom around the world;
> (4) to authorize the commitment of a substantial portion of United States Government resources to the continued development and implementation of technologies to counter the jamming of the Internet;
> (5) to utilize the expertise of the private sector in the development and implementation of such technologies, so that the many current technologies used commercially for securing business transactions and providing virtual meeting space can be used to promote democracy and freedom; and
> (6) to bring to bear the pressure of the free world on repressive governments guilty of Internet censorship and the intimidation and persecution of their citizens who use the Internet.

SEC. 4. DEVELOPMENT AND DEPLOYMENT OF TECHNOLOGIES TO DEFEAT INTERNET JAMMING AND CENSORSHIP.

> (a) Establishment of Office of Global Internet Freedom.—There is established in the National Telecommunications and Information Administration the Office of Global Internet Freedom (hereinafter in this Act referred to as the "Office"). The Office shall be headed by a Director who shall develop and implement, in consultation with the International Broadcasting Bureau, a comprehensive global strategy for promoting technology to combat state-sponsored and state-directed Internet jamming and persecution of those who use the Internet.

> (b) Authorization of Appropriations.—There are authorized to be appropriated to the Office $30,000,000 for each of the fiscal years 2003 and 2004.

> (c) Corporation of Other Federal Departments and Agencies.—Each department and agency of the United States Government shall cooperate fully with, and assist in the implementation of, the strategy developed by the Office and shall make such resources and information available to the Office as is necessary to the achievement of the purposes of this Act.

> (d) Report to Congress.—On March 1 following the date of the enactment of this Act and annually thereafter, the Director of the Office shall submit to the Congress a report on the status of state interference with Internet use and of efforts by the United States to counter such interference. Each report shall list the countries that pursue policies of Internet censorship, blocking, and other abuses; provide information concerning the government agencies or quasi-governmental organizations that implement Internet censorship; and describe with the greatest particularity practicable the technological means by which such blocking and other abuses are

accomplished. In the discretion of the Director, such report may be submitted in both a classified and nonclassified version.

(e) Limitation on Authority.—Nothing in this Act shall be interpreted to authorize any action by the United States to interfere with foreign national censorship for the purpose of protecting minors from harm, preserving public morality, or assisting with legitimate law enforcement aims.

SEC. 5. SENSE OF CONGRESS.

It is the sense of the Congress that the United States should—

(1) publicly, prominently, and consistently denounce governments that restrict, censor, ban, and block access to information on the Internet;

(2) direct the United States Representative to the United Nations to submit a resolution at the next annual meeting of the United Nations Human Rights Commission condemning all governments that practice Internet censorship and deny freedom to access and share information; and

(3) deploy, at the earliest practicable date, technologies aimed at defeating state-directed Internet censorship and the persecution of those who use the Internet.

Mr. KYL. Mr. President, I rise today to introduce, with Senator Wyden, the Global Internet Freedom Act.

The Internet is one of the most powerful tools to promote the exchange of ideas and to disseminate information. In that regard, it is a key component in our efforts to reach populations living under undemocratic governments that continue to restrict freedom of speech, the press, and association. Unfortunately, however, many authoritarian governments including the regimes in the People's Republic of China, Saudi Arabia, Syria, Vietnam, Cuba, and North Korea aggressively block and censor the Internet, often subjecting to torture and imprisonment those individuals who dare to resist the controls.

In Vietnam, for example, the Prime Minister issued a decree in August 2000 that prohibits individuals from using the Internet "for the purpose of hostile actions against the country or to destabilize security, violate morality, or violate other laws and regulations." The Communist government owns and controls the sole Internet access provider, which is authorized to monitor the sites that subscribers use. It erects firewalls to block sites it deems politically or culturally inappropriate. And it is seeking additional authority to monitor some 4,000 Internet cafes in Vietnam, and hold responsible the owners of these cafes for customer use of the Internet.

The situation in Syria is no better. Like Vietnam, that country has only one government-run Internet service provider. The Government blocks access to Internet sites that contain information deemed politically sensitive including pro-Israel sites and also periodically blocks access to servers that provide free e-mail services. In 2000, the Syrian Government which monitors e-mail detained one individual for simply forwarding via e-mail a political cartoon.

The Chinese Government is one of the worst offenders. Beijing has passed sweeping regulations in the past 2 years prohibiting news and commentary on Internet sites in China that are not state-sanctioned. The Ministry of Information Industry regulates Internet access, and the Ministries of Public and State Security monitor its use. According to the State Department's most recent Country Reports on Human Rights Practices.

Despite the continued expansion of the Internet in the country, the Chinese government maintained its efforts to monitor and control content on the Internet. . . . The authorities block access to Web sites they find offensive. Authorities have at times blocked politically sensitive Web sites, including those of dissident groups and some major foreign news organizations, such as the VOA, the Washington Post, the New York Times, and the BBC.

The U.S.-China Security Review Commission noted in its recent report that China has even convinced American companies like Yahoo! to assist in its censorship efforts, and others, like America Online, to leave open the possibility of turning over names, e-mail addresses, or records of political dissidents if the Chinese Government demands them.

Those who attempt to circumvent Internet restrictions in China are often subject to harsh punishment. For example, Huang Qi, the operator of an Internet site that posted information about missing persons, including students who disappeared in the 1989 Tiananmen massacre, was tried secretly and found guilty of "subverting state power." According to the State Department, Huang was bound hand and foot and beaten by police while they tried to force him to confess.

These are but a few examples of the incredible lengths that authoritarian governments will go to in order to preserve control over their populations and prevent change. Voice of America, Radio Free Asia, Amnesty International, and the National Endowment for Democracy—just to name a few—all utilize the Internet to try to provide news, spread democratic values, and promote human rights in these countries. But the obstacles they face are great.

The U.S. private sector is developing a number of techniques and technologies to combat Internet blocking. Unfortunately, however, the U.S. Government has contributed few resources to assist these efforts and to put the new techniques to use. For example, Voice of America and Radio Free Asia have budgeted only $1 million for technology to counter Chinese Government Internet jamming, and that funding has now expired.

This is why I am pleased to introduce the Global Internet Freedom Act. This bill will take an important step toward promoting Internet freedom throughout the world. Specifically, it establishes, within the Commerce Department's National Telecommunications and Information Administration, the Office of Global Internet Freedom. It authorizes $30 million per year in fiscal years 2003 and 2004 for this office, which would be responsible for developing and implementing a comprehensive global strategy to combat state-sponsored Internet jamming and persecution of Internet users. Additionally, the director of the office would be required to submit to Congress an annual report on U.S. efforts to counter state interference with Internet use.

Similar legislation has already been introduced in the House of Representatives by Congressmen Cox and Lantos.

I cannot stress enough the importance of the Internet in promoting the flow of democratic ideas. If the benefits of the Internet are able to reach more and more people around the globe, repressive governments will begin to be challenged by individuals who are freely exchanging views and getting uncensored news and information.

The United States should take full advantage of the opportunities inherent in worldwide access to the Internet, and should make clear to the international community that fostering Internet freedom is a top priority. Creation of an Office of Global Internet Freedom will enable us to do just that.

I ask unanimous consent that the bill be printed in the Record.

Public Domain: accessed at http://www.fas.org

About the FCC

Summary

The Federal Communications Commission (FCC) is an independent United States government agency, directly responsible to Congress. The FCC was established by the Communications Act of 1934 and is charged with regulating interstate and international communications by radio, television, wire, satellite and cable. The FCC's jurisdiction covers the 50 states, the District of Columbia, and U.S. possessions.

Organization

The FCC is directed by five Commissioners appointed by the President and confirmed by the Senate for 5-year terms, except when filling an unexpired term. The President designates one of the Commissioners to serve as Chairperson. Only three Commissioners may be members of the same political party. None of them can have a financial interest in any Commission-related business.

As the chief executive officer of the Commission, the Chairman delegates management and administrative responsibility to the Managing Director. The Commissioners supervise all FCC activities, delegating responsibilities to staff units and Bureaus.

Bureaus and Offices

The Commission staff is organized by function. There are six operating Bureaus and ten Staff Offices. The Bureaus' responsibilities include: processing applications for licenses and other filings; analyzing complaints; conducting investigations; developing and implementing regulatory programs; and taking part in hearings. Our Offices provide support services. Even though the Bureaus and Offices have their individual functions, they regularly join forces and share expertise in addressing Commission issues.

<u>Consumer & Governmental Affairs Bureau</u> - educates and informs consumers about telecommunications goods and services and engages their input to help guide the work of the Commission. CGB coordinates telecommunications policy efforts with industry and with other governmental agencies — federal, tribal, state and local — in serving the public interest.

<u>Enforcement Bureau</u> - enforces the Communications Act, as well as the Commission's rules, orders and authorizations.

<u>International Bureau</u> - represents the Commission in satellite and international matters.

<u>Media Bureau</u> - regulates AM, FM radio and television broadcast stations, as well as Multipoint Distribution (i.e., cable and satellite) and Instructional Television Fixed Services.

<u>Wireless Telecommunications</u> - oversees cellular and PCS phones, pagers and two-way radios. This Bureau also regulates the use of radio spectrum to fulfill the communications needs of businesses, local and state governments, public safety service providers, aircraft and ship operators, and individuals.

<u>Wireline Competition Bureau</u> - responsible for rules and policies concerning telephone companies that provide interstate, and under certain circumstances intrastate, telecommunications services to the public through the use of wire-based transmission facilities (i.e., corded/cordless telephones).

<u>Office of Administrative Law Judges</u> - presides over hearings, and issues Initial Decisions.

<u>Office of Communications Business Opportunities</u> - provides advice to the Commission on issues and policies concerning opportunities for ownership and contracting by small, minority and women-owned communications businesses.

<u>Office of Engineering And Technology</u> - allocates spectrum for non-Government use and provides expert advice on technical issues before the Commission.

<u>Office of The General Counsel</u> - serves as chief legal advisor to the Commission's various Bureaus and Offices.

<u>Office of Inspector General</u> - conducts and supervises audits and investigations relating to the operations of the Commission.

<u>Office of Legislative Affairs</u> - is the Commission's main point of contact with Congress.

Office of The Managing Director - functions as a chief operating official, serving under the direction and supervision of the Chairman.

Office of Media Relations - informs the news media of FCC decisions and serves as the Commission's main point of contact with the media.

Office of Strategic Planning & Policy Analysis - works with the Chairman, Commissioners, Bureaus and Offices to develop strategic plans identifying policy objectives for the agency.

Office of Work Place Diversity - advises the Commission on all issues related to workforce diversity, affirmative recruitment and equal employment opportunity.

Public Domain: accessed at http://www.fcc.gov/aboutus.html/

Chapter 11
Questions

1. Why do both the legislative and executive branches of the U.S. government have a say in communications policy? Given what you see in these readings, do you believe that Congress or the bureaucracy would be better able to regulate your electronic communications?

2. The "digital divide" has to do with the fact that some Americans (probably including you) have a lot more access to the Internet and other electronic resources and know how to use them more effectively than others (say, your parents). What effect, if any, do you think this has on politics and government in the United States, and why?

CHAPTER 12
THE CONGRESS

The role that the United States Congress plays in politics and government today is explained in these reading selections. In "Congress in American Society," prepared by The Center on Congress at Indiana University, you get a pretty good idea of the wide array of topics that Congress deals with. One important function of the members of Congress is to "bring home the bacon" to their constituents. An example of this porkbarrel activity is shown in the information provided from Florida Congressman Ander Crenshaw's Web page in which he takes credit for emergency funding to restore beach property. Congress has internal mechanisms to investigate possible unethical behavior by its members, as is shown in the statement of the House Committee on Standards of Official Conduct (which often is referred to as the House Ethics Committee) about a complaint against Representative Tom DeLay, the Texas Republican leader of the majority party in the House.

Congress in American Society
by The Center on Congress, Indiana University

Cynics and doubters will find plenty of evidence to support their view that the United States Congress is not everything it should be. But amidst all the conflict and confrontation in Congress are episodes of cooperation and consensus. These may not be as well publicized as the disagreements, but they have led to many extraordinary legislative achievements over the years. Anyone who doubts that Congress remains a relevant and significant institution need look no further than the following list.

When it takes up issues like the education of our children, or the quality of the water we drink, or our ability to respond to emergencies and natural disasters, Congress is doing its best to reflect and to improve the quality of our lives as individuals and to strengthen our nation as a whole.

How many of the following acts of Congress affect your daily life?

Aerospace

Research and development of air and space technologies funded by Congress, primarily through NASA, have resulted in technological innovations in:
- communications
- navigation
- geological studies
- weather forecasting

- consumer items, like cordless power tools, bar code scanners, and joysticks
- national defense systems

Agriculture

Americans spend 10% of their personal income on food, far less than the rest of the world must spend. By funding agricultural research programs, Congress has enabled the nation's farmers to increase farm output nearly two-and-a-half times what it was in 1950.

Stable U.S. food commodity prices in a world-wide market are the result of Congress:
- granting subsidies to farmers
- expanding foreign aid programs as a market for American agricultural products
- increasing export opportunities
- providing controls on surplus production.

Art and Culture

To encourage artistic and cultural expression, Congress has passed copyright laws to give those with original ideas rights and protection for their intellectual property. Copyright laws have been expanded over the years from protecting the written word to now also protecting:
- movies
- sound recordings
- television shows
- computer software
- semiconductor chips

Automobile Safety

Congress has passed laws to promote auto safety. It required:
- car manufacturers to meet minimum safety standards in their designs, including seat belts and air bags, and it
- created the National Highway Traffic Safety Administration to promote highway safety.

Air Safety

Congress created the Federal Aviation Agency [FAA] which manages and regulates all U.S. commercial aviation to assure air safety.

Banking

Congress established the national insurance policies which guarantee the safety of deposits made in banks and savings and loan institutions.

Civil Rights

Congress passed the Civil Rights Act of 1964, outlawing racial discrimination:

- in employment
- in all public places
- in any programs receiving federal funds.

Clean Air

Congress enacted laws providing national pollution control standards, including:
- mandatory requirements on automakers to reduce car emissions
- restrictions on power plant pollution
- regulation of toxic pollutants

Consumer Safety

Congress has established various programs to regulate and monitor the safety of items used by consumers. For example, it established:
- a program of government inspections of the purity of food, such as meat and dairy products
- regulations to monitor toiletries, cosmetics, and medicines to prevent toxic ingredients from harming consumers
- regulations to monitor advertising for fraudulent claims
- the Consumer Product Safety Commission to monitor the safety of toys and other consumer products
- regulations on local and state governments to assure the safety of municipal drinking water.

Crime

Congress passed the Crime Control and Safe Streets Act, giving law enforcement grants to states and local governments to increase the number of officers and improve crime prevention.

Defense

All the branches of the U.S. military, which provide for the nation's security and protection from foreign invasion, were created and are funded by the Congress. It established:
- our national security and intelligence agencies
- defense research programs to keep pace with rapid technological changes in weaponry
- defense research programs which led to the invention of Global Positioning Systems. GPS is now available to consumers as well as the Department of Defense

Disaster Relief

The Federal Emergency Management Agency [FEMA] can trace its beginnings to the Congressional Act of 1803. Congress now provides over $2 billion a year for emergency disaster funds.

- It partners with FEMA to create Project Impact communities in every state to mitigate disasters through prevention programs

- It provides yearly emergency supplemental funding for disaster relief
- It provides funds for long-term recovery
- It provides buy-out assistance for victims

Drug and Alcohol Abuse

Congress created the Office of National Drug Abuse Policy [the Drug Czar] to educate the public about the hazards of alcohol and drug abuse and develop prevention programs.

Educational Opportunities

Congress created:
- Pell Grants to fund an expanded higher education scholarship program
- A system of federal loans and scholarships for undergrads, which amounts to about 75% of all financial aid available to students
- Fulbright Scholarships for college and faculty exchanges abroad
- Federal grants for improved math, science, and foreign language programs
- the Head Start program to enable disadvantaged children to better prepare for school
- Funds for libraries and special ed programs in low-income elementary school districts.
- Funds to help schools meet equal access requirements so that students with disabilities can attend school
- the school-to-work program to develop apprenticeships and occupationally relevant content in high school curriculums.

Energy Conservation

With passage of the Energy Security Act, Congress allocated billions toward the development of synthetic, alternative, and renewable fuel in preparation for the day when the earth's supply of natural fuel diminishes. It also:
- mandated conservation standards for major appliances
- required utility companies to give consumers information about conservation
- provided schools and hospitals with grants to install energy saving equipment.

Family Leave

Congress granted unpaid leave to workers for up to 12 weeks per year for the birth or adoption of a child or due to the illness of a close family member.

Family Support

Congress required the states to:
- provide education, training, and work programs for welfare mothers
- provide extended child care and medical benefits to parents who left welfare to work
- created a national alert program for missing children
- create programs for family preservation efforts, such as emergency counseling.

Food Safety

Congress established a program of government inspections of the purity of food, meat, and medicines.

Handicapped Access

Congress expanded employment opportunities for the handicapped by passing the Americans with Disabilities Act, requiring that access to the workplace and public spaces be made available to those with physical disabilities.

Hazardous Waste

Congress established federal controls on hazardous waste management and set standards for land disposal of waste.

Health and Medicine

Congress has provided funds for:
- research into the cause and prevention of diseases such as cancer, AIDS, and heart disease through passage of the Public Health Service Act
- a system to check the safety and potency of vaccines, serums, and medicinal drugs.
- research at the National Institutes of Health to help develop new and more effective medicines
- programs to develop nutritional science and require nutritional labeling and education about diet and health
- training and educational programs for medical professionals
- subsidies for hospital and medical school construction.

Housing

Congress passed the Civil Rights Act of 1968, outlawing racial discrimination in the sale or rental of housing units. In 1988, it extended the discrimination ban to families with children and to the handicapped. Congress has also authorized funds for:
- homeless shelters
- trusts to help low-income home buyers
- subsidies for low-income renters

Internet

The two federal agencies instrumental in creating the computer protocols which became today's Internet are funded by the U.S. Congress.
- The Department of Defense Advanced Research Projects Agency [DARPA] created Arpanet, an experimental prototype computer network for defense work in 1969.
- The National Science Foundation built on that work in 1986 to create NSFnet, linking

computer centers for their community of researchers, and creating the same protocols used by the Internet today.

Labor Safety and Wages

Congress:
- created the concept of a federal minimum wage and votes periodic increases in the wage rate
- passed the Occupational Safety and Health Act to set safety and health standards in the workplace
- established an agency [OSHA] to inspect work sites and enforce health and safety rules.
- banned job discrimination based on age, race, gender, or disability
- established a federal unemployment compensation program to pay workers who have lost their jobs for a temporary period as they transition to another job.

Medicare

Congress provided federal health insurance for the aged and poor with passage of the Medicare Act in 1965.

Poverty

Congress established a public assistance program for families with dependent children, and it:
- provided for food stamps and nutritional assistance to the eligible poor
- encouraged poverty prevention and assistance programs by creating community action agencies which provide services and training for the poor
- encouraged community volunteers in programs such as VISTA and Upward Bound
- instituted tax credits for low-income families
- created Job Corps training for public service employment
- created transition programs for people moving from welfare to work

Privacy

Congress has:
- banned schools from disclosing records to third parties without permission
- granted students rights to access their own records and the right to correct information in them
- enacted laws prohibiting video stores from disclosing their customers' names and selections to outside parties
- banned lie detector tests as a prerequisite for employment, except in selected cases.
- required banks to inform their customers of their right to request privacy for their records
- limited federal government access to banking records.

Retirement

Congress:
- lowered the age for young workers to qualify to start earning pension credits
- expanded pension coverage for those who leave but subsequently return to a job.
- set up a program to protect retired workers' pensions and insure they will continue to receive their pension checks if their former companies go under.

Social Security

Congress passed the Social Security Act in 1935, which established:
- income insurance for the elderly and disabled
- survivors' benefits
- a system of unemployment compensation.

School Lunch

Congress passed the National School Lunch Act to:
- support school lunches in public and private schools
- improve the diet of school children
- provide use for surplus farm commodities.

Transportation

Congress created the nation's interstate highway system in 1956 and:
- created a fund from user and gasoline taxes to support highway construction and maintenance for years to come, leading to the over 45,000 miles of convenient interstate Americans enjoy today
- provided federal government loans and grants for construction and maintenance of mass transit systems across the country by passing the Urban Mass Transportation Act.

Water Safety

Congress has mandated national drinking water standards and created groundwater protection programs.

Women's Rights

Congress banned:
- discrimination in school sports programs based on sex, passing Title IX of the Education Amendments Act in 1972
- sex discrimination in the granting of credit cards and consumer loans
- sex discrimination in military academies by opening up appointments to women
- different wage scales for women and men, by implementing equal pay for equal work laws.

Voting Rights

Congress passed the Voting Rights Act of 1965. It banned:

- interference with an individual's right to register or vote, making it a federal crime
- the use of literacy tests as a barrier to voting, and
- Congress established the right to vote absentee, requiring states to accept mail ballots from military personnel and other U.S. citizens living abroad

http://congress.indiana.edu/backgrounders/role_of_congress.php
Reprinted with permission from © The Center on Congress, Indiana University
The Center on Congress
Indiana University
SPEA 316
Bloomington, IN 47405
Phone: (812) 856-4706
Fax: (812) 856-4703
email: congress@indiana.edu

Congressional Ethics Complaint Against Rep. Tom DeLay
House Committee on Standards of Official Conduct, October 6, 2004

Editors **Note**: One of the most important elements of representative government is the trust people have in the system and their leaders. Congress has a long history of reprimanding its members for improprieties that affect the performance of the institution and also the legitimacy and credibility of public office. As we edited this reader, the House Ethics Committee admonished Congressman Tom DeLay. The following is a headline from the news. The official letter of reprimand follows.

> *"WASHINGTON (CNN)—For the second time in two weeks, the House Ethics Committee has issued admonishments to Majority Leader Tom DeLay over his conduct, warning the Texas Republican to "temper" his future actions to comply with House rules and standards of conduct.*
>
> *The committee announced Wednesday evening that it had unanimously admonished DeLay on two counts of an ethics complaint filed against him by Rep. Chris Bell, a Texas Democrat who lost his re-election bid after Texas legislators passed a redistricting plan engineered by the No. 2 House Republican."*

108TH CONGRESS, 2nd SESSION
U.S. House of Representatives
Committee on Standards of Official Conduct

Statement of the Committee regarding disposition of the complaint filed against Representative

Tom DeLay

October 6, 2004

The Honorable Tom DeLay
Majority Leader
U.S. House of Representatives
Suite H-107, The Capitol
Washington, D.C. 20515

Dear Colleague:

As you are aware, the Committee has made a number of decisions regarding the allegations made in the complaint that was filed against you by Representative Bell on June 15, 2004. This letter implements determinations made by the Committee that you be admonished for your conduct in two respects:

- your participation in and facilitation of an energy company golf fundraiser at The Homestead resort for your leadership PACs on June 2-3, 2002. Those actions were objectionable under House standards of conduct because, at a minimum, they created an appearance that donors were being provided special access to you regarding the then-pending energy legislation.

- your intervention in a partisan conflict in the Texas House of Representatives using the resources of a Federal agency, the Federal Aviation Administration. This action raises serious concerns under House standards of conduct that preclude use of governmental resources for a political undertaking.

The bases of these Committee determinations are as follows.

Your actions regarding the energy company golf fundraiser at The Homestead resort on June 2-3, 2002. With regard to the solicitation and receipt of campaign contributions, the Committee has clearly stated that a Member may not make any solicitation that may create even an appearance that, because of a contribution, a contributor will receive or is entitled to either special treatment or special access to the Member in his or her official capacity. This point is made on p. 34 of the *Campaign Activity* booklet that the Committee issued in December 2001.[1] In the same vein, a Member should not participate in a fundraising event that gives even an appearance that donors will receive or are entitled to either special treatment or special access.

On the basis of the information before the Committee, the Committee concluded that your participation in and facilitation of the energy company golf fundraiser at The Homestead resort on June 2-3, 2002 is objectionable in that those actions, at a minimum, created such an improper appearance. As a general matter, fundraisers directed to a particular industry or to others sharing a particular federal interest are permissible, and at such events Members are free to talk about their record and positions on issues of interest to the attendees. In addition, of course, a Member has no control over what the donors at a fundraising event spontaneously say to or ask of the Member with regard to their legislative interests. Nevertheless, there are a number of considerations regarding this particular fundraiser that make your participation in and facilitation of the fundraiser objectionable under the above-stated standards of conduct.

In particular, there was the timing of the fundraiser, *i.e.*, it took place just as the House-Senate conference on major energy legislation, H.R. 4, was about to get underway. Indeed, one of the communications between organizers of the fundraiser that you provided to us—an e-mail of May 30, 2002 from Mr. Maloney to Mr. Perkins that notes the legislative interests of each of the attendees—includes a specific reference to the conference. That legislation was of critical importance to the attendees. In addition, there was the fact that you were in a position to significantly influence the conference, both as a member of the House leadership and, by action taken about a week and a half after the fundraiser, your appointment as one of the conferees.

In view of these considerations, other aspects of the fundraiser that would have been unobjectionable otherwise had the effect, in these specific circumstances, of furthering the appearance that the contributors were receiving impermissible special treatment or access. One of these aspects was the presence at the fundraiser of two of your key staff members from your leadership office: Jack Victory, who handled energy issues, and your office counsel, Carl Thorsen. In addition, there were the limited number of attendees, and the fact that the fundraiser included several events at a resort over a two-day period, both of which facilitated direct contact with you and your congressional staff members.

We also note the description of the event that was provided to the Committee by counsel for the attendees of one of the contributors, Westar Energy, Inc. That description includes the following:

On Sunday, June 2, 2002 Douglas Sterbenz and Doug Lawrence [Westar executives] attended a reception and dinner with fifteen to twenty others at the Homestead. Representative Tom DeLay was present for the reception and dinner. Mr. DeLay asked the group to advise him of any interest we had in Federal Energy Legislation. Mr. Lawrence advised Mr. DeLay that Westar supported repeal of the P.U.C.H.A. [sic] provision in the Energy Bill, provided that Westar's restructuring wouldn't be harmed by the [r]epeal. Lawrence advised that Westar needed a grandfather clause to continue as a safe harbor if P.U.C.H.A. was to be repealed. The following day, Mr. Lawrence provided a staff aide to Rep. DeLay a bound briefing book that Westar had put together on this issue. [emphasis added]

On June 3rd, 2002, Mr. Lawrence attended a golf outing at the Homestead where he played golf with the attendees. Mr. Lawrence shared a cart with an aide to Congressman Delay and advised the aide he would give him the materials in the briefing book and later did. At lunch that day, Mr. Sterbenz, Mr. Lawrence and others participating in the golf outing had lunch. During the lunch Mr. Lawrence restated to Rep. DeLay Westar's position regarding the need for a grandfather clause if P.U.H.C.A. was to be repealed.

When we brought the above-quoted statement to your attention and requested your response to it, you stated that you gave a general briefing on energy issues at that event, but that you have no recollection of your specific remarks. You also stated that "it would not be typical" for you to have made such a statement at a fundraiser, and that this is not at all consistent with the manner in which you "normally would interact with attendees at such an event." In view of your response, the Committee's determination on this matter is not based on Mr. Lawrence's characterization of your remarks. Rather, the other circumstances of the event, as set forth above, are more than sufficient to support the Committee's determination.

In addition, while the views of any one donor are not dispositive on whether a fundraising activity creates an appearance of impropriety, the documents we obtained indicate that the individuals who were active on Westar's behalf were of the view that the company's participation in the fundraiser provided special access to you. In this regard, later in June 2002, when Mr. Lawrence was proposing that Westar executives make additional contributions, he stated that Westar had made "significant progress" with you and Representative Barton, and that, "The contributions made in the first round were successful in opening the appropriate dialogue." When we asked Mr. Lawrence about that statement, he said he was referring to the presentations he was able to make at the fundraiser earlier that month. In addition, the following month, when Westar's lobbyist, Mr. Richard Bornemann, sent a memorandum to your staff seeking an appointment with you for the company's CEO, he noted Westar's participation in The Homestead fundraiser.

Your use of governmental resources for a political undertaking. The Committee has long taken the position that House standards of conduct prohibit Members from taking (or withholding) any official action on the basis of the partisan affiliation (or the campaign support) of the individuals involved. This is the point made in an advisory memorandum that the Committee issued to House Members, officers and employees on May 11, 1999. In addition, a provision of the Code of Ethics for Government Service, which the Committee deems to be fully applicable to House Members and staff, requires that federal officials "[u]phold the Constitution, laws, and legal regulations of the United States and of all governments therein and never be a party to their evasion." These laws include, of course, those that generally prohibit the use of governmental resources for political purposes—particularly 31 U.S.C. § 1301, which provides that official funds are to be used only for the purposes for which appropriated, and, with regard to executive branch personnel, the Hatch Act, which prohibits those employees from engaging in political activity while on duty or in a government building.

Your intervention in a partisan conflict in the Texas House of Representatives using the resources of a Federal agency, the Federal Aviation Administration, raises serious concerns under these standards of conduct. Your contacts with the FAA were in connection with the dispute over congressional redistricting in the Texas House of Representatives that occurred in May 2003. The purpose of these contacts was to obtain information on the whereabouts of Democratic Members of the Texas House who had absented themselves from Austin for the purpose of denying the House a quorum. You have stated to us that you made these contacts at the request of the Speaker of the Texas House of Representatives, who was seeking information on the location of an airplane that was shuttling the absent legislators, and that you relayed the information you had obtained on the location of the airplane solely to the Texas House Speaker.

The submissions that you made to the Committee argue that those contacts with the FAA were proper, but those arguments are not persuasive.

First, your submissions assert that the Inspector General of the U.S Department of Transportation (DOT IG) found no wrongdoing in this matter. It is correct that the statement that the DOT IG submitted to the House Transportation and Infrastructure Committee states, "We did not find that actions [taken by the FAA official whom your office contacted] in this matter to have violated any rules or regulations." However, the assertion made in your submissions disregards a number of important considerations. To begin with, the DOT IG's statement raises specific concern about the FAA official's failure to inquire of your staff member as to why she was requesting information on the location of the particular airplane, "[W]e do not understand why he did not ask the staffer about the purpose of her request—particularly since he told us he thought it might involve a safety issue." In addition, there are the statements made by the FAA official to the DOT IG regarding his views of the requests of your office and his handling of them after he learned about the absent Texas legislators on May 13th:

I figured out why they were calling. . . I just felt like I had been used. . . I don't do anything for political purposes. . . and I just did not like. . . somebody calling me for political reasons. . . I would never use my office to help somebody politically, for any political reasons, period.

He also stated that in hindsight, "he would have handled the staffer's request differently, by coordinating with the FAA Chief Counsel's Office and senior agency officials, along with asking the requestor for background about the request." In short, without being apprised of the reason for the request, the FAA was denied the opportunity to make a prior, reasoned determination on whether collecting and providing the requested information would be both permissible and appropriate under the laws, rules and policies governing the FAA at the time.

Yet another pertinent point here is that on July 15, 2003, upon the recommendation of the DOT IG, the FAA issued an order setting out a specific policy regarding disclosure of aircraft and flight data from FAA information systems. That policy includes the following basic provision:

No request for Flight Track Data shall be granted unless it is first determined that the request is being made in the interest of aviation safety or efficiency, or for an official purpose by a United States Government agency or law enforcement organization with respect to an ongoing investigation.

In sum, the statements made by the FAA official regarding his views of his actions after he had learned the purpose of the requests, and the FAA's later establishment of a restrictive policy on responding to such requests, indicate a larger concern about the propriety of the FAA's response to your requests for information, regardless of whether, in the specific circumstances, the actions of the FAA official did not violate the FAA rules or regulations that were in effect at the time.

Second, it is asserted that the House Committee on Transportation and Infrastructure found no wrongdoing in this matter. In this regard, the report that the Transportation Committee issued on this matter states with regard to the DOT IG's report, "[T]here were no findings that federal resources were misused or that agency personnel violated any departmental rules or regulations." Because the Transportation Committee report merely characterizes the findings of the DOT IG, the materials set out above regarding the DOT IG's report respond to this assertion as well. It should also be noted that it is the Committee on Standards of Official Conduct, and not the Transportation Committee, that has the jurisdiction to make determinations regarding the official conduct of House Members and staff.

Third, your submissions assert that the information that you sought and that was provided to you is publicly available over the Internet. Indeed, according to the statement of the DOT IG, "[C]omparable information—including near real-time aircraft locator data—is currently available to the general public through commercial databases accessible via the internet." However, the issues discussed here have arisen because you did not obtain the information on the location of the particular aircraft from one of the commercial databases, but instead you obtained it from FAA databases using the services of FAA personnel.

Finally, your submissions assert that these contacts were proper because they were made in the context of a "legitimate law enforcement issue." While acknowledging that this matter arose out of a political dispute, one of your submissions states that it "was a proper matter for the law enforcement authorities of Texas," citing certain letters of the Sergeant-at-Arms and the Texas Attorney General on the matter. However, review of those documents establishes that to the extent that there was any "enforcement" issue here, it was solely a matter of enforcement of rules of the Texas House of Representatives that govern its Members.

Indeed, this consideration highlights a separate basis on which the contacts with the FAA were objectionable, and that is that such use of federal executive branch resources to resolve an issue before a state legislative body raises serious concerns under the fundamental concepts of separation of powers and federalism. The enforcement of the rules of the Texas House—like enforcement of the rules of the U.S. House of Representatives or any other legislative body—is the responsibility of the Members, officers and employees of that body.

Insofar as enforcing the rules of the Texas House on Member attendance is concerned, the rules of that body provide that this is the responsibility of "the sergeant-at-arms or an officer appointed by the sergeant-at-arms." Whether it is permissible and appropriate for the Texas House Sergeant-at-Arms to appoint every official of the Texas Department of Public Safety as such an officer, as occurred here, is a matter to be resolved by Texas authorities under Texas law. However, the invocation of Federal executive branch resources in a partisan dispute before a state legislative body is a different matter entirely, and such action raises the serious concerns that are set out here.

* * *

We note that your response to the Committee's decision of last week included the statement, "During my entire career I have worked to advance my party's legislative agenda." Your actions that are addressed in this letter, as well as those addressed in the Committee's decision of last week and in prior Committee actions, are all ones that, in a broad sense, were directed to the advancement of your legislative agenda. Those actions are also ones that your peers who sit on this Committee determined, after careful consideration, went beyond the bounds of acceptable conduct.

As you are aware, it does not suffice for any House Member to assert that his or her actions violated no law, or violated no specific prohibition or requirement of the House Rules. The House Code of Official Conduct broadly requires that every House Member, officer and employee "conduct himself at all times in a manner that shall reflect creditably on the House." It is particularly important that members of the House leadership, who are the most publicly visible Members, adhere to this requirement scrupulously. The fact that a violation results from the overaggressive pursuit of one's legislative agenda simply does not constitute a mitigating factor.

In addition, a state criminal investigation of the 2002 election activities of the Texans for a Republican Majority PAC, with which you were involved during the period in question, is underway. While Committee action on Count II of the complaint regarding those activities has been deferred pending further action in the state cases and investigation, the Committee will act on the underlying allegations at an appropriate time.

In view of the number of instances to date in which the Committee has found it necessary to comment on conduct in which you have engaged,[2] it is clearly necessary for you to temper your future actions to assure that you are in full compliance at all times with the applicable House Rules and standards of conduct. We remind you that the House Code of Official Conduct provides the Committee with authority "to deal with any given act or accumulation of acts which, in the judgment of the committee, are severe enough to reflect discredit on the Congress."[3]

Sincerely,

Joel Hefley   Alan B. Mollohan
Chairman   Ranking Minority Member

[1] More generally, under House standards of conduct as set out in Committee publications, a Member may not make any solicitation for campaign or political contributions that is linked with any specific official action taken or to be taken by that Member. In addition, a Member may not accept any contribution that is linked with any specific official action taken or to be taken by that Member.

[2] In addition to the two matters addressed in this letter and the conduct addressed in the Committee report of last week, there was the Committee letter to you of November 7, 1997 that concerned, in part, statements that may create the impression that official access or action are linked with campaign contributions, and a confidential Committee letter to you of May 7, 1999.

[3]*House Ethics Manual* at 12 (reprinting excerpt from the 1968 committee report on the House Code of Official Conduct (emphasis added)).

Public Domain.

Congressman Crenshaw Praises Emergency Beach Renourishment Funding

---

Editors Note: This is one the pages from a Florida member of Congress. Four major hurricanes had just swept across Florida creating a great deal of damage. A very hotly contested presidential election between George W. Bush and John Kerry was moving toward the November 2 election day. Like all members of the House, Congressman Crenshaw was up for election. Read the material we have reproduced below and think about the connections between all of these factors.

Crenshaw Praises Emergency Beach Renourishment Funding

2004-10-15

(WASHINGTON) - Congressman Ander Crenshaw today announced that with President Bush's signing of H.R. 4837 this week, approximately $15 million will be coming to Duval County for beach renourishment projects.

"In talking with the Army Corps of Engineers, we are going to need about $15 million to restore Duval County's projects," said Crenshaw, a member of the House Appropriations Committee that hammered out the final details of the emergency supplemental. "These funds are critical. That's why I pushed to put the money in the bill and I am pleased to report that is what has been signed into law."

Federally approved beach renourishment projects in Duval County are eligible for emergency federal monies. The House approved these emergency funds on Friday, October 8th. The Senate approved the funds on October 10th. President Bush signed the bill into law on Wednesday, October 13th. This law includes a $62 million dollar section for "Beach Replenishment and Dredging funds" to restore navigation channels, repair and rehabilitate coastal areas, beach renourishment, and address other projects in affected areas. An estimated $15 million of the $62 million has been designated by the Army Corps of Engineers to restore the Duval County shore protection project.

Congressman Crenshaw has been working with the Army Corps to direct the emergency funding to the First Coast. The law requires that any federal funds coming to the First Coast must receive a local matching amount.

"I commend the Army Corps of Engineers for their quick response to this very serious situation," said Crenshaw. "Properties are in danger. Jobs are in danger. The future of local economies depends on keeping these beaches whole."

"A significant amount of this emergency funding has been appropriated for Duval County beach renourishment," said Richard Bonner, Deputy District Engineer for Program Management, Jacksonville District. "The cost of replacing sand is many times less than the cost of repairing property damaged by a storm. We cannot prevent all storm damage but we can certainly mitigate its effects in the future."

Congressman Crenshaw toured the damaged beach areas on October 4th with Jerry Scarborough with the Army Corps of Engineers, Chief of the Coastal/Navigation Branch, Steve Ross Army Corps of Engineers Project Manager, Atlantic Beach Mayor John Meserve, Jim Hanson Atlantic Beach City Manager, and Roy Paxson Assistant City Manager for Jacksonville Beach.

Crenshaw Announces Disaster Relief Bill Signed Into Law

2004-10-14

(WASHINGTON) - Congressman Ander Crenshaw today announced President Bush has signed the fiscal year 2005 Military Construction appropriations bill into law. In the legislation are $61 million in military construction projects specifically requested for Northeast Florida. The measure also includes an $11.6 billion disaster aid package to help Florida and other states hit by hurricanes Frances, Ivan, and Jeanne.

"This is substantial help for our communities. These dollars will go directly to where we need them most," said Crenshaw, a member of the House Appropriations Committee. "In the area of disaster relief, there's money in there for impacted families, damaged infrastructure, small business assistance loans, and beach renourishment."

In addition to disaster relief, the bill invests over $10 billion in military construction projects including $61 million for Northeast Florida projects. The overall measure includes $5.3 billion for Active Duty construction, Guard and Reserve construction, troop housing, hospitals and medical clinics, schools, and new weapons systems. The measure also invests $4.2 billion in family housing projects that will result in the elimination of over 34,500 inadequate housing units.

"These investments are critical to our national security," said Crenshaw. "The projects coming to Northeast Florida will keep our bases modern, cutting edge, and ready to accept new missions. These are the sorts of investments that will help our region in the upcoming round of Base Closure and Realignment."

The $11.6 billion hurricane disaster relief package attached to the Military Construction law addresses a number of areas throughout Florida including:

FEMA—The law provides $6.5 billion for disaster recovery efforts of the Federal Emergency Management Agency (FEMA). FEMA uses these resources for a variety of disaster relief activities including direct assistance to impacted individuals and families, paying for debris removal and utility and infrastructure repairs and emergency food and shelter, and to mitigate future damage to public and private property.

SBA Disaster Relief loans—The disaster relief activities of the Small Business Administration are funded at $929 million. This funding level will leverage $5.5 billion in low interest loans to individuals and businesses.

Beach Replenishment and Dredging—Includes $362 million for the **Army Corps of Engineers** to restore navigation channels, repair and rehabilitate coastal areas, beach renourishment, and address other projects in affected areas. Congressman Crenshaw is working with the Corps to direct a portion of this to the First Coast.

Highway and Infrastructure Repairs—$1.2 billion for the **Federal Highway Administration's Emergency Relief Program** for emergency repairs to eligible highways and roads affected by Hurricanes Charley, Frances, Ivan, Jeanne, and Gaston. Also includes $30 million for repair for airports and aviation facilities.

Agricultural and Rural Assistance—Includes $608 million for assistance to rural areas. These funds will be used to repair storm damage to community facilities, damaged waterways and watersheds and rural housing developments.

Economic Development—Provides $150 million for **Community Development Grants** for emergency expenses to help replace damaged homes, including replacement of destroyed farm labor housing and housing for other low-income persons, properties, and businesses, and for economic redevelopment projects.

American Red Cross receives $70 million for their mission to shelter, feed and otherwise support victims of the recent natural disasters in Florida and other affected areas.

Defense damage and recovery—$1.1 billion for DOD for costs associated with the evacuation, base preparation, base recovery, and damage to structure and equipment at various military facilities.

"I commend my colleagues and President Bush for quick action on this much needed relief," said Crenshaw, a member of the conference committee responsible for drafting the final version of the bill. "This relief goes a long way to helping a wide range of people and communities who are taking huge financial hits due to storm damage."

Northeast Florida Projects Contained in the FY 2005 MilCon Appropriations Bill:
- **$4.0 million WAS ADDED** for a new Corrosion Control Facility for the Florida Air National Guard 125th Fighter Wing located at Jacksonville International Airport. The 125th Maintenance Squadron is responsible for day-to-day maintenance of 19 F-15 Air-to-Air Fighter Aircraft. However, they have no facility to perform corrosion control on

the aircraft, which includes washing, surface preparation and painting. The unit must have an adequate facility to maintain the aging F-15 fighters as well as be ready to accept the future F-22 and/or Joint Strike Fighter aircraft.

- **$150,000 WAS ADDED** to begin the planning and design of the second phase of a new aircraft parking apron at Naval Air Station Jacksonville. Due to the current lack of adequate parking-apron space, aircraft are being parked inside hangars, on taxiways, the secondary runway, and the hot cargo pad. This project will continue to add to the parking apron space to allow all aircraft stationed at NAS Jacksonville to be parked outside airfield safety zones and in proximity to their respective maintenance hangars. NAS Jacksonville received $6.0 million in the fiscal year 2004 Military Construction Appropriations and Defense Authorization Bills for phase one of this project.

- **$150,000 WAS ADDED** to begin the planning and design of a Consolidated Operational Support Facility at NAS Jacksonville. This facility will consolidate all of NAS Jacksonville's base support services and demolish four remotely located, deteriorated, WWII era facilities.

- **$12.0 million WAS ADDED** for the construction of a new Regional Training Institute (RTI) facility at Camp Blanding. Due to size and age of the current facility, it is very difficult to house, feed, teach and train the more than 800 students that attend RTI per cycle. The readiness of the entire state and the National Guard will be affected if the school cannot adequately accomplish its mission due to inadequate facilities.

- **$28.4 million** for an addition to the Fleet Hospital at Naval Air Station Jacksonville. The existing facility was constructed in 1967. Critical inpatient functions such as surgery and obstetrics have never been upgraded. The operating rooms are significantly undersized and fall far short of current DoD criteria and modern standards. Naval Hospital Jacksonville requires the capability to deliver efficient and modern surgical and obstetrics care to its beneficiaries, and greater demand for ambulatory services cannot be satisfied within the constraints of the existing facility.

- **$6.2 million** for a new Airfield Control Tower at Naval Station Mayport. The existing air traffic control tower was constructed in 1954, and its height does not provide adequate line of sight to all airfield surfaces as required by FAA. Yearly, NAVSTA Mayport averages 90 days of carrier divert services and hosts over 650 transient aircraft supporting 3 flag staffs, 1 aircraft carrier, and 21 ships home ported ships.

- **$9.3 million** for a new U.S. Marine Corps Reserve Center in Jacksonville. Currently, the 4th Assault Amphibian Battalion maintains two separate facilities for their equipment and personnel. These facilities are located more than 25 miles apart and a one-way drive can sometimes take upwards of an hour. In addition to the loss of training hours for the reserve Marines traveling between sites, both facilities are in a very poor state of repair.

Chapter 12
Questions

1.   In the 2004 elections, the Republican Party strengthened its majorities in both the U.S. House and Senate. What effect do you expect this might have on the decisions that Congress makes in the next couple of years?

2.   Do you think that porkbarrel legislation is unethical, or is this just a case of "business as usual" with government officials saying "thank you" to the voters and groups that helped get them elected? Why, or why not?

The background of candidates for President of the United States (POTUS to the president's Secret Service protectors) often come under close scrutiny during the campaign, and their characteristics and possible character flaws can play a big role in who wins the election. In the 2004 presidential contest, the personal histories of George W. Bush and John F. Kerry became the stuff of headlines. In "How Kerry Became a Girlie-Man," a *New York Times* essay explores how the mass media were employed to make decorated war veteran Kerry into a less adept military figure than President Bush, who had no military combat experience and at best a questionable record in the National Guard. What a president plans to do is often outlined in the president's inaugural address; Bush's second inauguration speech is reproduced here.

How Kerry Became a Girlie-Man
By Frank Rich, *The New York Times*, September 5, 2004

Only in an election year ruled by fiction could a sissy who used Daddy's connections to escape Vietnam turn an actual war hero into a girlie-man.

As we leave the scripted conventions behind us, that is the uber-scenario that has locked into place, brilliantly engineered by the president of the United States, with more than a little unwitting assistance from his opponent. It's a marvel, really. Even a $10,000 reward offered this year by Garry Trudeau couldn't smoke out a credible eyewitness to support George W. Bush's contention that he showed up to defend Alabama against the Viet Cong in 1972. Yet John F. Kerry, who without doubt shed his own blood and others' in the vicinity of the Mekong, not the Mississippi, is now the deserter and the wimp.

Don't believe anyone who says that this will soon fade, and that the election will henceforth turn on health-care policy or other wonkish debate. Any voter who's undecided by now in this polarized election isn't sitting around studying the fine points. In a time of fear, the only battle that matters is the broad-stroked cultural mano a mano over who's most macho. And so both parties built their weeklong infotainments on militarism and masculinity, from Mr. Kerry's toy-soldier "reporting for duty" salute in Boston to the special Madison Square Garden runway for Mr. Bush's acceptance speech, a giant phallus thrusting him into the nation's lap, or whatever. ("To me that says strength" is how his media adviser, Mark McKinnon, forecast the set's metaphorical impact to The Times.) Though pundits said that Republicans pushed moderates center stage last week to placate suburban swing voters, the real point was less to soften the president's Draconian image on abortion than to harden his manly bona fides. Hence Mr. Bush was fronted by a testosterone-heavy lineup led by a former mayor who did not dally to read a children's book on 9/11, a senator who served in the Hanoi Hilton rather than the "champagne unit" of the Texas Air National Guard, and a governor who can play the role of a warrior on screen more convincingly than can a former Andover cheerleader gallivanting on an aircraft carrier.

Not that Mr. Bush is ignorant of the ways of Hollywood. Unlike Mr. Kerry, whose show business pals he constantly derides, the president actually worked in the film business. In the 1980's he lined his pockets as a board member of Silver Screen, which financed Disney movies. Maybe he even picked up a few tricks of the trade along the way. The elevation of Mr. Bush to Rambo, as The New York Daily News dubbed him last weekend, and the concurrent demotion of Mr. Kerry to Corporal Klinger, is a major production, requiring meticulous preparation. It did not begin with the Swift Boat ads.

The early drafts of the script pre-date 9/11. In "A Charge to Keep," his 1999 campaign biography crafted by Karen Hughes, Mr. Bush implies that he just happened to slide on his own into one of the "several openings" for pilots in the Texas Air National Guard in 1968 and that he continued to fly with his unit for "several years" after his initial service. This is fantasy that went largely unchallenged until 9/11 subjected it to greater scrutiny. Since then, the mysterious gaps in the president's military résumé have been finessed by the dialogue and wardrobe departments, from the invocation of "Wanted: Dead or Alive" (whatever did happen to that varmint, Osama, anyway?) to the "Mission Accomplished" rollout of what an approving Wall Street Journal column described as his "hot" and "virile" flight suit. Of late, Mr. Bush's imagineers have publicized his proud possession of Saddam Hussein's captured pistol, which, in another of their efforts at phallic stagecraft, is said to be kept in the same study where the previous incumbent squandered his own weapon of masculinity on Monica Lewinsky.

But with the high stakes of an election at hand, it's not enough to stuff socks in the president's flight suit. Mr. Kerry must be turned into a girl. Such castration warfare has been a Republican staple ever since Michael Dukakis provided the opening by dressing up like Snoopy to ride a tank. We've had Bill Clinton vilified as the stooge of a harridan wife and Al Gore as the puppet of the makeover artist Naomi Wolf. But given his actual history on the field of battle, this year's Democratic standard bearer would, seemingly, be immune to such attacks, especially from the camp of a candidate whose most daring feat of physical courage was tearing down the Princeton goalposts.

No matter. Once Mr. Kerry usurped Howard Dean, whose wartime sojourn in Aspen made the president look like a Green Beret, the Bush campaign's principals and surrogates went into overdrive. Mr. Kerry was said to appear "French." (That's code for "faggy.") His alleged encounters with Botox and a Christophe hairdresser were dutifully clocked on Drudge. For Memorial Day weekend, the redoubtable New York Post published hypothetical barbecue memos for the two contenders, with Mr. Bush favoring sausage and beer (albeit nonalcoholic) and Mr. Kerry opting for frogs legs, chardonnay and crème brûlée. Ann Coulter, that great arbiter of the marriage bond, posted a column titled "Just a Gigolo" in which the presumptive Democratic candidate was portrayed as "a poodle to rich women." Eventually John Edwards would become "the Breck girl," and Dick Cheney would yank an adjective out of context to suggest that Mr. Kerry wanted to fight a "sensitive" war on terror. (For a translation of "sensitive" in this context, see "French" above.)

But there was still this Vietnam problem. One guy went there, one may have gone AWOL. Enter Karen Hughes. Having helped fictionalize Mr. Bush's wartime years, she now resurfaced to undermine Mr. Kerry's, using her April book tour (for her memoir "Ten Minutes From Normal") to introduce the rhetorical insinuations of mendacity that would surface in the Swift Boat Veterans for Truth assault four months later.

The rest is the rewriting of history. Democrats are shocked that the Republicans have gotten away with it to the extent they have. After all, John O'Neill, the ringleader of the Swifties, didn't serve "with" Mr. Kerry anywhere except on "The Dick Cavett Show." Other members of this truth squad include a doctor who claims to have treated Mr. Kerry's wounds even though his name isn't on a single relevant document and a guy who has gone so far as to accuse Jim Rassmann, whom Mr. Kerry saved from certain death, of being a liar. How could such obvious clowns fool so many? It must be Karl Rove's fault, or Fox's, or a lack of diligence from the non-Fox press.

To some extent, this is true. The connections between the Swifties and the Bushies would be obvious even if the current onslaught didn't mimic the 2000 Bush attack on John McCain, or even if each day didn't bring the revelation of overlapping personnel. When Marc Racicot, the Bush-Cheney chairman, says (dishonestly) that Mr. Kerry has called American troops "universally responsible" for Abu Ghraib, his message sounds coordinated with the Swifties' claim (equally dishonest) that Mr. Kerry once held American troops universally responsible for the atrocities committed in Vietnam.

By turning spurious, unchecked smears into a mediathon, Fox has given priceless nonstop hype to commercials that otherwise would have been seen only in seven small to medium markets, where the total buy of airtime amounted to a scant $500,000. Though the major newspapers, including this one, did vet and challenge the Swifties' claims, aggressive reporting on TV was rare.

But Mr. Kerry, having joined the macho game with Mr. Bush on the president's own cheesy terms, is hardly innocent in his own diminishment. From the get-go he's tried to match his opponent in stupid male tricks. If Mr. Bush clears brush in Crawford, then Mr. Kerry rides a Harley-Davidson onto Jay Leno's set. When the Democrat asks "Who among us does not love Nascar?" and lets reporters follow him around on a "day off when his errands include buying a jock strap, he is asking to be ridiculed as an "International Man of Mystery." In the new issue of GO, you can witness him having a beer (alcoholic) with a reporter as he confesses to a modicum of lust for Charlize Theron and Catherine Zeta-Jones. Presumably the only reason he excluded the demographically desirable Halle Berry is that her Catwoman outfit too closely resembles his own costume for windsurfing.

The flaw in Mr. Kerry is not, as Washington wisdom has it, that he asked for trouble from the Swifties by bringing up Vietnam in the first place. Both his Vietnam service and Vietnam itself are entirely relevant to a campaign set against an unpopular and ineptly executed war in Iraq that was spawned by the executive branch in similarly cloudy circumstances. But having brought Vietnam up against the backdrop of our 2004 war, Mr. Kerry has nothing to say about it except that his service proves he's more manly than Mr. Bush. Well, nearly anyone is more manly than a president who didn't have the guts to visit with the 9/11 commission unaccompanied by a chaperone.

It's Mr. Kerry's behavior now, not what he did 35 years ago, that has prevented his manliness from trumping the president's. Posing against a macho landscape like the Grand Canyon, he says that he would have given Mr. Bush the authority to go to war in Iraq even if he knew then what we know now. The setting may be the Old West, but the words do sound as if they've been translated from the French. His attempt to do nuance, as Mr. Bush would put it, makes him sound as if he buys the message the Republicans hammered in last week: the road from 9/11 led inevitably into Iraq.

The truth is that Mr. Kerry was a man's man not just when he volunteered to fight in a losing war but when he came home and forthrightly fought against it, on grounds that history has upheld. Unless he's man enough to stand up for that past, he's doomed to keep competing with Mr. Bush to see who can best play an action figure on TV. Mr. Kerry doesn't seem to understand that it takes a certain kind of talent to play dress-up and deliver lines like "Bring it on." In that race, it's not necessarily the best man but the best actor who will win.

President Sworn In To Second Term

Vice President Cheney, Mr. Chief Justice, President Carter, President Bush, President Clinton, reverend clergy, distinguished guests, fellow citizens:

On this day, prescribed by law and marked by ceremony, we celebrate the durable wisdom of our Constitution, and recall the deep commitments that unite our country. I am grateful for the honor of this hour, mindful of the consequential times in which we live, and determined to fulfill the oath that I have sworn and you have witnessed.

At this second gathering, our duties are defined not by the words I use, but by the history we have seen together. For a half century, America defended our own freedom by standing watch on distant borders. After the shipwreck of communism came years of relative quiet, years of repose, years of sabbatical - and then there came a day of fire.

We have seen our vulnerability—and we have seen its deepest source. For as long as whole regions of the world simmer in resentment and tyranny - prone to ideologies that feed hatred and excuse murder—violence will gather, and multiply in destructive power, and cross the most defended borders, and raise a mortal threat. There is only one force of history that can break the reign of hatred and resentment, and expose the pretensions of tyrants, and reward the hopes of the decent and tolerant, and that is the force of human freedom.

We are led, by events and common sense, to one conclusion: The survival of liberty in our land increasingly depends on the success of liberty in other lands. The best hope for peace in our world is the expansion of freedom in all the world.

America's vital interests and our deepest beliefs are now one. From the day of our Founding, we have proclaimed that every man and woman on this earth has rights, and dignity, and matchless value, because they bear the image of the Maker of Heaven and earth. Across the generations we have proclaimed the imperative of self-government, because no one is fit to be a master, and no one deserves to be a slave. Advancing these ideals is the mission that created our Nation. It is the honorable achievement of our fathers. Now it is the urgent requirement of our nation's security, and the calling of our time.

So it is the policy of the United States to seek and support the growth of democratic movements and institutions in every nation and culture, with the ultimate goal of ending tyranny in our world.

This is not primarily the task of arms, though we will defend ourselves and our friends by force of arms when necessary. Freedom, by its nature, must be chosen, and defended by citizens, and sustained by the rule of law and the protection of minorities. And when the soul of a nation finally speaks, the institutions that arise may reflect customs and traditions very different from our own. America will not impose our own style of government on the unwilling. Our goal instead is to help others find their own voice, attain their own freedom, and make their own way.

The great objective of ending tyranny is the concentrated work of generations. The difficulty of the task is no excuse for avoiding it. America's influence is not unlimited, but fortunately for the oppressed, America's influence is considerable, and we will use it confidently in freedom's cause.

My most solemn duty is to protect this nation and its people against further attacks and emerging threats. Some have unwisely chosen to test America's resolve, and have found it firm.

We will persistently clarify the choice before every ruler and every nation: The moral choice between oppression, which is always wrong, and freedom, which is eternally right. America will not pretend that jailed dissidents prefer their chains, or that women welcome humiliation and servitude, or that any human being aspires to live at the mercy of bullies.

We will encourage reform in other governments by making clear that success in our relations will require the decent treatment of their own people. America's belief in human dignity will guide our policies, yet rights must be more than the grudging concessions of dictators; they are secured by free dissent and the participation of the governed. In the long run, there is no justice without freedom, and there can be no human rights without human liberty.

Some, I know, have questioned the global appeal of liberty - though this time in history, four decades defined by the swiftest advance of freedom ever seen, is an odd time for doubt. Americans, of all people, should never be surprised by the power of our ideals. Eventually, the call of freedom comes to every mind and every soul. We do not accept the existence of permanent tyranny because we do not accept the possibility of permanent slavery. Liberty will come to those who love it.

Today, America speaks anew to the peoples of the world:

All who live in tyranny and hopelessness can know: the United States will not ignore your oppression, or excuse your oppressors. When you stand for your liberty, we will stand with you.

Democratic reformers facing repression, prison, or exile can know: America sees you for who you are: the future leaders of your free country.

The rulers of outlaw regimes can know that we still believe as Abraham Lincoln did: "Those who deny freedom to others deserve it not for themselves; and, under the rule of a just God, cannot long retain it."

The leaders of governments with long habits of control need to know: To serve your people you must learn to trust them. Start on this journey of progress and justice, and America will walk at your side.

And all the allies of the United States can know: we honor your friendship, we rely on your counsel, and we depend on your help. Division among free nations is a primary goal of freedom's enemies. The concerted effort of free nations to promote democracy is a prelude to our enemies' defeat.

Today, I also speak anew to my fellow citizens:

From all of you, I have asked patience in the hard task of securing America, which you have granted in good measure. Our country has accepted obligations that are difficult to fulfill, and would be dishonorable to abandon. Yet because we have acted in the great liberating tradition of this nation, tens of millions have achieved their freedom. And as hope kindles hope, millions more will find it. By our efforts, we have lit a fire as well - a fire in the minds of men. It warms those who feel its power, it burns those who fight its progress, and one day this untamed fire of freedom will reach the darkest corners of our world.

A few Americans have accepted the hardest duties in this cause—in the quiet work of intelligence and diplomacy ... the idealistic work of helping raise up free governments ... the dangerous and necessary work of fighting our enemies. Some have shown their devotion to our country in deaths that honored their whole lives—and we will always honor their names and their sacrifice.

All Americans have witnessed this idealism, and some for the first time. I ask our youngest citizens to believe the evidence of your eyes. You have seen duty and allegiance in the determined faces of our soldiers. You have seen that life is fragile, and evil is real, and courage triumphs. Make the choice to serve in a cause larger than your wants, larger than yourself—and in your days you will add not just to the wealth of our country, but to its character.

America has need of idealism and courage, because we have essential work at home - the unfinished work of American freedom. In a world moving toward liberty, we are determined to show the meaning and promise of liberty.

In America's ideal of freedom, citizens find the dignity and security of economic independence, instead of laboring on the edge of subsistence. This is the broader definition of liberty that motivated the Homestead Act, the Social Security Act, and the G.I. Bill of Rights. And now we will extend this vision by reforming great institutions to serve the needs of our time. To give every American a stake in the promise and future of our country, we will bring the highest standards to our schools, and build an ownership society. We will widen the ownership of homes and businesses, retirement savings and health insurance—preparing our people for the challenges of life in a free society. By making every citizen an agent of his or her own destiny, we will give our fellow Americans greater freedom from want and fear, and make our society more prosperous and just and equal.

In America's ideal of freedom, the public interest depends on private character—on integrity, and tolerance toward others, and the rule of conscience in our own lives. Self-government relies, in the end, on the governing of the self. That edifice of character is built in families, supported by communities with standards, and sustained in our national life by the truths of Sinai, the Sermon on the Mount, the words of the Koran, and the varied faiths of our people. Americans move forward in every generation by reaffirming all that is good and true that came before—ideals of justice and conduct that are the same yesterday, today, and forever.

In America's ideal of freedom, the exercise of rights is ennobled by service, and mercy, and a heart for the weak. Liberty for all does not mean independence from one another. Our nation relies on men and women who look after a neighbor and surround the lost with love. Americans, at our best, value the life we see in one another, and must always remember that even the unwanted have worth. And our country must abandon all the habits of racism, because we cannot carry the message of freedom and the baggage of bigotry at the same time.

From the perspective of a single day, including this day of dedication, the issues and questions before our country are many. From the viewpoint of centuries, the questions that come to us are narrowed and few. Did our generation advance the cause of freedom? And did our character bring credit to that cause?

These questions that judge us also unite us, because Americans of every party and background, Americans by choice and by birth, are bound to one another in the cause of freedom. We have known divisions, which must be healed to move forward in great purposes—and I will strive in good faith to heal them. Yet those divisions do not define America. We felt the unity and fellowship of our nation when freedom came under attack, and our response came like a single hand over a single heart. And we can feel that same unity and pride whenever America acts for good, and the victims of disaster are given hope, and the unjust encounter justice, and the captives are set free.

We go forward with complete confidence in the eventual triumph of freedom. Not because history runs on the wheels of inevitability; it is human choices that move events. Not because we consider ourselves a chosen nation; God moves and chooses as He wills. We have confidence because freedom is the permanent hope of mankind, the hunger in dark places, the longing of the soul. When our Founders declared a new order of the ages; when soldiers died in wave upon wave for a union based on liberty; when citizens marched in peaceful outrage under the banner "Freedom Now"—they were acting on an ancient hope that is meant to be fulfilled. History has an ebb and flow of justice, but history also has a visible direction, set by liberty and the Author of Liberty.

When the Declaration of Independence was first read in public and the Liberty Bell was sounded in celebration, a witness said, "It rang as if it meant something." In our time it means something still. America, in this young century, proclaims liberty throughout all the world, and to all the inhabitants thereof. Renewed in our strength—tested, but not weary—we are ready for the greatest achievements in the history of freedom.

May God bless you, and may He watch over the United States of America.

Public Domain: accessed at http://www.whitehouse.gov/news/releases/2005/01/20050120-1.html

Chapter 13
Questions

1. Would you want to run for POTUS? Why, or why not? To what extent does your answer hinge on something about your background that might come out in a campaign?

2. Whether or not you would run for President yourself, what do you look for in a presidential candidate? Which do you think matters most: the issues that are raised in the campaign, the party of the candidate, the candidate's personal qualities, or something else? Why?

CHAPTER 14
THE BUREAUCRACY

The agencies that populate the executive branch of the United States government tend to be difficult to understand without some careful effort. In particular, we are supposed to be living in an era of smaller and more restricted national government, but you might be surprised to learn from the "Federal Bureaucracy Thickening" article that by at least some measures the executive branch actually has been growing recently. The most recently created Cabinet-level federal agency is the Department of Homeland Security, formed in response to the terrorist attacks of September11, 2001. In "President Highlights a More Secure America on First Anniversary of Department of Homeland Security," you get a good idea of what that agency does and what the Bush administration wants it to do.

Federal Bureaucracy Thickening, Study Finds
by Amelia Gruber

July 22, 2004

The federal bureaucracy has expanded over the past six years, according to research published Friday by a Brookings Institution scholar.

"Despite the president's promise to bring businesslike thinking to the federal government, the Bush administration has overseen, or at the very least permitted, a significant expansion in the both the height and width of the federal hierarchy," said Paul Light, director of the Center for Public Service at Brookings and a professor at New York University. "There have never been more layers at the top of government, nor more occupants at each layer."

Light based this conclusion on an analysis of positions listed in *The Federal Yellow Book* directory. With the help of a colleague at Brookings, Light compiled an inventory of managers supporting secretaries, deputy secretaries, undersecretaries, assistant secretaries and administrators at each of the Cabinet departments. Such leadership support positions included chief of staff to the secretary, deputy chief of staff to the secretary, chief of staff to the undersecretary and deputy assistant secretary.

In 2004, there were 64 different support titles across the government. Six years ago, there were 51; in 1992, there were 33. A survey completed in 1960 found just 17.

Of the 64 titles in 2004, many existed at only one or two departments. But 19 were listed in at least seven departments, and six were listed at four to seven departments. "Having a chief of staff has become a signal of one's importance in the bureaucratic pecking order," Light wrote in the report.

Historically, titles have tended to proliferate across the government once introduced in one department, Light noted. For instance, in 1981, one department hired a chief of staff to the secretary. By 1992, 10 departments adopted the position, and by 2004, 14 of the 15 cabinet departments listed the title.

The breadth of the bureaucracy has also increased, Light found. In 2004, 2,592 employees held senior government positions, almost a 9 percent increase over 1998, when there were 2,385.

While the Bush administration has slowed the rate of increase in layers of bureaucracy, the administration hasn't focused enough attention on streamlining government, Light said. Streamlining of bureaucracy is not listed as a priority in the President's Management Agenda, but should be, according to Light.

"The Bush management agenda cares nothing about the hierarchical structure of departments . . . and I think that's a big mistake," he said. "If you're not paying attention to it, [an expansion] happens naturally."

According to Light, the long-term trend toward a broadening of bureaucracy stems from the "ever-expanding federal agenda," agencies' tendency to offer senior career executives promotions in lieu of pay increases, efforts to control the bureaucracy through "ever-denser networks" of political appointees, and Congress' creation of new titles such as chief information officer and inspector general.

Over the past six years, the thickening of bureaucracy can be attributed partly to homeland security efforts, Light concluded. The Homeland Security Department has 21 managerial layers with 146 employees filling them, as opposed to the three layers and three occupants planned in the winter of 2003, he stated.

But the jump in homeland security-related work doesn't fully account for the recent expansion of bureaucracy, Light said. "Thickening has occurred in almost every department, including many that are not involved in homeland security or the war on terrorism," he stated in his report.

At the same time, the Defense and Treasury departments have demonstrated that agencies can streamline management, Light said. Treasury underwent a 30 percent reduction in titleholders over the past six years, declining from 239 to 168 largely because of the transfer of Customs and the Secret Service to the Homeland Security Department.

The Defense Department made a concerted effort to streamline management, Light said. Though it still has 30 executive titles—the most in the government—it has reduced its total number of senior titleholders by 21 percent since 1998.

Other federal agencies should follow Defense and Treasury's lead, Light said, adding that they also should look the private sector as a model, he said.

"Unlike the private sector, which extols the virtues of 'less is more' when it comes to management layers, Congress and presidents continue to behave as if new layers of management, and more managers at each layer, somehow improvement accountability and performance," Light wrote. "In fact, more is actually less when it comes to making sure the front lines of government have the resources and guidance they need to faithfully execute the laws."

Amelia Gruber
agruber@govexec.com

Public Domain: accessed at http://www.govexec.com/dailyfed/0704/072204a1.htm

---

President Highlights a More Secure America on First Anniversary of Department of Homeland Security

---

Today's Presidential Action

In remarks celebrating the Department of Homeland Security's first anniversary, President Bush highlighted the accomplishments of DHS and the significant progress being made at the Federal, state, and local level in making America more secure.

On March 1, 2003, approximately 180,000 personnel from 22 different organizations around the government became part of the Department of Homeland Security—completing the largest government reorganization since the beginning of the Cold War. As a result, our efforts to defend the homeland are more effective, efficient, and organized.

Background: Securing the Homeland

The Department of Homeland Security was created with one single overriding responsibility: to make America more secure. Along with the sweeping transformation within the FBI, the establishment of the Department of Defense's U.S. Northern Command, and the creation of the multi-agency Terrorist Threat Integration Center and Terrorist Screening Center, America is better prepared to prevent, disrupt, and respond to terrorist attacks than ever before.

Border and Transportation Security: DHS has unified the agencies responsible for securing our borders—many now wearing the same uniform—to keep out terrorists, criminals, and dangerous material. To do so, DHS is implementing a layered security strategy—including an increased DHS presence at key foreign ports, improved visa and inspection processes, strengthened seaport security, and improved security technology at airports and border crossings. DHS is implementing background checks on 100% of applications for U.S. citizenship and has registered over 1.5 million travelers into the U.S. VISIT program. The Coast Guard also has seized over 136,000 pounds of cocaine and arrested more than 280 drug smugglers in 2003 with this layered approach.

Critical Infrastructure: DHS has worked to better protect our communications systems, power grids, and transportation networks. During the holiday terror alert, DHS coordinated with private and civic partners to upgrade security at key facilities around the country. DHS also established a National Cyber Security Division to examine cyber-security incidents, track attacks, and coordinate response.

Chemical and Biological Threats: DHS has established the BioWatch program, which protects many large U.S. cities by monitoring the air for biological agents that could be released by terrorists. Additionally, with the funding of the President's Project BioShield, America is able to develop and acquire more advanced vaccines and treatments for biological agents.

Helping our First Responders: The Federal Government has provided more than $13 billion to equip and train local officials such as firefighters, police officers, and EMS workers to respond to terrorism and other emergencies and created a National Incident Management system. Over 500,000 responders have been trained in weapons of mass destruction awareness and response since September 11, 2001.

The USA PATRIOT Act: The PATRIOT Act has played a vital role in protecting the homeland, enabling the Federal government to better track terrorists, disrupt their cells, and seize their assets. By breaking down unnecessary barriers between intelligence and law enforcement officers, the PATRIOT Act is helping to ensure that the best available information about terrorist threats is provided to the people who need it most.

Public Domain: accessed at http://www.whitehouse.gov/homeland/index.html

Chapter 14
Questions

1.   Why would Republican administrations preside over a "thickening" of the federal bureaucracy? Why would a Democratic administration (President Clinton's) claim that "the era of big government is over?"

2.   What do President Bush's comments on the new Department of Homeland Security tell you about how a federal bureaucratic agency works? To what extent do you believe that the president's statements are accurate, and to what extent do you believe they represent hoped-for, rather than actual, achievements?

The federal courts often are referred to as different from the "political" legislative and executive branches, particularly in that judicial power lies in the ability to slap down the other branches, as is shown in the article, "In Classic Check and Balance, Court Shows Bush It Also Has Wartime Powers," by Todd Purdham. One of the most important ruling by the U.S. Supreme Court is *Brown v. Board of Education,* in 1954, which played a major role in the civil rights revolution and in the spread of government support for some degree of societal equality; the history of that landmark judicial ruling is provided here.

In Classic Check and Balance, Court Shows Bush It Also Has Wartime Powers
by Todd S. Purdum, The New York Times, June 29, 2004

Washington, June 28—In the fall of 2001, President Bush justified his decision to treat some captured terrorist suspects as "enemy combatants" without access to lawyers, courts or other long-established legal rights on the grounds that he could not let the United States' "enemies use the forums of liberty to destroy liberty itself."

On Monday morning, the Supreme Court upended a good-sized chunk of that logic, and offered a powerful reminder that in the United States, even in wartime, no prisoner is ever beneath the law's regard, and no president above its limits.

It was Justice Robert H. Jackson who first noted 52 years ago this month, in another wartime election summer, that a president is not commander in chief of the country, only of the military. Justice Jackson wrote that in his concurring opinion overturning Harry S. Truman's seizure of the American steel industry during the Korean war, and Justice David H. Souter cited those words approvingly in his concurrence on Monday.

The effect of the current court's ruling in two related cases was to place a classic institutional and political check on Mr. Bush's effort to keep some citizens and aliens held as the most dangerous "enemy combatants" from ever having their day in any court. It is precisely the right to some such hearing, the court held, that defines the constitutional separation of powers and by extension the American governing creed.

While Mr. Bush will now have to seek explicit Congressional authorization in dealing with these terrorist suspects, that should not be an insurmountable task for this president. But it falls to him at a time when he is already facing challenges on many fronts, including the handover of sovereignty in a still-dangerous Iraq, questions about his administration's policies on interrogation of prisoners of war and polls that show slipping public support for his handling the war on terrorism and uncertain prospects for his re-election.

"It is a clear demonstration of how much our system of checks and balances, of separation of powers, continues to be an effective brake on any one branch," said the historian Robert Dallek. "After all, this is not a left-leaning court, or one dominated by justices who are left of center. But ultimately the court has a unique degree of independence from the executive and legislative branches, that even in times of great difficulty it does not lightly give up."

Justice Antonin Scalia dissented from the majority in the case of Yaser Esam Hamdi, an American citizen picked up in Afghanistan and held mostly without access to the outside world ever since, only because he disagreed with its finding that Mr. Hamdi's imprisonment might be justified after a hearing. "The very core of liberty secured by our Anglo-Saxon system of separated powers has been freedom from indefinite imprisonment at the will of the executive," wrote Justice Scalia, who argued that Mr. Hamdi should either be charged with treason or released.

The White House chose to emphasize the parts of the majority opinion in the Hamdi case, and another involving foreign detainees at Guantánamo Bay, Cuba, that supported the president's ability to detain "enemy combatants" without trial.

"The president's most solemn obligation is to defend the American people, and we're pleased that the Supreme Court has upheld the president's authority to detain enemy combatants, including citizens, for the duration of the conflict," said a White House spokeswoman, Claire Buchan. "The administration is committed to fashioning a process that addresses the court's concerns and permits the president to continue to exercise his constitutional responsibility as commander in chief to protect this nation during times of war."

In a statement, Mark Corallo, a Justice Department spokesman, said the department was pleased that the court "upheld the authority of the president as commander in chief of the armed forces to detain enemy combatants, including U.S. citizens." The statement added that the court "also held that individuals detained by the United States as enemy combatants have certain procedural rights to contest their detention. But the court recognized that those procedures must reflect the unique context of the detention of enemy combatants and the need of the executive to prosecute the war."

Much other reaction broke down along predictably partisan lines. Senator John Kerry of Massachusetts, the presumptive Democratic presidential nominee, praised the decision, saying: "I have argued all along with respect to detainees that it is vital to uphold the Constitution of the United States, to respect civil liberties and civil rights, even as we protect our country. I've suggested many ways you can do that, including judicial review, different kinds of review structures."

By contrast, Senator John Cornyn, Republican of Texas, the chairman of the Judiciary Committee's subcommittee on the constitution, civil rights and property rights, called the decisions "a bit of a disappointment," and added: "I am a little concerned about the new constraints that the Supreme Court has placed on the president as commander in chief. I hope that they don't represent handcuffs."

Some historians were not surprised by the court's decisions. Alonzo Hamby, a scholar of the presidency at Ohio University, noted wryly that "once upon a time, it was not assumed that presidents necessarily had to pay attention to Supreme Court decisions."

In the 1830's, when the Supreme Court declared the government's forced removal of Indian tribes from their lands illegal, President Andrew Jackson famously dismissed the ruling by the chief justice by saying: "John Marshall has made his decision. Now let him enforce it."

Mr. Hamby said, "But in the world we live in now, it's literally impossible for a president to ignore a Supreme Court decision, no matter how wrong or dangerous he may think it is."

History of Brown v. Board of Education

The Plessy Decision

Although the Declaration of Independence stated that "All men are created equal," due to the institution of slavery, this statement was not to be grounded in law in the United States until after the Civil War (and, arguably, not completely fulfilled for many years thereafter). In 1865, the Thirteenth Amendment was ratified and finally put an end to slavery. Moreover, the Fourteenth Amendment (1868) strengthened the legal rights of newly freed slaves by stating, among other things, that no state shall deprive anyone of either "due process of law" or of the "equal protection of the law." Finally, the Fifteenth Amendment (1870) further strengthened the legal rights of newly freed slaves by prohibiting states from denying anyone the right to vote due to race.

Despite these Amendments, African Americans were often treated differently than whites in many parts of the country, especially in the South. In fact, many state legislatures enacted laws that led to the legally mandated segregation of the races. In other words, the laws of many states decreed that blacks and whites could not use the same public facilities, ride the same buses, attend the same schools, etc. These laws came to be known as Jim Crow laws.

Although there were many people who felt that these laws were unjust, it was not until the 1890s that they were directly challenged in court. In 1892, an African-American man named Homer Plessy refused to give up his seat to a white man on a train in New Orleans, as he was required to do by Louisiana state law. For this action he was arrested. Plessy, contending that the Louisiana law separating blacks from whites on trains violated the "equal protection clause" of the Fourteenth Amendment to the U.S. Constitution, decided to fight his arrest in court. By 1896, his case had made it all the way to the United States Supreme Court.

By a vote of 8-1, the Supreme Court ruled against *Plessy*. In the case of *Plessy v. Ferguson*, Justice Henry Billings Brown, writing the majority opinion, stated that: "The object of the [Fourteenth] amendment was undoubtedly to enforce the equality of the two races before the law, but in the nature of things it could not have been intended to abolish distinctions based upon color, or to endorse social, as distinguished from political, equality. . . If one race be inferior to the other socially, the Constitution of the United States cannot put them upon the same plane."

The lone dissenter, Justice John Marshal Harlan, interpreting the Fourteenth Amendment another way, stated, "Our Constitution is color-blind, and neither knows nor tolerates classes among citizens." Justice Harlan's dissent would become a rallying cry for those in later generations that wished to declare segregation unconstitutional.

Sadly, as a result of the Plessy decision, in the early Twentieth Century the Supreme Court continued to uphold the legality of Jim Crow laws and other forms of racial discrimination. In the case of *Cumming v. Richmond (Ga.) County Board of Education* (1899), for instance, the Court refused to issue an injunction preventing a school board from spending tax money on a white high school when the same school board voted to close down a black high school for financial reasons. Moreover, in *Gong Lum v. Rice* (1927), the Court upheld a school's decision to bar a person of Chinese descent from a "white" school.

The Road to Brown

(Note: Some of the case information is from Patterson, James T. Brown v. Board of Education: A Civil Rights Milestone and Its Troubled Legacy. Oxford University Press; New York, 2001.)

Early Cases

Despite the Supreme Court's ruling in *Plessy* and similar cases, many people continued to press for the abolition of Jim Crow and other racially discriminatory laws. One particular organization that fought for racial equality was the National Association for the Advancement of Colored People (NAACP) founded in 1909. For about the first 20 years of its existence, it tried to persuade Congress and other legislative bodies to enact laws that would protect African Americans from lynchings and other racist actions. Beginning in the 1930s, though, the NAACP's Legal Defense and Education Fund began to turn to the courts to try to make progress in overcoming legally sanctioned discrimination. From 1935-1938, the legal arm of the NAACP was headed by Charles Hamilton Houston. Houston, together with Thurgood Marshall, devised a strategy to attack Jim Crow laws by striking at them where they were perhaps weakest—in the field of education. Although Marshall played a crucial role in all of the cases listed below, Houston was the head of the NAACP Legal Defense and Education Fund while *Murray v. Maryland* and *Missouri ex rel Gaines v. Canada* were decided. After Houston returned to private practice in 1938, Marshall became head of the Fund and used it to argue the cases of *Sweat v. Painter* and *McLaurin v. Oklahoma Board of Regents of Higher Education*.

Murray v. Maryland (1936)

Disappointed that the University of Maryland School of Law was rejecting black applicants solely because of their race, beginning in 1933 Thurgood Marshal (who was himself rejected from this law school because of its racial acceptance policies) decided to challenge this practice in the Maryland court system. Before a Baltimore City Court in 1935, Marshall argued that Donald Gaines Murray was just as qualified as white applicants to attend the University of Maryland's School of Law and that it was solely due to his race that he was rejected. Furthermore, he argued that since the "black" law schools which Murray would otherwise have to attend were no where near the same academic caliber as the University's law school, the University was violating the principle of "separate but equal." Moreover, Marshall argued that the disparities between the "white" and "black" law schools were so great that the only remedy would be to allow students like Murray to attend the University's law school. The Baltimore City Court agreed and the University then appealed to the Maryland Court of Appeals. In 1936, the Court of Appeals also ruled in favor of Murray and ordered the law school to admit him. Two years later, Murray graduated.

Missouri ex rel Gaines v. Canada (1938)

Beginning in 1936, the NAACP Legal Defense and Education Fund decided to take on the case of Lloyd Gaines, a graduate student of Lincoln University (an all-black college) who applied to the University of Missouri Law School but was denied because of his race. The State of Missouri gave Gaines the option of either attending an all-black law school that it would build (Missouri did not have any all-black law schools at this time) or having Missouri help to pay for him to attend a law school in a neighboring state. Gaines rejected both of these options, and, employing the services of Thurgood Marshall and the NAACP Legal Defense and Education Fund, he decided to sue the state in order to attend the University of Missouri's law school. By 1938, his case reached the U.S. Supreme Court, and, in December of that year, the Court sided with him. The six-member majority stated that since a "black" law school did not currently exist in the State of Missouri, the "equal protection clause" required the state to provide, within its boundaries, a legal education for Gaines. In other words, since the state provided legal education for white students, it could not send black students, like Gaines, to school in another state.

Sweat v. Painter (1950)

Encouraged by their victory in the Gaines' case, the NAACP continued to attack legally sanctioned racial discrimination in higher education. In 1946, an African American man named Heman Sweat applied to the University of Texas' "white" law school. Hoping that it would not have to admit Sweat to the "white" law school if a "black" school already existed, elsewhere on the University's campus, the state hastily set up an underfunded "black" law school. At this point, Sweat employed the services of Thurgood Marshall and the NAACP Legal Defense and Education Fund and sued to be admitted to the University's "white" law school. He argued that the education that he was receiving in the "black" law school was not of the same academic caliber as the education that he would be receiving if he attended the "white" law school. When the case reached the U.S. Supreme Court in 1950, the Court unanimously agreed with him, citing as its reason the blatant inequalities between the University's law school (the school for whites) and the hastily erected school for blacks. In other words, the "black" law school was "separate," but not "equal." Like the Murray case, the Court found the only appropriate remedy for this situation was to admit Sweat to the University's law school.

McLaurin v. Oklahoma Board of Regents of Higher Education (1950)

In 1949 the University of Oklahoma admitted George McLaurin, an African-American, to its doctoral program. However, it required him to sit apart from the rest of his class, eat at a separate time and table from white students, etc. McLaurin, stating that these actions were both unusual and resulting in adverse effects on his academic pursuits, sued to put an end to these practices. McLaurin employed Thurgood Marshall and the NAACP Legal Defense and Education Fund to argue his case, a case which eventually went to the U.S. Supreme Court. In an opinion delivered on the same day as the decision in Sweat, the Court stated that the University's actions concerning McLaurin were adversely affecting his ability to learn and ordered that they cease immediately.

Brown v. Board of Education (1954, 1955)

The case that came to be known as *Brown v. Board of Education* was actually the name given to five separate cases that were heard by the U.S. Supreme Court concerning the issue of segregation in public schools. These cases were *Brown v. Board of Education of Topeka, Briggs v. Elliot, Davis v. Board of Education of Prince Edward County* (VA.), *Boiling v. Sharpe*, and *Gebhart v. Ethel*. While the facts of each case are different, the main issue in each was the constitutionality of state-sponsored segregation in public schools. Once again, Thurgood Marshall and the NAACP Legal Defense and Education Fund handled these cases. Although it acknowledged some of the plantiffs' claims, a three-judge panel at the U.S. District Court that heard the cases ruled in favor of the school boards. The plantiffs then appealed to the U.S. Supreme Court.

When the cases came before the Supreme Court in 1952, the Court consolidated all five cases under the name of Brown v. Board of Education. Marshall personally argued the case before the Court. Although he raised a variety of legal issues on appeal, the most common one was that separate school systems for blacks and whites were inherently unequal, and thus, violate the "equal protection clause" of the Fourteenth Amendment to the U.S. Constitution. Furthermore, relying on sociological tests, such as the one performed by social scientist Kenneth Clark, and other data, he also argued that segregated school systems had a tendency to make black children feel inferior to white children, and thus, such a system should not be legally permissible.

Meeting to decide the case, the Justices of the Supreme Court realized that they were deeply divided over the issues raised. While most wanted to reverse Plessy and declare segregation in public schools to be unconstitutional, they had various reasons for doing so. Unable to come to a solution by June 1953 (the end of the Court's 1952-1953 term), the Court decided to rehear the case in December 1953. During the intervening months, however, Chief Justice Fred Vinson, died and was replaced by Gov. Earl Warren of California. After the case was reheard in 1953, Chief Justice Warren was able to do something that his predecessor had not—i.e. bring all of the Justices to agree to support a unanimous decision declaring segregation in public schools unconstitutional. On May 14, 1954, he delivered the opinion of the Court, stating that "We conclude that in the field of public education the doctrine of 'separate but equal' has no place. Separate educational facilities are inherently unequal. . ."

Expecting opposition to its ruling, especially in the southern states, the Supreme Court did not immediately try to give direction for the implementation of its ruling. Rather, it asked the attorney generals of all states with laws permitting segregation in their public schools to submit plans for how to proceed with desegregation. After still more hearings before the Court concerning the matter of desegregation, on May 31, 1955, the Justices handed down a plan for how it was to proceed; desegregation was to proceed with "all deliberate speed." Although it would be many years before all segregated school systems were to be desegregated, Brown and Brown II (as the Courts plan for how to desegregate schools came to be called) were responsible for getting the process underway.

Public Domain: accessed at http://www.uscourts.gov/outreach/brown_journey.htm

---

Chapter 15
Questions

1. It's been said that "the Supreme Court follows the election returns." What evidence do you see that this statement is true, and what evidence do you see to the contrary?

2. Which branch of government—legislative, executive, or judicial—is most powerful? Why? Which is least powerful? Why?

CHAPTER 16
DOMESTIC POLICY

The federal government has run up a very large national debt by spending more than it takes in as revenue, and this fiscal imbalance has become a major partisan issue. In "Budget and Deficit," Republicans and Democrats in Congress emphasize their differences on how to deal with this problem. In "War's Burden Must be Shared," New York Democratic Representative Charles Rangel defends his proposal for a new military draft with alternative national service, and a Republican counterargument is presented saying that a draft isn't needed in Terry Everett's "Rumors of Impending Military Draft are Unfounded." The way that federal spending responds to natural disasters and to other forms of pressure from the public is addressed in the article, "In Defense of Hurricanes."

Budget and Deficit, from the Senate Republican and House Democratic Budget Committees

Editor's Note: Rarely has the federal budget and deficit been a more politically explosive issue as it became at the end of the 2004 and just weeks before the elections. Below are two pieces that talk about the budget and the deficit one from the Senate Budget Committee controlled by the Republican majority and the second from the House Committee, also controlled by the majority Republicans, but we've reprinted the perspective of the minority Democrats. These reflect the very different perspectives on the same issue as filtered through the partisan political lenses of members of Congress.

Editor's Note: The following is from the Republican Majority Senate Committee

FY05 BUDGET RESOLUTION...SECURITY, OPPORTUNITY, RESPONSIBILITY

Fiscal Discipline

Spending trends cannot continue if Congress is to eliminate red ink...
In a January Congressional Budget Office Report outlining budget options, the unavoidable danger sign was about spending. If Congress continues allowing spending to grow excessively (discretionary spending has grown 6.9 percent annually on average the past five years) the 10-year deficit will be two and a half times larger ($4.57 trillion up from $1.89 trillion).

Federal Reserve Chairman Alan Greenspan agrees...
When asked during a February hearing of the House Budget Committee how much he would cut in terms of discretionary spending to help lower the deficit, Greenspan responded, "I would cut

as much as feasible, largely because the longer-term fiscal outlook is assured if we resolve most, if not all, of the problem on the outlay side."

THEREFORE OUR BUDGET FOCUSES ON FISCAL DISCIPLINE AND SPENDING RESTRAINT BY...

Cutting the deficit in half in three years...
Deficits are projected to fall from $477 billion in FY 2004 to $223 billion in FY 2007, and continue to fall throughout the five-year budget window to $202 billion in FY 2009. As a percentage of the overall economy, the deficit falls from 4.2 percent in FY 2004 to 2.0 percent by FY 2006. By FY 2009, deficits would represent just 1.4 percent of GDP.

Building on a history of slowed spending growth by holding growth in non-defense, nonhomeland security spending to less than 1 percent...
In the 2001 budget, the last before President Bush took office, spending outside of defense and homeland security grew by nearly 15 percent. The President and Congress have cut spending growth in this area to 6 percent in FY 2002, 5 percent in FY 2003 and 3 percent in FY 2004. Our budget continues that pattern of fiscal discipline by this year holding non-defense, non-homeland security spending growth to less than 1 percent, forcing government bureaucracy to trim the fat.

Requiring Congress to crack down on waste, fraud and abuse...
Federal coffers provide a tempting target for fraud and abuse. Our budget instructs the Senate to attack waste, fraud and abuse in mandatory spending programs, and provides a modest savings target of $3.4 billion.

Maintaining budget enforcement tools to protect against unbudgeted spending...
Last year, Senate Republicans used budget enforcement tools to stand firm for fiscal discipline against 59 budget-busting amendments, saving taxpayers a combined $804.5 billion over 10 years in discretionary spending alone. These budget tools are again included in the FY 2005 budget and will provide added protection against unchecked spending in the coming year.

Editor's Note: The following piece is from the Democrats in the House.

The national debt on October 14: $7,430,950,110,669.97
Your share of the national debt: $25,229.92

Administration Announces 2004 Deficit An All-Time Record
Thursday, October 14, 2004—For Immediate Release

Contact: Chuck Fant, 202-225-5501
Spratt Statement on New Deficit Numbers
WASHINGTON — U.S. Rep. John Spratt (D-SC) issued the following statement on the final 2004 deficit figure released today by the Administration.

"Today the Administration announced that the 2004 deficit will be the largest in history—$413 billion—breaking last year's record $377 billion deficit by $36 billion. This deficit represents a remarkable deterioration from the $268 billion *surplus* that the Administration projected (including the cost of its proposed policies) when it took office in 2001—a $681 billion swing in the wrong direction for 2004 alone.

"While the 2004 deficit is an all-time high, the full picture is even worse. When the Social Security Trust Fund surplus is removed from the figures, the 2004 deficit is actually $564 billion, or more than 5 percent of GDP.

"This announcement is the latest in a long series of troubling news items about the budget. Just this morning, the Administration announced that rising debt has hit the statutory limit for the third time in three years, and that the Secretary of the Treasury is avoiding a default only by undertaking extraordinary actions such as disinvesting from a Federal Employees Retirement System investment fund. The debt limit now must be raised again, despite the fact that only 17 months ago the limit was raised by a record $984 billion.

"The Administration may attempt to tout today's numbers as somehow representing an 'improvement' over the inaccurate estimates that it offered earlier in the year. But there is simply no credible way to represent the largest deficit in history as good news.

"Republicans control the House, the Senate, and the White House; but today's release shows that they have failed to control the budget, and cannot escape responsibility for these results. Every year on their watch, the bottom line of the budget has gotten worse and worse."

Public Domain: accessed at http://www.senate.gov/~budget/republican/ and http://www.house.gov/budget_democrats/

War's Burden Must Be Shared
by Congressman Charles Rangel, January 7, 2003

Some people have questioned my motives for introducing legislation to reinstitute the military draft and requiring alternative national service by young people who cannot serve.

In brief, my bill would replace the existing Selective Service law to establish a system in which all American men and women, as well legal permanent residents, aged 18 to 26, would be subject to compulsory military service or alternative civilian service. The President would determine the numbers needed and the means of selection. Deferments would be limited to those completing high school, up to the age of 20, with no exemptions for college or graduate school.

There are some who believe my proposal is really meant to show my opposition to a unilateral preemptive attack against Iraq by the U.S. Others believe that I want to make it clear that, if there is a war, there should be a more equitable representation of all classes of Americans making the sacrifice for this great country.

The fact is, both of these objectives are mine. I truly believe that decision-makers who support war would more readily feel the pain of conflict and appreciate the sacrifice of those on the front lines if their children were there, too. I don't make too much of the fact that only four members of the 107th Congress, which voted overwhelmingly in favor of war with Iraq, had children in the military. That is only a symptom of a larger problem, in which it is assumed that the defense of our country is the sole responsibility of paid volunteers.

But what if I am wrong in my desire for peace and in my doubts that Iraq is an imminent threat? If President Bush, the Congress and other supporters of an invasion are right and war is inevitable, then everyone who loves this country is bound by patriotic duty to defend it, or to share in the sacrifice of those placed in harm's way.

The disproportionately high representation of the poor and minorities in the enlisted ranks is well documented. Minorities comprise 35 percent of the military and Blacks 20 percent, well above their proportion of the general population. They, along with poor and rural Whites do more than their fair share of service in our ground forces. Yet the value of our foot soldiers is demeaned by those who promote the unproven notion that high-tech warfare will bring a quick and easy victory in Iraq.

I fear that the Bush administration's apparent determination to invade Iraq could thrust us into all-out war, perhaps a religious war, in the Middle East. I do not share Defense Secretary Rumsfeld's certainty that the U.S. has the capacity to defeat Iraq and North Korea in quick succession. Most dismaying is the absence of any discussion of the potential loss of life and the principle of shared sacrifice—in both the military and economic spheres.

In fact, the administration is using the rhetoric of war while engaging in politics as usual. While deploying thousands of troops to the Middle East, the President is promoting $600 billion in additional tax cuts which will primarily benefit the most affluent Americans, those whose sons and daughters are least likely to set foot on the sands of Iraq.

If objections to his economic proposal are "class warfare," as the President has said, then President Bush himself has started the war.

Public Domain: accessed at
http://www.house.gov/apps/list/hearing/ny15_rangel/sharedsacrifice010703.html

Rumors of Impending Military Draft are Unfounded
by Congressman Terry Everett, October 11, 2004

In the age of the Internet and lightning fast communication, rumors spread like wildfire and are too often taken as truth by many who choose not to verify them. A classic example is the rumor of an impending return of the military draft. It has assumed a life of its own and has become so widespread that Congress took an unusual step last week to address it.

The chatter among on-line groups and on college campuses about a revival of mandated national military service may have been partially started by the politically-motivated efforts of a New York Democrat Congressman. In January of 2003, liberal lawmaker Charles Rangel of Harlem introduced the Universal Service Act. His bill, if passed, would obligate every U.S. citizen, both men and women, between the ages of 18 and 26 to perform a two-year period of national service.

Rangel's bill would, in effect, reinstitute the draft. This legislation, HR 163, was never popular in the U.S. House and Rangel only garnered five cosponsors—all fellow liberal democrats. Despite this fact, rumors began flying that Congress is preparing to reinstitute the draft.

There have been no calls from President Bush, Vice President Dick Cheney, Secretary of Defense Donald Rumsfeld, or the conservative leadership of Congress for a reinstatement of the draft. As a senior member of the House Armed Services, Intelligence, and Veterans Affairs committees, I have heard no interest in reviving the draft. Indeed, the consensus is just the opposite.

In April, Secretary of Defense Rumsfeld spoke out publicly on the matter noting that he believed a draft to be unnecessary and inappropriate. Similarly, the chairman of the House Armed Services Committee, Rep. Duncan Hunter, R-California, has also made clear he has no intention of considering any legislation to bring back the draft. And on the campaign trail just a few weeks ago, President Bush spoke to the rumors saying they are completely unfounded.

I share in this assessment. A military draft is not only unneeded, but unwise. We have the best trained and motivated armed forces in our nation's history because our military personnel are comprised entirely of volunteers who have chosen to serve their country. A draft would only undermine that cohesion.

Talk of a draft might be taken seriously if our military were running well short of recruitment goals with no change in sight, but such is simply not the case. As Secretary Rumsfeld recently pointed out, the Army and Marine Corps both exceeded their active forces recruiting goals through September 2004 and retention of those already serving is going well. The reserve is also above target in recruitment.

Despite these facts, rumors about a new draft persist and are fueled by President Bush's political opponents who know them not to be true, but nonetheless wish to exploit them for political advantage. Last week, the U.S. House took the usual step of calling up Rep. Rangel's draft bill for a vote to put the matter and the rumors to rest. His legislation failed miserably with 402 lawmakers voting against it. Even Rangel himself voted to kill it.

Just as there are those who choose to believe that man never landed on the Moon, there will be a sizeable number of people who simply choose to believe rumors of an impending draft. Congress and the Administration have presented the facts. There is no need or desire to bring back the military draft. End of story.

Public Domain: accessed at http://wwwc.house.gov/everett/news/columns/col_101104.asp

In Defense of Hurricanes

Hurricanes are not so bad.

In fact, if it weren't for big, active hurricanes people would do dumb things they'd regret later. Like, building flimsy homes or trailer parks close to the shoreline and in low-lying areas that flood. Like, putting up huge pink condos right on the beaches of shifting barrier islands. Like, putting basement parking lots in those condos for their $60,000 Porsches. Like, tying up million dollar boats in long pearly strings with only a piece of rope wrapped around a small cleat on a floating wooden dock. Like, building roads, sticking power poles, and laying boardwalks on the ever-shifting sands along the beaches. Or build America's premier space center on a barrier island, Cape Canaveral.[1]

Of course this is precisely what has happened over the past 30+ years of diminished hurricane activity along the coast of Florida, other Gulf States, and all along the East Coast. After seeing 99% of buildings in his neighborhood damaged, one Floridian said that living on the coast "…is a numbers game. We've been here for 30 years and have dodged all these storms," to which his daughter added, "It's just the price you pay for living in paradise."[2] While this is an admirable resilience, it may unfortunately be true that in the coming 30 years there will be a much greater price to pay for living in paradise.

Understand that I'm personally pained by hurricanes, because I lived in Florida for seven years, I visit South Florida at least five times a year to sail, scuba dive and do research, and because I have many friends living exactly in those places, with boats, sports cars in the basements of their condos, and cute houses in low lying areas. I know personally, people living in trailer parks near the beach. When the big storms of 2004 hit Florida like the Four Horsemen of the Apocalypse, I hurt at the fear and suffering of my friends and the millions of others I saw on TV. And as a coastal policy scientist I'm sympathetic with the local, state and federal

166

authorities who faced a massive task of putting people's lives back together and getting government services up-and-running.

The 2004 hurricane season damaged one in five homes in Florida and early estimates put the cost of all damage at $25-30 billion, which I believe is low. When all the power lines, roads, homes, trailer parks, boats, airplanes, cars and trucks, buildings, beaches, palm trees, docks and piers, oil rigs, transmission towers, signage, bridges, smashed windows, and other man-made things are replaced or repaired, and all the psychological counseling and health care of traumatized people is over, the bill will be a least $150 billion. I've extrapolated this from reviewing many cost estimates of previous storms, insurance company studies, and from risk-management assessments.

But they all should have known they were in a risk area. Memory fades in the absence of experience. The past 30+ years have seen unusually small numbers of hurricanes so people either don't know or had forgotten what these weather systems do.

More interesting is the fact that the coastal zone is by far the fastest growing population area of the United States. The beach, the sea, a boat, lazy days strolling along the dunes, listening to the surf pound in the distance, lounging at the palm-roofed bar sipping margaritas, are by all accounts, the popular culture definition of a great vacation and the "good life." I once had a group of students track the number of times the ocean and the beach appears in movies, TV shows, magazines, and commercials. The general consensus was that this is **the** preferred environment depicted. As a huge tidal wave of "baby boomers" retires in the coming years, we estimate that tens of millions will move to the coast.

If they haven't seen a big eruption in 100 years, people will build cabins on the slopes of volcanoes. If they haven't experienced the horror of massive tremors, building codes in earthquake-prone areas become lax. If there has been drought for 40 years, people build in the ravines and washes of riverbeds.

Anyway, hurricanes are not a choice. They are a reality.

Given their size and fury, hurricanes are an opportunity for people and especially policy-makers to design around. By that I mean that it is possible to behave smartly in the face of hurricanes and to reduce their toll on lives and property and to plan so that in the aftermath of hurricanes the natural environment is protected from toxic spills contamination, and degradation.

The problem is that any prolonged period of "normalcy" without significant hurricane activity reduces the policymaking tools for proactive design or regulation. If it hasn't snowed or iced up for a while, people forget how to deal with snow and ice. If there haven't been many hurricanes for years, neither citizens nor governments remember to be careful what they do and where they do it. Moreover, unless people see and feel the need for aggressive (and expensive) policies, the voters won't pay for it, there is no political support, and thus no political will. Politicians at all levels simply will find it impossible to make hard, unpopular decisions unless they can make a good, credible case.

The active hurricanes of 2004 give us the opportunity to reconsider many policy decisions both along the high risk storm paths on the coast and also in the interior of the Eastern Seaboard states where the deadly tail-ends of the storms end up killing people and destroying homes and communities mostly as a result of flooding and mud-slides.

As the damage from the hurricanes was still being cleaned up and people's lives put back in order, I asked a group of over 30 coastal policy students at Nova Southeastern University Oceanographic Center in Dania Beach, (Ft. Lauderdale), Florida with whom I work on various coastal management projects, to comment on the following question:

"What practical lessons and positive decisions can come from the experience of these storms? What might people, private sector companies, and governments at all levels do to avoid such devastation when the next series of storms hit?"

"I believe that insurance should not cover homes that are in prime areas where natural disasters occur. If the people want to take the cost of their home and move elsewhere, that is fine, but not in the same spot. Like in the Keys, and in floodplain areas along the Mississippi River (the two areas I know most about) insurance companies in both areas do not cover flooding, and in the Keys, they do not cover hurricane damage. Do you see people stopping to build? No…, actually there are people rich enough to not care. Like many others I do no feel that because of their stupidity in where they live, it should cost all of us more. They could make this very simple; if you live so many feet from the coastline, you're NOT covered by insurance. This is how it works in the Midwest floodplains, why can't it work here along the coasts?"

"Living in South Florida (West Palm Beach), and recently experiencing the aftermath of Jeanne and Frances, I believe future hurricane damage would be lessened if the government would regulate shutters. Shutters should be free to low income families, as well as generators. These are the people who did not just have damage but lost their houses and were without power the longest."

"The government should implement codes for all ocean front houses and condos requiring them to have built in generators and built in shutters. I also believe that trailers should be illegal in Florida. They are just too dangerous. If you can't afford a house then apartments are available. Building near the coastline and old construction should be required to have yearly inspections to look for areas that leak, faulty roofs, etc. On a positive note, the hurricanes caused people to come together, in a time of need. With a loss of power, neighbors were getting to know each other, children were playing board games instead of watching TV; there were football games in the street and barbeques. The hurricane caused a lot of us to realize the importance of old fashioned values."

"Probably some kind of more effective structures like concrete pillar/pilings drilled in bedrock, if there were any to be found, with concrete building on top would be helpful. These buildings should have roofs with no overhangs. Trailer parks, which proliferate in Florida, should be prohibited. We can use an example of what works in the Caribbean islands. People will not move out, but the people most hurt are the ones in the wooden shacks right near the ocean. I think a combination of setbacks and sturdier buildings would be the most appropriate response to water based disasters. Erosion is going to take place no matter what (and so what?); I can see that here in just 9 months of living in St. Kitts. People have to take individual responsibility for their behavior. You build on a flood plain or in the path of a hurricane and you're going to get water in your basement once in a while."

"I'm not big on doomsday predictions. I think the most important thing said in the article was [the] quotation by Dr. Mileti: The average person cannot take on worrying about or making very salient for themselves a high consequence/low probability event. Life is full of unpredictable events. Shouldn't we just get over that fact that we have little control?"

"I think that zoning on beaches should only be for recreation—city use (open beaches). Homes and businesses should be a certain distance from the waterfront to allow dunes to develop naturally. The dunes and beaches are our best defense against hurricanes. And if a home is destroyed on the water, insurance shouldn't pay for the rebuilding of a larger structure or even one of the same size. Especially public insurance shouldn't be used for this purpose. It was the owner's choice to build or live on the water and a policy holder inland should not pay for the higher risk decision made by the waterfront property owner. The waterfront property owner should pay for the rebuilding of a structure if they choose to do so and if not, then insurance should be happy to allow the owner to build elsewhere that is not as risky. When new structures are built, they should be designed to have winds go around them not just hit a structure and stop. This can be accomplished by rounding edges of buildings and having flat roofs or very low lying roofs—and not tar/shingled roofs—that just flies away in the winds."

"Some of you may be familiar with this already, but in an attempt to restrict future development along the coast, the Florida Legislature created the Coastal Construction Control Line Program. The program "protects the coastal system from improperly sited and designed structures which can destabilize or destroy the beach and dune system. Once destabilized, the valuable natural resources are lost, as are their important values for recreation, upland property protection and environmental habitat. Adoption of a coastal construction control line establishes an area of jurisdiction in which special siting and design criteria are applied for construction and related activities. These standards may be more stringent than those already applied in the rest of the coastal building zone because of the greater forces expected to occur in the more seaward zone of the beach during a storm event." So the government is trying to help the situation through permitting and zoning, but unfortunately money talks. Many developers either know the loopholes in the program or know the right people to help them along with their project."

"Also thinking about the trailer park comments (above) I am not sure if we should really ban them and live in apartments. As an outsider of Florida looking to move there, the apartments are very expensive. Some thoughts on how to make the trailers sturdier are to build them on better foundations and make them out of stronger material. Also regulate how close they can be to the coast. I do feel that the government should take an active role in all of this and make regulations on where we can build and what the buildings are made of. However, I see a problem with this too, and that is if storms do get worse and worse as people predict, then inland areas need to be regulated as well. I believe this because with bigger storm systems, they get wind damage, tornadoes, as well as local flooding. So I feel as though they should not only regulate coastal buildings but all building to coincide with the increase in severe weather. They should have a list of what materials to use to build in certain areas, and regulate better where people can build and how big they can build."

View all the discussion at: http://coastalpolicy.blogspot.com/

The discussions of policy responses to natural disasters and long-term planning to anticipate problems are interesting because Americans clearly are uncomfortable with "excessive" government regulation. That's clear from the political position of Pres. Bill Clinton when he said in the State of the Union address, "The era of big government is over." The Republican Party also underscores it, which at least since Pres. Ronald Reagan have made "smaller government" their mantra.

Yet, we see time and again (as we did, for example, with the September 11, 2001 terrorist attacks) that the only referee for the management of crisis decisions and action regarding public safety, economic development, transportation and utilities infrastructure, security and law enforcement, and disaster relief itself is government! (I recognize that private agencies, churches, neighbors, and the Red Cross and other non-governmental entities play a huge role in helping communities in these times of crisis, but it's clear that governments at all levels are **the** critically important elements.)

Of course, much of the "smaller government" philosophy applied mainly to trying to slow the growth of the federal government. In fact, many programs and responsibilities were simply shoved down to state, county, and local levels. In a federal system such as the Unites States, we assume that the closer to "the people" the government is, the better it will respond to the community, the citizens, and voters. Thus, regulations and zoning related to coastal management should be smarter if they are done, say, at the state of municipality level. In fact, access to local government is often very uneven because most people are not engaged citizens. Therefore, highly motivated and interested parties such as developers, builders and other commercial interests often have much greater success influencing and helping shape policies. In particular along the coastal areas of the United States where real estate values are rising phenomenally, there has been an unprecedented building boom. In many cases this has been in places that are high risk.

No matter how hard we try, we can only **dominate** coastal areas to the extent that we can armor the beach, and stop storms, wind, and tide from washing away the foundations in which the armor rests. Policy makers would do well to lay out an agenda of both soft coexistence with the realities of coastal ecosystems as well as designing more smartly the "hard" resistance points on which we cannot, really, will not, yield to nature (for example highway A1A down the Florida Keys).

The hurricanes of 2004 are a tragedy. They are also an opportunity for policy makers and citizens to reexamine their priorities and make smarter decisions for the future. In the final analysis, however, these storms prove once again how small and relatively helpless we are in the face of nature's forces.

Hurricanes were here first. They own the coasts!

Chapter 16
Questions

1. How important is it for the federal budget to be balanced? Do you think it's worse for the federal government to have a budget deficit or a budget surplus, and why?

2. As a student, how do you benefit from federal spending? Hint: Think about student loans, scholarships, reduced-price high school meals, mass transportation, highway safety, or just about anything else you might do as a student.

Economic policy in the United States is concerned particularly with the tradeoff between government policy that favors the interests of those who own capital and those who work for the holders of capital. This tension is manifested specifically in policy decisions about how fast to foster job creation as opposed to limiting inflation or providing tax reductions for some groups or corporations. In "Kerry Says Bush is Wrong for Choosing Tax Breaks for Outsourcing Instead of Creating Jobs," you can see how the choices between reducing taxes and stimulating job growth played out in the Democratic Party's rhetoric of the 2004 presidential election campaign. In "Economic Growth and Job Creation," you see the counterargument provided by the Republican party and the Bush administration.

Kerry Says Bush is Wrong for Choosing Tax Breaks for Outsourcing Instead of Creating Jobs

Kerry Says Bush is Wrong for Choosing Tax Breaks for Outsourcing Instead of Creating Jobs Outlines Plan to Create and Keep Jobs in America during NC Town Hall

For Immediate Release: September 7, 2004

Greensboro, NC—Democratic presidential nominee John Kerry Tuesday held a town hall meeting in Greensboro, North Carolina, where he pledged to move America in a new direction by putting an end to tax breaks that reward companies for shipping American jobs overseas.

While George Bush has chosen to support a tax code that rewards outsourcing and moved America in the wrong direction with record job loss and low-paying jobs, Kerry stressed today that his plan will make America stronger at home by creating and keeping good-paying jobs in America.

"Because of George Bush's wrong choices, this country is continuing to ship good jobs overseas—jobs with good wages and good benefits," Kerry said. "All across America, companies have shut their doors, putting hardworking people out of a job, leaving entire communities without help or hope. And you know what George W. Bush's choice is? You know it's the wrong one. He's actually encouraging the export of American jobs."

When it comes to keeping jobs in America, George W. Bush has made the wrong choice for America. Under his watch, our nation is moving in the wrong direction and shipping jobs overseas in record numbers. Over the last three years, America has lost 2.7 million manufacturing jobs.

In the face of this failure, Bush administration officials have consistently defended outsourcing. Bush's Chairman of the Council of Economic Advisors N. Gregory Mankiw called outsourcing "a good thing," and just last week, Labor Secretary Elaine Chao said that it creates jobs. Treasury Secretary John Snow once ran a company that sent jobs abroad, and the president himself was caught trying to name a CEO who outsourced jobs to be the nation's manufacturing czar.

As Kerry noted today, the Bush Treasury Department has even wrongly proposed more tax breaks for companies that move jobs overseas, saying we should we should consider paying for these new tax breaks by raising taxes on companies that export U.S. products.

"Today, the tax code actually does something that's right," Kerry said. "It actually gives tax breaks to companies that export American products. If they sell more products overseas and create jobs here at home, they pay lower taxes so they can grow and expand and hire more people. Sounds like a pretty good idea, right? But George W. Bush doesn't think so. He's wrong again. He wants to end the good tax incentives that help US companies sell more and hire more."

John Kerry and John Edwards know America needs to move in a new direction, and they have a plan that ends tax breaks for companies that ship jobs overseas.

While Bush chooses tax breaks for outsourcing, the Kerry-Edwards plan will end the tax breaks that encourage companies to ship jobs overseas and use the savings to reward companies that create jobs in America. Under their plan, 99 percent of companies will pay lower taxes—but no company will pay lower taxes just because it creates jobs overseas.

"Let me say it plainly: it is wrong to give tax breaks to companies that ship our jobs overseas," Kerry said. "So we're going to set a new direction for America. We're going to close the tax loopholes that reward companies for shipping jobs overseas, and we're going to reward companies that believe that American workers do the best job in the world."

The Kerry-Edwards plan to create and keep jobs in America is a key part of their broader economic plan which includes enforcing our trade agreements, cutting the budget deficit, reining in the spiraling costs of health care, moving America towards energy independence and investing in education and technology.

Paid for and authorized by Kerry-Edwards 2004, Inc.

Public Domain: accessed at http://www.johnkerry.com/

From the White House Homepage

Economic Growth and Job Creation

"Today we are taking essential action to strengthen the American economy.... We are helping workers who need more take-home pay. We're helping seniors who rely on dividends. We're helping small business owners looking to grow and to create more new jobs. We're helping families with children who will receive immediate relief. By ensuring that Americans have more to spend, to save, and to invest, this [tax relief] legislation is adding fuel to an economic recovery. We have taken aggressive action to strengthen the foundation of our economy so that every American who wants to work will be able to find a job."

-President George W. Bush, May 28, 2003

The Accomplishments

A Growing Economy
- Since last summer, *the American economy has grown at the fastest rate of any major industrialized nation.*
- *America's economy has been growing at rates as fast as any in nearly 20 years.*
- *Nearly 1.5 million jobs have been created since August 2003* and 1.3 million new jobs have been created this year alone. The unemployment rate today is below the average unemployment rate of the 1970s, the 1980s, and the 1990s.
- From 2000 to 2003, *productivity grew at the fastest three-year rate in more than a half-century*, raising the standard of living for all Americans.
- The Conference Board's index of leading indicators has risen at an average annual rate of 4.2 percent since March 2003 - the fastest 15-month period of increase in 20 years - *suggesting vibrant economic growth in the near term.*
- The stock market regained more than $4 trillion in equity since its low in mid-2002. *In 2003 the Dow Jones Industrial Average rose 25 percent and the NASDAQ rose 50 percent.*
- *Manufacturing activity expanded in July 2004 for the 14th consecutive month.*
- Real after-tax incomes are *up 11 percent* since December 2000.
- Interest rates reached their *lowest levels in decades* during the Bush Administration.
- *Homeownership reached an all-time high and mortgage rates reached their lowest level in decades.*
- During the Bush Administration, we have experienced one of the *lowest core inflation rates (averaging two percent per year) in the past 40 years.*

Historic Tax Relief

- President Bush, working closely with Congress, *provided the largest tax relief in a generation.*
- The President secured enactment of *three major tax relief bills*, providing tax relief to every taxpayer who pays income tax while completely eliminating the income tax burden for nearly five million families.
- In 2004, taxpayers will receive, *on average, a tax cut of $1,586.*
- *The marriage penalty for low and moderate income taxpayers has been reduced.* In 2004, 49 million married couples will receive an average tax cut of $2,602.
- *The child tax credit has been doubled, increasing from $500 to $1,000.* In 2004, 43 million families with children will receive an average tax cut of $2,090.
- *Twenty-five million small business owners will receive tax relief averaging $3,001.* The President's tax relief also provides America's businesses with incentives to invest in new equipment to make their workers more productive and to create new jobs.
- President Bush, working with Congress, *is phasing out the death tax.*

Providing Job Training

- President Bush proposed the *Jobs for the 21st Century initiative*, providing more than a half-billion dollars in funding for new education and job training initiatives. The plan includes $250 million to fund partnerships between community colleges and employers to help Americans prepare for the higher-skilled, higher-paying jobs of the new century, and $33 million for expanded Pell Grants for low-income students.
- The Bush Administration proposed *$23 billion for job training and employment assistance in 2005.*
- The President proposed a *$50 million Personal Reemployment Accounts pilot program*, allowing unemployed workers who have the hardest time finding jobs to choose the services they need to return to work, including assistance with training, child care, and transportation costs.
- President Bush has supported *extension of Federal unemployment benefits* three times, providing more than $23 billion to help almost eight million American workers.
- President Bush proposed to *reform major Federal job training programs* to double the number of people trained, and to ensure more people receive flexible Innovation Training Accounts which allow workers to make choices about the skills they need.

Helping America's Small Businesses

- President Bush's *historic tax relief* reduced marginal income tax rates across-the-board, benefiting the more than 90 percent of small businesses that pay taxes at individual income tax rates. In 2004, 25 million small businesses will save, on average, $3,001 due to the President's tax relief.
- *President Bush raised from $25,000 to $100,000 the amount that small businesses can expense for new capital investments*, reducing the cost of purchasing new machinery, computers, trucks, and other qualified investments.
- *The number of women-owned businesses has continued to grow at twice the rate of all United States businesses.* Women are now the owners of 10.6 million businesses in the country, which generate $3.6 trillion in sales, and between 1997 and 2002, employment at majority-women-owned private companies increased by 30 percent.

- The Bush Administration *proposed and supports Association Health Plans* (AHPs) to help employees of small businesses afford health coverage.
- *The regulatory burden on small businesses has been reduced.* Small business owners have also been given a bigger voice on ways to improve regulations.
- The Administration has implemented *new regulations that help small businesses* compete for Federal procurement dollars and streamlined the appeals process.

Promoting Minority Small Businesses
- Business loans to minorities *increased by 40 percent* in 2003.
- President Bush proposed a *21 percent increase for the Minority Business Development Agency*, the largest increase in more than a decade.

Supporting Technological Innovation
- President Bush has proposed the *largest Federal research and development budget in history*.
- President Bush proposed *making permanent the research and experimentation tax credit* to promote private sector investment in new technologies and manufacturing techniques.
- The President created a *new math and science partnership program* to improve teacher training and student learning. The President's 2005 budget meets his commitment to fully fund his five-year, $1 billion goal.
- The Bush Administration set a national goal of *universal, affordable access to broadband technology* by the year 2007—and it has opposed all efforts to tax access to broadband.

Restraining Federal Spending and Improving Government Efficiency
- President Bush *brought the annual rate of growth in non-security discretionary spending down* from 15 percent in the last budget enacted during the Clinton Administration to a proposed 0.5 percent for next year.
- The President's budget will put the country on a path toward *cutting the deficit in half* from its peak over the next five years. And better progress is being made than anticipated just six months ago. Rising revenues, spurred by a growing economy, are decreasing the deficit faster than anticipated.
- The Bush Administration launched the President's Management Agenda (PMA) to *make the Federal government more results-oriented and accountable.* For the first time, a majority of agencies evaluate their employees based on how well they are performing relative to clear expectations. Departments and agencies have assessed the performance of more than 600 programs, representing approximately $1.4 trillion in Federal spending, And by working to eliminate more than $35 billion in improper payments and producing more timely and accurate financial information, more Federal agencies than ever are being held accountable for spending the taxpayers' money wisely.
- The Bush Administration has achieved *the biggest overhaul of the Federal civil service system in a quarter-century* and opened up hundreds of thousands of Federal jobs to competition. The result is that government provides better results at lower costs to taxpayers.

Chapter 17
Questions

1.   Which do you think is more important, to make sure that everyone can get a job or to reduce taxes? Why?

2.   Of the two arguments presented here, do you agree more with Kerry's views or those expressed by the Bush administration? What do these statements have in common, and to what extent do you think they are in opposition to each other?

It is important to know how the United States relates to the roughly 200 other countries on the planet, as well as the many nongovernmental organizations such as the United Nations, interest groups, and corporations that play a major role in international affairs. "U.S. Foreign Policy in the Second Bush Term" gives a broad overview of the foreign policy likely to be followed by a second Bush administration. "The Dark Side" assesses the global spread of what the United States regards as "terrorism" directed against its national interests and the interests of U.S.-supported governments and global organizations. An official statement of U.S. foreign policy, regarding women's rights and its role in the war in Afghanistan is provided in "US Commitment to Afghan Women: The U.S.-Afghan Women's Council."

U.S. Foreign Policy in the Second Bush Term

The most important objective is to protect the American people and spread freedom and democracy. (Bush 11/4)

"So the President is not going to, as has been said, trim his sails or pull back. It's going to be a continuation of his principles, his policies, his beliefs. And I think people will see that it is a foreign policy of national interests and the interests of our friends and alliances, multilateral in nature, willing, however, when necessary, to act if we have to act alone or with a willing coalition to defend our interests and our needs. And the President took that message to the American people and the American people accepted that message and gave him more than a marginal mandate to keep moving forward." (Powell 11/9)

Afghanistan: "The Afghan people, by going to the polls in the millions, proved ... that this administration's faith in freedom to change peoples' habits is worthy." (Bush 11/4)

"We will continue to consolidate the success that we have seen in Afghanistan as manifested in the presidential elections and get Afghanistan ready for the parliamentary elections next Spring, continue our reconstruction efforts, continuing the resettlement of the 3.7 billion Afghan refugees who have returned to the country and continue our efforts to work with Pakistan to defeat the Al Qaeda and Taliban elements that are working in the frontier areas of Pakistan, as well as continuing to fight those elements that come across into Afghanistan or in Afghanistan that are trying to stop this progress towards democracy." (Powell 11/8)

War Against Terrorism: We will persevere until the enemy is defeated and our nation is safe from danger. Every civilized country also has a stake in the outcome of this war. (Bush

On Cooperation with Europe: I'll continue to reach out to our friends and allies, our partners in the EU and NATO, to promote development and progress, to defeat the terrorists and to encourage freedom and democracy as alternatives to tyranny and terror. (Bush 11/4)

Iraq: "We will work with the Allawi government to achieve our objective, which is elections, on the path to stability, and we'll continue to train the troops." (Bush 11/4)

"With respect to Iraq, a regime that we determined was dangerous is gone. We still have a difficult insurgency to face, but there's no reason that Iraq cannot go down the path that Afghanistan has gone down. ... Now what we're going to do is complete the effort to give the Iraqi people a democracy." Powell 11/9

Iran: We and the Europeans continue to agree on the fundamentals that ... Iran needs to cooperate fully with the International Atomic Energy Agency; it needs to meet its nonproliferation obligations; and it needs to suspend fully and immediately all enrichment-related and reprocessing activities. (Boucher 11/8)

"I think the nuclear issue is an important one to resolve in one way or another, but there are other aspects of Iranian behavior that are troubling -- support for terrorist activity -- and we'll just have to see whether or not there are openings here or not." (Powell 11/9)

Middle East Peace: "I agree with him [U.K. Prime Minister Tony Blair] him that the Middle East peace is a very important part of a peaceful world. I have been working on Middle Eastern peace ever since I've been the President. I've laid down some -- a very hopeful strategy on -- in June of 2002, and my hope is that we will make good progress. I think it's very important for our friends, the Israelis, to have a peaceful Palestinian state living on their border. And it's very important for the Palestinian people to have a peaceful, hopeful future. That's why I articulated a two-state vision in that Rose Garden speech. I meant it when I said it and I mean it now." (Bush 11/4)

"The United States stands by to work very actively to get the Road Map moving forward." [Powell 11/8]

"What we have been looking for this whole period is responsible leadership on the part of the Palestinians so that we can get going. And we recognize that Israel has obligations as well with respect to outpost elimination and settlement activity. And in this period that we're in now, waiting to see what transpires with respect to Palestinian leadership, we hope that opportunities will come out of this transition period." (Powell 11/9)

Global Issues: "We have an obligation in this country to continue to work with nations to help alleviate poverty and disease. We will continue to press forward on the HIV/AIDS initiative, the Millennium Challenge Account. We will continue to do our duty to help feed the hungry." (Bush 11/4)

Climate Change: "The Administration, remains committed to a technically-sound and market-driven approach to combating climate change and in fact has $5.8 billion in this year's budget to support that approach." (Boucher 11/8)

Multilateralism: "The President's National Security policy ... [is] a policy of partnerships. It's a policy of reaching out. It's a policy of working with others on opening up trade around the world. It's a policy of dealing with the infectious diseases that are really killing many more thousands of people a day than any terrorist incident will. It's a policy of expansion of alliances. It's a policy of working multilaterally to deal with problems like the nuclear issue in Iran and the nuclear issue in North Korea." (Powell 11/9)

The Dark Side
by Roy Morrison

The Twin Towers unfortunately were just the beginning of the march of slaughter. The shroud has spread over a school in Russia, working class commuter trains in Madrid, buses in Israel, market places in Baghdad, nightclubs in Bali.

The brutality is calculated. The innocent are the target. The justifications, if any are offered, are blood for blood, or perhaps the redemptive righteousness of murder, or the mad claim of murder to help reconstitute a medieval theocracy.

War College professors attempt to parse a new doctrine of asymmetrical warfare and the weapons of the weak. Box cutters and farm fertilizer become effective tools against our high technology nation state still fixated on spending billions on star wars ballistic missile interceptors.

Two things are clear. First, mass terror has become the practice of a global grassroots movement. It is certainly not now, if it ever was, under the direction of Osama bin Laden and a coherent Al Queda network who once upon a time declared war against the United States.

Second, this movement is much more than simply an undifferentiated expression of terror. We are in conflict with a movement, not a tactic. We are struggling with a global Islamist movement that is best understood as an essentially fascist and reactionary political ideology, as cogently described by Paul Berman in his Terror and Liberalism. The Islamist movement embraces a theocratic authoritarianism, a cult of redemptive violence, and terror as a tactic. It is no more a representative expression of Islam and Islamic civilization than the Army of God bombing abortion clinics represents Christianity and the West. The Islamists are a mass movement that has embraced the dark side.

Guns and repression are not the weapons of choice to triumph over a diffuse, global grassroots movement. In the long run, the struggle will be won or lost not by killing or capturing the current generation of terror leaders, but by creating conditions where the support for and efficacy of succeeding generations of Islamists declines and where terrorism's new recruits effectively vanish as the fascist plague has run its course.

The security battle against terrorist cells that need be fought in the shadows is quite different from the concomitant political and social struggle that must, by its nature, take place in a largely public sphere. It's the politics, not the guns that will matter most in the end. We must understand the dynamics of diffuse global grassroots movements that share a common ideology and commitment.

We need to turn to people who may know little or nothing about war and violence. They are not self-styled terrorism experts. What matters most is not how to hatch plans to infiltrate terror cells or catch their leaders. What counts at least as much is understanding what makes movements thrive. What makes people flock to their cause? What turns people away? What's empowering? What makes movements turn away from radical demands and tactics and embrace conventional democratic practice? Practitioners of such movements, the activists, not just scholars and professors, may have important contributions to make to such considerations.

I have many years experience, for example, with the non-violent antinuclear and peace movements. In a little more than two years from 1976 to 78 a small group of New England anti-nuclear organizers, following the example of German farmers and activists occupying the Whyl nuclear power plant site, built the Clamshell Alliance, a mass nonviolent movement of tens of thousand in New England.

Clamshell and the Islamists are polar opposites. We embraced nonviolence. They exalt slaughter. We were open and public. They are closed and secretive. We used consensus. They are authoritarian. We embraced diversity and freedom. They preach exclusivity and obedience. We produced a Handbook for Nonviolent Action. They publish manuals for terror. We trained all participants be trained in nonviolence and followed nonviolent guidelines. They train people in black arts of terror and murder. We announced major actions in advance. They move by stealth. We were organized into nonviolent affinity groups. They form terror cells. We moved at our best toward the light. They represent the dark side. And yet we are both diffuse grassroots based mass movements subject to broadly common dynamics, albeit in radically differing circumstances and for diametrically opposed ends.

Clamshell inspired the formation of dozens of similar Alliances around the Country. Clamshell was joined by such as the Shad on Long Island, Abalone in California, Paddle Wheel on the Mississippi… Our movement continued to grow explosively for a few years, particularly following the Three Mile Island accident in 1979. But in the 1980s, the grassroots movement, while still a force, had lost much of its efficacy. Why and how did this happen?

In capsule, the strength of the anti-nuclear movement was undermined by our success. We helped stop the orders for new plants, contributed to the abandonment of more than 150 orders and projects, helped make the TMI accident and then Chernobyl catastrophe understood as events of global import confirming our arguments. At the same time, the movement was damaged by internal tactical disputes, encouraged, but not caused by police infiltration.

Meanwhile many of our positions were adapted, to greater or lesser extents, by main stream politicians. A calculus of successes and failures helped transform the energies of the grassroots antinuclear movement from a potentially radically transformative force toward more moderate reform. We need to undertake a similar calculus to project how we might affect Islamist energies in the future.

The stakes are high. The danger is not just that small bands of lunatics will inflict more and increasingly bloody acts of murder, or that they will obtain weapons of mass destruction to perpetrate truly titanic slaughter. The deeper danger is that the global grassroots Islamist movement will find legitimacy and come to represent, in the minds of people, the best and legitimate expression of their hopes and aspirations. Adolf Hitler, we should remember, did not seize power as a result of a failed beet hall putsch. He was elected. And then went about his murderous business.

In Palestinian politics Hamas, for example, has already become a competitor for power with Arafat's Fatah. The PLO is enormously corrupt; Hamas is at least comparatively virtuous as providers of social services while it conducts murderous terror attacks.

To effectively campaign against the global grassroots Islamist movement, we must disabuse ourselves of the false beliefs that we can behave as if we are at war with nation states, or that support of nation states is what is crucial for the health of this global grassroots movement.

The Bush administration doesn't seem to have a clue. Their war in Iraq has stoked the flames of resentment against the United States, helped build the global terror movement and aided in the global recruitment of a new generation of terrorists, and distracted the United States and our allies both from the battle against the Islamists and even the beginnings of an effective constructive global program to undermine the Islamists global mass movement.

Following Sept. 11, George Bush didn't put out a call for either participation or sacrifice in wake of the attack on the Twin Towers. He told us to shop, go back to work and let the experts take care of the problem. He was wrong then and he's wrong now. The U.S. response to 911 was a conquest of Afghanistan that both permitted the escape of bin Laden and key associates and failed to build a strong and democratic Afghan government.

This was followed by a superfluous, preemptive war against Iraq. Bush's failed plan is to bring democracy to the Middle East through the barrel of a gun and the blood of American soldiers. It is a recipe for building the strength of the Islamist terror movement, not defeating it.

The alternative is a commitment and partnership for peacemaking, democratization from below, and sustainable development. Instead of a military colossus raining bombs from the heavens we need to be partners in lifting the burden of debt from impoverished nations, in the equitable development of fair trade, in the embrace of renewable resources to free both ourselves and the petroleum exporting nations from the oil curse. So much to do and almost nothing is being done beyond the rain of bombs. If we turn toward an enlightened pursuit of our self-interest, pursuing peace and justice the United States will triumph in struggle against Islamist terror with the least cost in blood or in treasure. If we would only really act as a beacon for democracy, a partner in shared prosperity and freedom and not global military overlord...

George Bush is wrong. He still acts as if ordinary Americans can just sit on the sidelines and that Marines and National Guardsmen fighting in the streets of Najav are somehow winning his so-called war against terror. This is the road to ruin.

We need turn away from our own dark side. We need understand the dynamics of global mass movements and how through the pursuit of peace and justice and sustainable prosperity we can help lift the shroud of Islamist terror.

It's worth recalling what JFK said to us in January 1961, "Ask not what your country can do for you. Ask what you can do for your country." It's time.

Roy Morrison's latest book is *Tax Pollution, Not Income*. In 2004 he was a candidate for the Democratic nomination in N.H.'s 2nd CD.

U.S. Commitment to Afghan Women: The U.S.-Afghan Women's Council

Fact Sheet
Office of the Senior Coordinator for International Women's Issues
Washington, DC
February 22, 2005

After the fall of the Taliban, the United States launched a historic initiative to help elevate the status of women in Afghanistan. To accelerate progress, President George W. Bush and President Hamid Karzai announced the creation of the U.S.-Afghan Women's Council (USAWC) on January 28, 2002. The Council promotes public-private partnerships between U.S. and Afghan institutions and mobilizes private sector resources to help Afghan women. Specifically, the Council seeks to identify concrete actions to bring real and practical benefits to the women of Afghanistan and to enable them to participate and take leadership roles in the political and economic life of their country. To this end, the Council has made education and microfinance its top priorities.

Meetings
The Council meets twice a year, alternating between Kabul and Washington, D.C., to discuss programs and priorities for assisting Afghan women and to review progress. Under Secretary of State for Global Affairs Paula Dobriansky co-chairs the Council with the Afghan Foreign Minister and the Afghan Minister of Women's Affairs. See http://usawc.state.gov/c10666.htm for more information about Council members.

June 2004: The Council's fifth meeting was held in Washington, DC in the Treaty Room of the White House on June 15, 2004. Members and invited Afghan and American special guests discussed several key issues, including the Afghan national elections, health care, and jobs. President Bush, President Karzai, Secretary Powell, National Security Advisor Rice, and Secretary of Health and Human Services Thompson met with the group. First Lady Laura Bush honored the Council with a lunch. More than 20 Afghan women attended the meeting and the lunch, including four Afghan Fulbright scholars (a U.S. Department of State educational exchange program), four Afghan women judges on a USAWC training project, and 12 U.S. Department of Agriculture Cochran Fellows in the U.S. for a U.S. Department of Agriculture program for job training in agribusiness.

February 2004: The fourth meeting of the Council was held in Kabul, February 24-26, 2004. Discussions focused on education, specifically the Teacher Training Institute and Afghan Literacy initiative; microfinance; the new constitution; and the elections in Fall 2004. The delegation visited a women's center and met with project managers of programs supported by the U.S. Government and by the U.S.-Afghan Women's Council.

July 2003: The Council's third meeting, in Washington, D.C., July 15-16, 2003, focused on the educational needs of women and girls, job skills training, business development, and the upcoming elections. The delegation met with First Lady Laura Bush and National Security Advisor Condoleezza Rice at the White House. Secretary Powell hosted a luncheon in their honor.

January 2003: At the Council's second meeting in Kabul, the U.S. announced that it would provide $2.5 million for women's resource centers in 14 of Afghanistan's provinces. The Council also committed $1 million in education and exchange programs for the centers. Programs at these centers focus on basic education literacy, microfinance and small business opportunities, human rights education, and the development and management of non-governmental organizations (NGOs).

Inaugural Meeting: The inaugural meeting took place in Washington, D.C. in April 2002. In response to a request from the Afghan side, the Council later announced its first initiative would bring Afghan women who work in government ministries to the United States for an educational exchange program. The program focused on computer training, leadership, and management training, and other skills vital to their positions.

Accomplishments

Political Participation

Women's Resource Center: USAID is building 17 Women's Resource Centers in Afghanistan. Four centers have been completed and two more are scheduled to finish in the near future. The centers will support outreach, advocacy, and policy formation of the Ministry of Women's Affairs, and create a space in rural provinces for training women in education, health, job skills, leadership, legal awareness, and political participation. Through USWAC women executives of AOL(Time Warner) donated $60,000 for the construction of the resource center in Parwan.

Afghan Women Leaders Connect (AWLC) ($10,000): This contribution supported a conference in Kabul in Fall 2004 hosted by the Women and Children Legal Research Foundation focusing on legal rights. This is in addition to the Summer 2004 grant of $10,000 that AWLC provided to the International Association of Women Judges to supplement the $75,000 grant by the State Department's International Narcotics and Law Enforcement Bureau, which trained four Afghan women judges in civil and family law.

Digital Video Conference: The Council has used digital videoconference (DVC) technology to connect Kabul, Washington, DC and New York, setting up links for discussions and mentoring sessions between women in these cities. The DVC in November 2003 focused on women's political participation in Afghanistan's draft constitution and the Afghan elections in 2004. The DVC in April 2003 focused on the topic of women and business.

Economic Opportunities

Community Banks: The Council views microcredit as an important means of helping women gain self-sufficiency through starting their own businesses. Through an original $10,000 donation to the Council from Daimler-Chrysler, the Foundation for International Community Assistance (FINCA), a leading NGO in microfinance, helped start two village banks in Herat. Daimler-Chrysler contributed an additional $25,000 in February 2004 to construct another five community banks to support microfinance loans for women in Herat province. With Additional funding from the U.S. Government and other donors, FINCA expects to assist more than 30,000 clients in Afghanistan over the next 5 years.

U.S. Bureau of Educational and Cultural Affairs/USAWC Department of State Grants ($750,000): Five grants were awarded to organizations for proposals that include: business and political leadership training (grant to World Learning); entrepreneurship training (grant to Women for Afghan Women); education and literacy training (grants to American Council for International Education and Institute for Training and Development); and women's leadership training (grant to University of Delaware). Seventy-one women have taken leadership training under the University of Delaware grant thus far.

Thunderbird Graduate School of International Management: Fifteen Afghan women successfully completed an advanced entrepreneurship training in January 2005. The participants aim to start businesses that would create jobs for women and to serve as mentors/teachers in Afghanistan.

Global Summit of Women ($40,000): Supported by USAID, a delegation of nine Afghan women attended the 2004 Global Summit in Seoul, Korea, in May to discuss trade opportunities and receive entrepreneurship training.

Arzu Carpet Initiative ($530,000): This program provides training and literacy skills to Afghan women in the hand-knotted carpet industry. Connie Duckworth, a USAWC member, provided the seed money to get the project started. Arzu placed its first carpet order on International Women's Day (March 8, 2004). The project Arzu (which means "Hope" in Dari) not only creates jobs and a cottage industry, it also re-circulates some of its profits to support microcredit initiatives and additional training for women.

U.S. Department of Agriculture Cochran Fellowships: Twelve women representing five provinces came to the United States in Spring 2004 for job training as managers and technicians in agribusiness.

Handicraft Training ($130,000): The Global Summit of Women (July 2002 in Barcelona, Spain) donated approximately $10,000 for job-skills training for women. Through this program, Shuhada, a local organization, is training women in weaving skills. At the conclusion of the program, the women will receive their own looms to produce textiles for market.

Media

Women Journalists: The PBS broadcast in November 2004 of the film "Afghanistan Unveiled" created an opportunity for mentoring for another Afghan journalist, the fourth that PBS, through USAWC auspices, has trained in the U.S. PBS provided modern digital video production and editing equipment for the women video filmmakers to use in Afghanistan and training videos for use at AINA, a Kabul-based NGO devoted to media training. The film "Afghanistan Unveiled" for which PBS paid $20,000 in royalties and rights depicts life under the Taliban and the journalist's' journey for the truth. PBS has also optioned the rights for AINA's next film about women's human rights called "If I Stand Up." These films and several short videos to encourage women to vote were made by the "women's project" at AINA with Department of State and USAID funding (from Summer 2002 through the October 2004 elections). The Asia Foundation (TAF) was a partner on the original "Afghanistan Unveiled" project in 2002 and continues to host trainings and screenings of the film (California, Maryland and Sundance Festivals.)

Health

Health Advisory Committee: On July 26, 2004 the Council's newly formed Health Advisory Committee sponsored a special session to discuss health issues and create public/private partnerships to utilize resources for greater impact and sustainability. Under Secretary Paula Dobriansky hosted the organizing meeting for the committee.

Midwife Training: The $5-million Rural Education and Community Health Care Initiative (REACH) provides health-related accelerated learning and basic literacy training for women and girls. Training will take place in the Women's Centers and will target provinces with the highest maternal mortality rates such as Ghazni, Baghlan, and Badakhshan. In April 2004, REACH graduated its first 25 midwives from the program, after they completed an 18-month program in Jalalabad. This pilot program is being replicated across Afghanistan. For each new midwife, the U.S. is supporting a lifetime of lives saved.

Afghan Family Health Book: In Fall 2004, U.S. Health and Human Services (HHS) Secretary Tommy Thompson initiated the roll-out of the "Afghan Family Health Book" across Afghanistan. This "talking book" provides useful and practical information about health practices and hygiene, focusing on health promotion and disease prevention. The books are being distributed via hospitals, clinics, and women's. The project was developed with Leapfrog Enterprises Inc., a developer, designer, and manufacturer of technology-based educational products.

Education

Fulbright Scholarships: Five Afghan women were awarded Fulbright scholarships for the academic year 2004-2005 for advanced graduate-level study in the U.S.

Women's Teacher Training Institute ($4 million): In cooperation with USAID, First Lady Laura Bush announced a USAWC Initiative to establish a Women's Teacher Training Institute in Kabul in tandem with The Afghan Literacy Initiative, designed to help teach basic literacy to Afghan women in rural areas of Afghanistan. The Institute opened in September 2004. The Institute's first program, Afghan Literary Initiative for 200 rural villages, is in progress.

Teacher Training: In 2002, the USAWC initiated a teacher-training exchange to bring 30 Afghan women teachers to Nebraska every six months for training. In turn, these women will train other teachers in Afghanistan.

Adopt-a-school Program: Church communities in Texas are providing their adopted school with supplies, textbooks, and training.

U.S. Leadership Management and Computer Education: The Council's first major program, in September and October 2002, brought 14 women from various Afghan government ministries to the United States for an educational exchange program. During their four-week stay, they received training in computer skills, proposal writing, communications, and leadership management. Each participant received a laptop computer to use while training in the United States and to take home to use in Afghanistan. The women met with President George W. Bush and National Security Adviser Condoleezza Rice at the White House, and with Secretary of State Colin L. Powell at a Department reception held in their honor. They also had the opportunity to interact with senior policymakers, Members of Congress, government agency officials, and representatives of non-governmental organizations. In Austin, Texas, they studied the interaction among federal, state, and local entities. Their program concluded in New York City where the participants met with representatives of the United Nations.

Public Domain: accessed at http://www.state.gov/g/wi/rls/42532.htm

Chapter 18
Questions

1. It has been said that the United States (or other countries) does not have permanent friends or permanent allies—only permanent interests. Do you agree or disagree with this "realist" statement of American foreign policy?

2. When do you think it is justifiable for the United States to go to war? How is the U.S.'s "war on terror" different from other wars the country has waged?

CHAPTER 19
STATE AND LOCAL GOVERNMENT

One of the "hot-button" issues in the 2004 national elections was whether same-sex marriage, or "gay marriage," would be banned in 11 states, but that was not the only issue on state ballots. The readings selected for this chapter discuss three issues that were addressed in the November vote at the state level. "Initiatives and Constitutional Amendments in 2004" provides an overview of several leading state legislative initiatives decided by the voters, and focuses on the passage of California's stem cell research proposal. "Protect Arizona Now" analyzes the outcome and possible consequences for immigrants of the passage of that state's initiative to require proof of U.S. citizenship when a state resident registers to vote. "Gay Marriage Amendment—The Case of Georgia" explains the circumstances behind the vote to amend the constitution to recognize only different-sex marriages as legal by the state.

Initiatives and Constitutional Amendments in 2004

One of the most interesting tools for Federalism and State and local government power in the United States is the initiative. This tool allows many (but not all) state and local governments (but **not** the federal government) to directly place items on the ballot for voters to approve or turn down. The 2004 election was no exception with a diverse menu of issues, including the following:

Alaska's Measure 2 Legalizing Marijuana
This would legalize the cultivation, use and sale of marijuana for persons 21 and older; the state and local government would regulate marijuana like alcohol and tobacco; doctors would be able to prescribe drugs to all patients, including children; public use laws could be enacted by the government as well as laws in the interest of public safety. (Failed Yes 43% No 57%)

Oregon's Measure 33 on Medical Marijuana
Amends and expands Oregon's medical marijuana laws; registered persons may possess up to 10 marijuana plants and one pound of usable marijuana (unless the person registers that he is growing one crop per year, in which case possession of up to six pounds per patient is allowed); marijuana dispensaries will be regulated and authorized by the state and must be non-profits; allows naturopaths and nurse practitioners to sign a medical marijuana card application. (Failed Yes 42% No 58%)

Arizona's Proposition 200 on Proof of Citizenship
This initiative would amend the state constitution to require persons in Arizona to provide proof of U.S. citizenship when registering to vote; any state or local agency that provides benefits not federally mandated would require proof of citizenship. (Passed Yes 56% No 44%)

Same-Sex Marriage Amendments for example in Arkansas Amendment 3

Amend the state constitution to define marriage as the union of one man and one woman; Arkansas would not recognize same-sex marriages or partnerships from another state; would recognize common-law marriages from other states; the Arkansas Legislature would determine rights of married couples. (These varied from state to state in the 11 where it was approved)

California's Proposition 66 also called the "Three Strikes" Law

This would amend California's "Three Strikes" law to require increased sentences only when current conviction is for a specified violent or serious crime; redefines violent or serious felonies; only previous convictions for violent or serious felonies, brought and tried separately, would qualify for second and third "strike" sentence increases; increased penalties for specific sex crimes involving children. (Failed Yes 47% to No 53%)

Colorado's Amendment 36 which would change the allocation of electoral votes in that state

This would have amended the state constitution to allow the selection of Electoral College voters based on the popular vote; changes from the winner-takes-all system of nine electoral votes to proportional system; electoral votes would be awarded based on the percentage of the state's popular vote won by each presidential candidate; if approved, amendment would take effect for the 2004 presidential election; uses the power of the Colorado constitution to allow the people to act as the state general assembly to enact this amendment. (Failed Yes 35% no 65%)

Florida's Amendment 1 on parental notification

Amendment 1 would change the Florida Constitution to require notification of the parent or guardian of a minor before an abortion; Florida Legislature would be required to provide exemptions and create a process for having notification waived. (Passed Yes 65% No 35%)

Maine's Question 1 on Property Tax Cap

The top amount for property and personal property taxes would be capped at 1 percent of the full cash value of the property; value would be based on 1996-97 assessment; base value may be adjusted a maximum of 2 percentage points lower or higher per year; no district, county or user fee taxes may be imposed; if approved, measure would go into effect on April 1, 2005. (Failed 37% No 63%)

California had one of the most interesting initiatives on the ballot Proposition 71 on stem cell research

On October 28, 2004, Steve Westly of the Sacramento Bee in California wrote,

"On Election Day, Californians can help lead the next revolution in technology—and help our state's economy grow—by voting Yes on Proposition 71, the California Stem Cell Research and Cures Initiative. The potential is enormous. More than 100 million Americans suffer from diseases such as Alzheimer's, Parkinson's, cancer, AIDS and diabetes - diseases that stem-cell therapies might treat and cure. But partisan politics is blocking funding for the most promising areas of stem-cell research."

The Oakland Tribune on October 23, 2004 had a story titled "Prop. 71 invests in future of California, mankind." The paper wrote:

NOTHING in medical science spells HOPE more emphatically for victims of a multitude of debilitating diseases and ailments than stem cell research.

That is why California is attempting to establish itself as the stem cell research capital of the world. Biosciences are already an integral part of our economy that we can't afford to lose.

Proposition 71 would assure our future role in that research. It also is the one initiative on the Nov. 2 ballot guaranteed to attract national and international attention.

The day after the 2004 election results were in the California Stem Cell Research & Cures Initiatives, wrote:

We Did It!
Proposition 71 Wins Decisive Victory
State Sends Clear Message About Finding Cures and Saving Lives With Stem Cells

With a clear mandate—and with the tireless efforts of our volunteers and supporters—the voters of California overwhelmingly approved Proposition 71, the California Stem Cell Research and Cures Initiative, by a margin of 59% to 41%. Californians demonstrated their support for stem cell research and life-saving cures. In passing Proposition 71, voters agreed to fund stem cell research at California hospitals, medical schools and universities, to develop lifesaving therapies and cures for diseases that could save the lives of millions of California children and adults, reduce state health care costs and provide a boost to regional economies and the state at large.

Proposition 71 establishes a state-sponsored stem cell research group using bonds totaling up to $3 billion; annual limit on the bonds is $350 million with General Fund money being using to pay for the bonds; department will fund stem cell research in California; prohibits human cloning by groups that receive funds.

The initiative passed by 59% to 41% after Governor Arnold Schwarzenegger strongly supported this law as a means of finding new cures for diseases and by also touting it as a way to put the state of California at the forefront of medical and genetic research. (In fact, the Boston Globe reported that the state of Massachusetts was very concerned when the proposition passed because it would put the state at a distinct disadvantage in its competition with California for high tech business and research).

Stem cell research has been a very political issue in the United States. Pres. Bush approved a limited line of adult stem cells that could be used in research to find cures for Alzheimers, spinal injuries and many other diseases and injury-based medical problems. Stem cell research on aborted fetuses in particular has been strongly opposed by pro-life groups and by those who believe that life beings at conception. The issue became a matter of national debate when former President Ronald Reagan died in 2004 (he had been ill with Alzheimers). Reagan's son Ron, as well as Nancy Regan, were supporters of stem cell research. Ron was a speaker at the Democratic convention in Boston in the summer of 2004 (even though, of course, Pres. Reagan was a conservative Republican.

The death of actor Christopher Reeve, who was paralyzed in a horseback riding accident and was a supporter of Sen. John Kerry in his bid for president in 2004 (Kerry supported stem cell research) and the involvement of actor Michael J. Fox who, suffers from Parkinsons disease, significantly raised the level of political debate on this matter.

In California actors Brad Pitt, Reeve, and a vast number of Hollywood stars, civil rights leaders and groups, science and educational leaders, private business had lobbied and campaigned hard for this initiative.

The following exit poll information presents a picture of how people voted. This information provides an interesting mosaic of an issue that combines medicine, morality, and money.

VOTE BY GENDER

TOTAL	Yes	No
Male (49%)	58%	42%
Female (51%)	61%	39%

VOTE BY RACE

TOTAL	Yes	No
White (66%)	58%	42%
African-American (6%)	61%	39%
Latino (20%)	63%	37%
Asian (4%)	64%	36%

VOTE BY EDUCATION

TOTAL	Yes	No
No High School (4%)	50%	50%
H.S. Graduate (16%)	56%	44%
Some College (34%)	60%	40%
College Graduate (29%)	59%	41%
Postgrad Study (17%)	66%	34%

VOTE BY PARTY ID

TOTAL	Yes	No
Democrat (39%)	80%	20%
Republican (34%)	36%	64%
Independent (27%)	60%	40%

VOTE BY IDEOLOGY

TOTAL	Yes	No
Liberal (26%)	83%	17%
Moderate (46%)	63%	37%
Conservative (28%)	32%	68%

VOTE BY CHURCH ATTENDANCE

TOTAL	Yes	No
Weekly (31%)	42%	58%
Occasionally (43%)	67%	33%
Never (22%)	70%	30%

VOTE BY SIZE OF COMMUNITY

TOTAL	Yes	No
Urban (47%)	62%	38%
Suburban (40%)	57%	43%
Rural (13%)	49%	51%

Policy Research Reports #67, © SEAS, 2004

"Protect Arizona Now": Proposition 200 and the 2004 Election

By a vote of 56% to 44% Arizona passed proposition 200 which amends the state constitution to require persons in Arizona to provide proof of U.S. citizenship when registering to vote; any state or local agency that provides benefits not federally mandated would require proof of citizenship. This was also called the anti-immigrant initiative by its opponents.

Proof of who you are and especially proof of citizenship has been a controversial issue in American elections. The Arizona case is interesting and deserves our scrutiny because the issues of privacy, verifiable identification, voter intimidation, and immigrant rights, are all extremely important can contentious issues in the United States. Proposition 200 touches in some ways on all of these.

When we look at the vote by race we see the highest support by white men and the lowest by non-white men. It's interesting that non-white women were the second highest supporters of Prop 200.

VOTE BY RACE AND GENDER

TOTAL	Yes	No
White Men (37%)	60%	40%
White Women (42%)	52%	48%
Non-White Men (11%)	51%	49%
Non-White Women (11%)	58%	42%

One hypothesis on who would oppose and support this initiative revolved around a generational gap. On the surface we would assume that younger (more tolerant, more civil libertarian) voters would oppose the proposition but that was not the case. In fact, the younger tow voter sets were more supportive while the two older clusters were slightly more opposed.

VOTE BY AGE

TOTAL	Yes	No
18-29 (15%)	56%	44%
30-44 (28%)	58%	42%
45-59 (32%)	54%	46%
60 and Older (25%)	54%	46%

"Vote by income" offers a very interesting perspective. The lowest income voters by far were the most strongly supportive of this law (72%). There is a reason for this (can you extrapolate what that is?). However, other income groups were more widely distributed and did not follow an income-centered path.

VOTE BY INCOME

TOTAL	Yes	No
Under $15,000 (8%)	72%	28%
$15-30,000 (13%)	49%	51%
$30-50,000 (20%)	56%	44%
$50-75,000 (20%)	54%	46%
$75-100,000 (15%)	61%	39%
$100-150,000 (12%)	49%	51%
$150-200,000 (3%)	41%	59%
$200,000 or More (4%)	59%	41%

When we examine voting patterns on this initiative we see a familiar pattern for the 2004 election. Liberals voted strongly against this initiative (67%) while conservatives voted even more strongly for it (70%). The problem clearly is that only 19% of the voters polled considered themselves Liberal while 37% see themselves as conservative. The balance lay with moderates who, by a small but crucial margin (55%), were in favor of Prop 200.

VOTE BY IDEOLOGY

TOTAL	Yes	No
Liberal (19%)	33%	67%
Moderate (43%)	55%	45%
Conservative (37%)	70%	30%

Finally, lets examine votes by party identification. Democrats, who in 2004 we assume tend to be more liberal than other party identifiers, opposed the law by 50% to 42% in favor. Republicans, who we presume are more conservative supported Prop 200 by 70% while independents (who may also be 'moderates" ideologically) were in favor by a slim 51%.

VOTE BY PARTY ID

TOTAL	Yes	No
Democrat (30%)	42%	58%
Republican (43%)	70%	30%
Independent (27%)	51%	49%

In the next section we have the evaluation of Prop 200 by the Arizona Legislative Council, which provides research for state lawmakers. This is followed by a small selection of statements supporting and opposing Prop 200.

ANALYSIS BY LEGISLATIVE COUNCIL
From the Arizona Secretary of State Web Site

Proposition 200 would require that evidence of United States citizenship be presented by every person to register to vote, that proof of identification be presented by every voter at the polling place prior to voting, that state and local governments verify the identity of all applicants for certain public benefits and that government employees report United States immigration law violations by applicants for public benefits.

Proposition 200 provides that for purposes of registering to vote, satisfactory evidence of United States citizenship includes:

- an Arizona driver or nonoperating identification license issued after October 1, 1996.
- a driver or nonoperating identification license issued by another state if the license indicates that the person has provided proof of United States citizenship.
- a copy of the applicant's birth certificate.
- a United States passport, or a copy of the pertinent pages of the passport.
- United States naturalization documents or a verified certificate of naturalization number.
- a Bureau of Indian Affairs card number, tribal treaty card number or tribal enrollment number.

- other documents or methods of proof that may be established by the federal government for the purpose of verifying employment eligibility.

The county recorder shall indicate this information in the person's permanent voter file for at least two years. A voter registration card from another county or state does not constitute satisfactory evidence of United States citizenship. A person who is registered to vote on the date that Proposition 200 becomes effective is not required to submit evidence of citizenship unless the person moves to a different county. Once a person has submitted sufficient evidence of citizenship, the person is not required to resubmit the evidence when making changes to voter registration information in the county where the evidence has been submitted.

Proposition 200 requires that prior to receiving a ballot at a polling place, a voter must present either one form of identification that contains the name, address and photograph of the person or two different forms of identification that contain the name and address of the person.

Proposition 200 requires that a state or local governmental entity that is responsible for administering "state and local public benefits that are not federally mandated" must:
- verify the identity and eligibility for each applicant for the public benefits.
- provide other state and local government employees with information to verify immigration status of applicants applying for public benefits and must also assist other state and local government employees in obtaining immigration status information from federal immigration authorities.
- refuse to accept any state or local government identification card, including a driver license, to establish identity or eligibility for public benefits unless the governmental entity that issued the card has verified the immigration status of the applicant.
- require all state and local government employees to make a written report to federal immigration authorities upon discovering a violation of federal immigration laws by an applicant for public benefits. An employee or supervisor who fails to make the required report is guilty of a class 2 misdemeanor, potentially punishable by a jail sentence of up to 4 months and a fine of up to $750, plus applicable surcharges.

Any resident of this state would have standing to bring a court action against the state, a local governmental entity or an agent of a state or local governmental entity to remedy a violation of the public benefits verification law including bringing an action to compel a government official to comply with the law.

Proposition 200 does not define the term "state and local public benefits that are not federally mandated".

ARGUMENTS "FOR" PROPOSITION 200
PAN'S Ballot Measure Argument

The Arizona Taxpayer & Citizen Protection Act requires only (1) proof of citizenship to register to vote, (2) photo I.D. when voting, and (3) proof of eligibility to collect welfare in Arizona.

(1) and (2): Arizona now allows people to declare themselves citizens without documentation to be qualified to vote. The Act utilizes forms of I.D. citizens already have. There is evidence of hundreds of thousands of unverified names on our voter rolls (and that's with nobody even checking citizenship verification). We have to provide adequate I.D. to cash checks, enroll children in little league, get a Blockbuster card, go to the Phoenix city dump, etc. Isn't voting as important as renting a video or going to the city dump?

(3): A.R.S. Title 46 covers only welfare, not public safety services such as police and fire. This Act amends only A.R.S. 46-140 to remove the welfare department's current practice of granting immunity from prosecution to illegal aliens. The current law already requires state employees (and their supervisors if applicable), to report fraud-even if committed "by mistake"- to the state department under penalty of a misdemeanor. Yet, AHCCCS's (Arizona Medicaid) application clearly states twice in bold letters that "AHCCCS will not report any information to ... (BCIS, formerly INS)." The AHCCCS further states that everyone applying for AHCCCS must furnish their Social Security number, but "immigrants who are not legally able to obtain a [SSN] are not required to provide one."

The welfare system in Arizona is obviously set up for fraud. It's no wonder AHCCCS costs increased from $200 million in FY 2001 to a staggering $1.2 billion in FY 2003 – a whopping 600% increase in just 3 years.

The Act does not change eligibility requirements to vote or collect welfare, and applies to everyone equally. What could be fairer?

Kathy McKee, Chairman, Protect Arizona NOW, Phoenix
Paid for by "Protect Arizona Now"

Citizens of Arizona,

The Arizona Taxpayer and Citizen Protection Act ("Initiative") simply protects the rights that are guaranteed by our constitution to all citizens. As stated in section 12 of the Arizona Constitution:

"There shall be enacted registration and other laws to secure the purity of elections and guard against abuses of the elective franchise."

The Initiative will prevent non-citizens from being able to register to vote in Arizona. Currently, no proof of citizenship is required. A person can register to vote by mail or over the Internet and have a ballot mailed to them. The Initiative will require all citizens to show proof of citizenship the first time they register to vote. The Initiative will require registered voters to provide proof of identity when obtaining a ballot whether in person or by mail.

The initiative also requires proof of eligibility for an applicant to receive non-federally mandated public benefits. Arizona statutes already require proof of eligibility when an applicant applies for state or local benefits. The initiative simply requires everyone to provide a specified and approved form of identification when applying for state and local benefits. It further requires government employees to provide a written report to federal immigration authorities for any violation of federal immigration laws by any applicant that is discovered by the employee.

I urge you to vote yes on the Arizona Taxpayer and Citizen Protection Act. It treats all Arizona citizens equally and fairly under the law.

Randy Pullen, Chairman, Yes on Proposition 200, Phoenix
Paid for by "Yes on Proposition 200"

ARGUMENTS "AGAINST" PROPOSITION 200

The League of Women Voters of Arizona believes this initiative is not just bad public policy but the politics of discrimination.

Voter fraud is the least of our problems. There have been as few as 10 cases in all of Maricopa County in the last ten years and none in Pima County. The provision that requires IDs at polling places will slow down the voting process, creating longer lines and reducing voter turnout as work of lengthy waits spreads. It will mean more provisional ballots, driving up the cost of elections and delaying the counting process, holding up election results. We should not make it more difficult for two million honest citizens to vote just because a very few may be abusing this right.

The initiative does nothing to change immigration policy. What it does is turn local and state government employees into immigration agents. To be applied fairly, everyone seeking a government benefit, including firefighting assistance, a library book, and police protection must prove citizenship. This means all residents all the time and demands even enforcement.

This invitation to discriminate should be rejected. We urge a "No" vote.

Gini McGirr, President, League of Women Voters of Arizona, Tucson
Bonnie Sounders, 1st Vice President, League of Women Voters of Arizona, Sun City
Paid for by "League of Women Voters of Arizona"

I urge you to vote no on the Arizona Taxpayer and Citizens Protection Act because this legislation is mean-spirited and unnecessary.

This legislation requires that every Arizonan must present evidence of United States citizenship to register initially and every time you vote. This requirement implies that persons who are not United States citizens are registering and voting today in Arizona elections. This legislation addresses a problem that does not exist and it creates a financial and bureaucratic burden on all Arizona taxpayers. Existing state and federal laws impose harsh jail sentences and severe fines for voter fraud and false claim to United States citizenship. This legislation is clearly unnecessary.

This legislation requires that local governments verify citizenship before public services are provided. Again, this requirement implies that undocumented people are now receiving public benefits in Arizona. Undocumented people do not qualify for benefits such as public assistance and food stamps. Existing state and federal laws impose harsh jail sentences and severe fines for welfare fraud and false claim to U.S. citizenship. This legislation is so broad as to require proof of citizenship before local fire personnel can put out a house fire, save occupants or provide life-saving intervention at the scene of an accident. My mother is an 80-year-old citizen who does not speak English and I do not want someone withholding life saving aid from her while attempting to determine her citizenship. This is not the Arizona I want to live in. This is not who we are as a people. Arizonans care about each other; blind hate is not an Arizona value.

This legislation is mean-spirited and unnecessary. Vote no.

Raul M. Grijalva, Member of Congress, Tucson

The Green Party of Arizona refers to this ballot measure as the "Let's make it hard for Americans to vote Initiative." Under the guise of affecting public assistance to undocumented migrants, where its impact is negligible, it sneaks in requirements that will make it harder for citizens to exercise our right to vote. We Greens push to make it easier for Americans to vote, not harder, because we believe that the best government will come when we all participate.

Under this measure young people, eager to register and vote as they come of age, will have to send away for a copy of their birth certificate first, and maybe miss deadlines, if the document comes at bureaucratic pace. Likewise, persons registered in other states, rather than present their old registration when they want to become Arizona residents, must pay for the proof of citizenship that they'll have to present. And older citizens, who like to vote at the polls on election day, may find themselves hiking several blocks back home, maneuvering a walker or cane, if they forget to bring a picture ID.

This measure is designed to make voting and registration less convenient for citizens, to add to costly bureaucracy and delay, and to intimidate and harass the vulnerable. When Arizonans learn the real agenda behind this thing, they will vote it down.

Vote NO.

Maggie Silk, Co-Chair, Arizona Green Party, Mesa
Claudia Ellquist, Tucson
Richard Scott, Treasurer, Arizona Green Party, Scottsdale

In red states (Republican) and blue ones where democrats won, eleven states passed amendments banning same-sex marriage on November 2, 2004.

Arkansas, Georgia, Kentucky, Michigan, Mississippi, Montana, Ohio, Oklahoma, North Dakota, Utah, and even more liberal Oregon approved the bans on gay marriage often by extraordinarily large margins (an extraordinary 86% in Mississippi).

Georgia Amendment

The following information gives some insight into the state of Georgia's Amendment # 1 which will change the Georgia constitution so only a union between a man and a woman would be recognized as legal by the state. It was approved by a 76% yes to 24% no. Interestingly (see table), African-Americans supported the amendment in larger percentages (80%) than other race groups. This was generally attributed to the fact that many black churches especially in the South are quite traditional on social values (moral) issues.

VOTE BY RACE

TOTAL	Yes	No
White (70%)	76%	24%
African-American (24%)	80%	20%
Latino (4%)	74%	26%

When we examine support by age cohort we find that there is a strong association between age and support with older voters giving strongest approval (84%) to the amendment and younger voters the least but still overwhelming support (72%). The argument that opposition to gay marriage is a "generational" issue is correct, however, at least in Georgia, the data does not hold out much promise that gay marriage will be approved anytime soon.

VOTE BY AGE

TOTAL	Yes	No
18-29(19%)	72%	28%
30-44 (36%)	75%	25%
45-59(31%)	77%	23%
60 and Older (15%)	84%	16%

When we examine this issue by party identity of the voters we find that democrats least supported the amendment. Republicans were the strongest supporters and Independents fell somewhere in-between although still strongly (72%) supporting the initiative.

VOTE BY PARTY ID

TOTAL	Yes	No
Democrat (34%)	64%	36%
Republican (42%)	88%	12%
Independent (24%)	72%	28%

One of the political issues regarding gay marriage and the 2004 election is the debate of whether it was an important issue in the defeat of Senator John Kerry. While more analysis is needed on this issue nationwide, the following table shows how people who voted for Sen. Kerry voted on the amendment only 60% voted "yes" and how those voting for Bush voted on the amendment - 88% voted "yes".

VOTE FOR PRESIDENT

TOTAL	Yes	No
Kerry (41%)	60%	40%
Bush (59%)	88%	12%

Perhaps the most interesting question is whether political philosophy or ideology has any connection to how people voted on the marriage amendment in Georgia. As the following table indicates the conventional wisdom that liberals support gay marriage is borne out with 53% of people defining themselves as liberal in the 2004 election exit polls voting against the amendment. As expected, conservatives showed an overwhelming support of Amendment # 1 (92%). (For comparison, in Oregon only 17% of "Liberals" votes "Yes" while in Mississippi a whopping 72% of "Liberals" voted for the amendment).

VOTE BY IDEOLOGY

TOTAL	Yes	No
Liberal (14%)	47%	53%
Moderate (44%)	71%	29%
Conservative (41%)	92%	8%

A ruling of the Massachusetts Supreme court initially launched gay marriage as a political issue. That decision declared the right to marry by same sex couples to be constitutionally protected. Critics have called this a "liberal" agenda. The results of exit polls in Georgia certainly suggest that political ideology plays an important role in the way people feel about and vote.

The following is the text of the Georgia amendment on same sex marriage.
Source: http://www.sos.state.ga. us/elections/2004_constitutional_amendments.htm

PROPOSED CONSTITUTIONAL AMENDMENTS
GENERAL ELECTION - State of Georgia
NOVEMBER 2, 2004

This booklet contains copies of the two proposed amendments to the Constitution in their entirety. [Editor: only amendment # 1 is reproduced here]. These amendments will be submitted at the general election on November 2, 2004. As required by the Constitution, these proposed amendments in their entirety are on file in the office of the judge of the probate court in each county and are available for public inspection. This booklet also includes summaries of the two proposals as prepared by Attorney General Thurbert E. Baker, Secretary of State Cathy Cox, and Legislative Counsel Sewell R. Brumby and published in the newspaper which is each county's official legal organ. There are no state-wide referendum questions on the 2004 general election ballot.

- AMENDMENT 1 -

Senate Resolution No. 595
Resolution Act No. 841
Ga. L.2004, p.1111

A RESOLUTION

Proposing an amendment to the Constitution so as to provide that this state shall recognize as marriage only the union of man and woman; to provide for submission of this amendment for ratification or rejection; and for other purposes.

BE IT RESOLVED BY THE GENERAL ASSEMBLY OF GEORGIA:

SECTION 1.

Article I of the Constitution is amended by adding a new Section IV to read as follows:

"SECTION IV.
MARRIAGE

Paragraph I. **Recognition of marriage,** (a) This state shall recognize as marriage only the union of man and woman. Marriages between persons of the same sex are prohibited in this state.

(b) No union between persons of the same sex shall be recognized by this state as entitled to the benefits of marriage. This state shall not give effect to any public act, record, or judicial proceeding of any other state or jurisdiction respecting a relationship between persons of the same sex that is treated as a marriage under the laws of such other state or jurisdiction. The courts of this state shall have no jurisdiction to grant a divorce or separate maintenance with respect to any such relationship or otherwise to consider or rule on any of the parties' respective rights arising as a result of or in connection with such relationship."

SECTION 2.

The above proposed amendment to the Constitution shall be published and submitted as provided in Article X, Section I, Paragraph II of the Constitution. The ballot submitting the above proposed amendment shall have written or printed thereon the following:

"YES ( )
 NO ( )

Shall the Constitution be amended so as to provide that this state shall recognize as marriage only the union of man and woman?"

All persons desiring to vote in favor of ratifying the proposed amendment shall vote "Yes." All persons desiring to vote against ratifying the proposed amendment shall vote "No." If such amendment shall be ratified as provided in said Paragraph of the Constitution, it shall become a part of the Constitution of this state.

Electric Politics, © 2004

Chapter 19
Questions

1. The anti-"gay marriage" proposals in all 11 states passed, most by wide margins, and some also barred same-sex "civil unions" that provide fewer legal protections for the couple. What do think are the best reasons to favor such a proposal, and what are the best reasons for opposing such proposals?

2. Think of two ballot initiatives that you would like to see on your state's ballot in the next election. How would you go about trying to get those initiatives passed into law?

CHAPTER 20
MONEY AND POLITICS

"Money and Politics" gives you a quick introduction to the role of campaign finance in the outcome of elections and in structuring how the political system works in the United States, in particular the role played by "527" independent fundraising groups. The accompanying statement, "Supreme Court Decision Upholding Soft Money Ban is Major Victory for America," is from Common Cause, a public interest group that has fought to limit the impact on American politics and government of wealthy organizations, individuals, and families. "The McCain-Feingold-Cochran Campaign Reform Bill" gives you a summary of the recently enacted legislation designed to limit the impact of "soft money" that bypasses the existing limits on campaign finance contributions.

Supreme Court Decision Upholding Soft Money Ban is Major Victory for America
Common Cause Statement on Supreme Court Victory

The following is the Common Cause statement on the Supreme Court Ruling of 2003:

"The Supreme Court decision today [December 10, 2003] upholding nearly all elements of the Bipartisan Campaign Reform Act (BCRA) is a major victory for democracy and all Americans.

By agreeing that unlimited contributions to the political parties "can corrupt or, at the very least, create the appearance of corruption of federal candidates and office holders," the Supreme Court has again recognized the importance and constitutionality of limiting big money in the political process.

"The American people wanted this law, Congress enacted it and now the Supreme Court has ruled it constitutional," said Common Cause President Chellie Pingree. "The toxic link between donors who write six-figure checks and people in power at the highest levels of government has been severed for good."

Upholding the ban on soft money and the ban on corporations and labor unions directly funding some broadcast advertisements about federal candidates means that additional, meaningful campaign finance reforms can now follow.

Common Cause plans to pursue reform of the presidential public finance system, public financing for congressional elections and in the states and free and reduced-cost TV airtime for political candidates.

"This struggle took more than a decade, but it proves that citizens can trump the power of special interests," Pingree said. It is also a testament to the courage and dedication of BCRA's sponsors, Sens. John McCain (R-AZ), Russell Feingold (D-WI) and Reps. Martin Meehan (D-MA) and Christopher Shays (R-CT), she said.

Common Cause is working with other organizations to make certain that the activities of 527's do not undermine the soft money ban. See our comments to the Federal Election Commission."

In spite of the campaign finance law and the initial optimism about less soft money in the 2004 campaign, interest groups found so many loopholes in the law that 2004 became the most expensive and perhaps most negative campaign in history. One of the lessons of this election is that money has a tendency to find its way and flow to campaigns. Moreover, in the United States the right to use money to influence politics is to a large extent protected by the free speech provision of the constitution. Thus, even when laws are enacted they tend to leave open vast areas of legitimate spending which will be exploited by political groups and which permit vast sums to leak (pour actually) into American politics.

This information has been compiled by the editors of this book. The information on Common Cause above comes from the Common Cause Website: http://www.commoncause.org/site/pp.asp?c=dkLNK1MQIwG&b=202960

The McCain-Feingold-Cochran Campaign Reform Bill

The selection was excerpted from http://www.straighttalkamerica.com

The McCain-Feingold-Cochran campaign reform bill is similar to the bills that were debated in the 105th and 106th Congresses. A strong bipartisan majority of both the House and the Senate favors this reform. It contains the following major components:

A Ban on Soft Money. The bill would prohibit all soft money contributions to the national political parties from corporations, labor unions, and wealthy individuals. State parties that are permitted under state law to accept these unregulated contributions would be prohibited from spending them on activities relating to federal elections, including advertising that supports or opposes a federal candidate. In addition, federal candidates would be prohibited from raising soft money. These provisions would shut down the Washington soft money machine, prohibiting the $100,000, $250,000 and even $500,000 contributions that for the last decade have flowed to the political parties.

McCain-Feingold-Cochran would also double the amount of "hard" money individuals may contribute to state parties for use in federal elections, from $5,000 to $10,000. It would increase the amount of "hard" money an individual may contribute in aggregate to all federal candidates, parties, and PACs in a single year from $25,000 to $30,000.

Restrictions on "Phony Issue Ads" Run by Corporations and Unions (The Snowe-Jeffords Amendment). First adopted as part of McCain-Feingold during the Senate's February 1998 campaign finance debate, the Snowe-Jeffords amendment addresses the explosion of thinly-veiled campaign advertising funded by corporate and union treasuries. These ads skirt federal election law by avoiding the use of direct entreaties to "vote for" or "vote against" a particular candidate. Under the bill, labor unions and for-profit corporations would be prohibited from spending their treasury funds on "electioneering communications." "Electioneering communications" are defined as radio or TV ads that refer to a clearly identified candidate or candidates and appear within 30 days of a primary or 60 days of a general election. This definition does not include any printed communication, direct mail, voter guides, or the Internet. It would also not cover issue advertising that does not identify a specific candidate or appears outside of the 30/60 day pre-election window.

The Snowe-Jeffords amendment permits 501(c)(4) non-profit corporations to make electioneering communications as long as they use only individual contributions (not corporate or union funds) and make certain disclosures. The amendment thus prevents unions or corporations from laundering funds through non-profits to make electioneering communications.

The amendment also provides that a group making electioneering communications that total $10,000 or more in an election cycle must disclose its identity, the cost of the communication, and the names and addresses of all contributors of $1,000 or more to the sponsor of the communication within the cycle. If the group makes expenditures on electioneering communications from a separate bank account to which only individuals can contribute, it need only disclose the large donors to that account.

The Snowe-Jeffords amendment treats corporations and unions fairly and equally. It does not prohibit any election ad, nor does it place limits on spending by outside organizations. But it will give the public crucial information about the election activities of independent groups and prevent corporate and union treasury money from being spent to influence elections.

Strict Codification of the "Beck" Decision. The bill would require labor unions to notify non-union employees that if they file an objection, they are entitled to have their agency fees reduced by an amount equal to the portion of fees used for political purposes.

Foreign Money. McCain-Feingold-Cochran would strengthen current law to prohibit foreign nationals from making any contributions in a federal, state or local election. The foreign money abuses from the 1996 election that captured so much attention would be entirely shut down by this proposal.

Greater Disclosure and Stronger Election Laws. McCain-Feingold-Cochran contains a number of provisions designed to improve disclosure of campaign finance information and strengthen enforcement of the law. The bill would: (1) strengthen current law to make it clear that it is unlawful to raise or solicit campaign contributions on federal property, including the

White House and the United States Congress: (2) bar federal candidates from converting campaign funds for personal use, such as a mortgage payment or country club membership; (3) specify circumstances in which activities by outside groups or parties will be considered coordinated with candidates; and (4) provide more timely disclosure of independent expenditures.

Public Domain: accessed at http://www.campaignfinancesite.org/legislation/mccain.html

---

Chapter 20
Questions

1. Do you think it's a good idea to limit the amount of money anyone or any organization can contribute to influence campaigns and elections? Is this issue more one of free speech in the form of spending money to support who and what you want, or is it more a matter of equal access for everyone regardless of how much money they have?

2. How much money do you think it should take to run a campaign? Find out how much money was spent on the latest campaign in your state for state legislature, governor, U.S. House of Representatives, and U.S. Senate, and compare this against how much you think each campaign should cost. What do you conclude?

Just about everything you wanted to know about blogs (that is, Web logs) is explained in "From the e-Democracy Blog," which focuses on the public relations disaster for CBS News, and its *60 Minutes* broadcasters as well as its former news anchor, Dan Rather, over reports of what turned out to be faked records of President George W. Bush's military service in 2004. The faulty nature of the story was revealed initially by bloggers. The importance of electronic media in American government and politics today is amplified by the article, "Court, 5-4, Blocks Law Regulating Internet Access," by Linda Greenhouse, which shows the difficulty inherent in trying to regulate what information can be accessed through electronic communication.

From the e-Democracy Blog

In September of 2004 the CBS program 60 Minutes reported that President George W. Bush had been given special treatment during his Vietnam-era service in the Texas National Guard. Central to the story were documents written and signed by President Bush's late National Guard commander Lt. Col. Jerry B. Killian. In several of these documents Killian wrote that he had been pressured to "sugarcoat the performance ratings" of Bush who was at the time the son of a Texas congressman (George H. Bush). The memos also showed that Bush failed to follow orders to take a physical examination required by the National Guard. The documents, copies of originals, had been obtained from "unnamed" sources that CBS claimed were reliable.

If true, the allegations and these documents would be embarrassing to Pres. Bush as he entered the last two months of his reelection campaign since they raised questions about his military service and his use of family connections to get into the Guard, avoid getting drafted and probably sent to Vietnam. His Democratic opponent Sen. John Kerry of Massachusetts had made his own Vietnam service and heroism (3 Purple Hearts and other medals) a cornerstone of his campaign. Vietnam war veterans hostile to Kerry and allegedly linked to the Bush campaign had recently run attack ads questioning the veracity of Kerry's heroism and successfully damaging Kerry in the polls.

This story would have gone virtually unchallenged in the past because the power of CBS and the "reputation" of *60 Minutes* and veteran anchor and reporter Dan Rather, have been almost unassailable, although he has been excoriated by conservatives as a supporter of liberal leaders. His clash with Richard Nixon in 1974, his critical reporting on Ronald Reagan, and his dispute with President George H. W. Bush during an interview in 1988 are often cited as examples of Dan Rather's hostility to Republicans. (See http://www.Ratherbiased.com or Media Research Center for allegations of his bias.)

However, in this case something amazing happened literally within hours of the airing of the story.

Web loggers—Bloggers—began to raise questions about the documents' veracity. The first to enter the fray were http://www.freerepublic.com, http://www.powerlineblog.com, and http://www.littlegreenfootballs.com/weblog. Blogs are on-line journals or "publications" that allow for easy posting, are interactive, and sometimes investigative.

Bloggers claimed that some of the documents looked like they had been produced by a computer using modern software—probably Microsoft Word—neither of which were available in 1972 when the documents were supposedly written. In question were the type style, Times New Roman, the use of superscripts on the 111th (the number of the squadron Bush served in), and the spacing of the type. Also in doubt were the signatures of Col. Killian.

The *Dallas Morning News* asked Col. Killian's former secretary, an 86-year-old woman by the name of Marian Carr Knox, about the documents. Regarding the documents, she was quoted as saying "These are not real. They're not what I typed, and I would have typed them for him," but she said the content was true. Dan rather later interviewed her and clearly seemed delighted that she verified the spirit or message of the memos—never mind that they were probably fake!

Thus "Rathergate" was born. (Note; in the US any scandal is "gated" following the big enchilada of scandals, Richard Nixon's Watergate).

What I find extraordinary about this tale is that ordinary people, using the Internet and web logs, were able to challenge and seriously threaten the veracity and credibility of a multi-billion dollar news empire such as CBS. More amazing is the fact that these Bloggers have damaged and perhaps in the long run destroyed the credibility of Dan Rather who was the lead reporter on this story and who, in the face of these serious allegations of fake documents, clearly decided to sandbag questions from other news outlets about the credibility and origin of the memos. The venerable *60 Minutes* itself may be at risk.

Rather and CBS refused to reveal where or how they obtained the documents and also did not come forward with all the "experts" who had been consulted. Several document specialists, who came out on their own after the story broke, told CBS the documents were fake, but they were ignored. The program seems to have relied on only one document specialist who had, as it turns out, looked primarily at the signature of Col. Killian on the documents. When he was asked after the scandal broke, he said he'd only verified Killian's signature, but he said felt it was possible that a legit signature had been copied and pasted into the memos.

The arrival of Bloggers on the scene has totally changed the nature of media.

I attended the 2004 Democratic National Convention (DNC) in Boston. For the first time in history there was a Bloggers Section. Bloggers were accredited by the DNC just as they accredited TV, Radio, and the print media. In fact, so many Bloggers had applied for credentials that the Democrats had a difficult time sorting out a reasonable number to whom credentials were given. In the "Talk Radio Alley " where I was located for part of the convention, Bloggers were much sought out celebrities. Young men and women (and mature dudes like me!) who in the past might work their way up the traditional institutional media ladder for many, many years were now directly injected into the news and commentary stream. All of them were producing commentary and descriptions that were far more exciting, novel, passionate, intense, interesting, and often brilliant than the usual fare we read or hear. Many others were trivial, opinionated, self-serving, nasty, disrespectful, or just wrong!

Millions of American and indeed people all over the world are now writing and also reading Blogs as their primary source of information, commentary, and communication. Bloggers are building virtual communities of people who share interests ranging from food, sexual orientation, surfing, human rights, health, information technology, to environmentalism, sailing, Scuba diving, and politics, which are my four passions (I have four Blogs, one on each of the latter topics, but, of course my political material http://cyberpolitics.blogspot.com/ is the most active and has been quoted by many mainstream electronic and print media).

Blogs are the "new media" and as challengers to the established, previously unrivaled, and arrogant "mainstream"—BIG and Powerful media—I think Blogs are one of the most amazing and significant developments of the information technology revolution.

The *Orlando Sentinel*'s Kathleen Parker had a column titled "Bloggers do job better than media" (9-16-04). She refers to the blogosphere as an "... intellectual ecosystem wherein the best specimens from various disciplines descend from the ether, converge on an issue and apply their talents."

Ok, maybe not.

I have seen Blogs that represent the worst specimens descend on the blogosphere—racists, misogynists, stupid and misinformed people, predators, identity thieves, and, I would assume, even terrorists.

Still, from where I sit right now in 2004 looking over the vast battleground of American politics, it's a remarkable thing to watch the *New York Times*, *Washington Post*, the major networks, *Newsweek*, and CNN pull up the rear on this scandal. And by the way, all the evidence tells **me** it was not a mistake, not an oversight, not "sloppy journalism," but a deliberate act. My proof? CBS rejected the expert advice of several of their own document expert consultants who said the papers were probably fake and "expert shopped" until they found one who agreed with them (and it turns out he got his "degree" in documentation from a correspondence school!).

Blogs are the ultimate democratization of information. They represent "disintermediated empowerment," the direct connection between people without the old information "brokers" (intermediaries) who have spun their tale and told us not just **what** is news but also **how to think about events**, and who often represented the views and interests of a small, national cultural media elite. If you've ever watched any of the network programming, you realize that it's all the same—the sequence of stories, who's interviewed, the message we're supposed to get. Anyone who watches mainstream TV news or political talk programs can't help but wonder why the same people are the "experts" on all the shows and why they come from New York or Washington, D.C. but rarely from San Diego, Des Moines, or Tuscaloosa. Even Public Radio and television use the same commentators and in many cases they also write columns for the *New York Times* or *Washington Post*. It often looks as if all of mainstream media political news is produced in one large warehouse and then delivered, like so many Krispy Kreme donuts to all the outlets.

Granted, The Fox Network and media mogul Rupert Murdoch's newspapers, Rush Limbaugh and conservative talk radio in general add a conservative and often blistering, simplistic, and divisive perspective on events. In fact, the absence of a successful liberal talk radio alternative makes this medium disturbingly monochromatic.

Bloggers are the "bottom up revolution" of media. For better or worse they add ideological and philosophical diversity to news and commentary. They reflect the divided, fragmented, and interesting plurality of American society. *E pluribus unum* has been misused by the political, cultural, and media elites. The *unum* is what they define it as. Bloggers are the *pluribus*!

Bloggers also represent a serious challenge to the arrogance of the establishment who now must be very, very careful what they print, transmit, or articulate because the Bloggers will be looking over their shoulders. This will make news reporting and analysis more complete, more diverse, and ultimately more precise. In the final analysis, Bloggers will make this a more democratic and accountable nation and improve the quality of our political discourse.

Postscript I—A day after I wrote these comments the *Washington Post* reported that a retired Texas National Guard officer, Lt. Col. Bill Burkett had posted comments on several *Yahoo* and other discussion groups (including *Online Journal*) urging the Democrats to wage "war" against the Republican ticket of Bush/Chaney. He had also laid out a strategy for justifying "down and dirty" tactics. So, once again, the Internet enters the picture, this time as a "digital paper trail" of someone involved.

Postscript II—On September 21, 2004, Dan Rather and CBS admitted on the evening news that they had made a mistake and apologized for using unverified documents. However, they also interviewed the source of the documents, Bill Burkett the retired officer, in an obvious ploy to shift some of the blame to him. Burkett admitted that he deliberately misled the network but refused to reveal his sources of the fake documents. However, the firestorm surrounding the incident continued and there were calls for Rather to apologize directly to President Bush and to resign or retire. CBS set up an independent investigation of the scam. It was alleged by many observers that the Kerry presidential campaign or independent Democratic groups backing the Kerry campaign were involved in or connected to this operation. The Kerry campaign denied any connection even though CBS had, as part of their deal, given Burkett the name and number of a contact in the Kerry campaign, who then had at least one phone conversation with the Kerry team. Conservatives and Republicans used the incident to electrify their political base by arguing that it's further proof of a Liberal media conspiracy against Republicans.

My conclusion is that this incident temporarily hurt Kerry and helped Bush, permanently diminished greatly the *60 Minutes* program and Dan Rather, further eroded the overall credibility of all the mainstream media, and temporarily elevated Bloggers to status of investigative mavens, fact-checkers, and guarantors of media honesty.

Later in the cycle many Bloggers discredited the validity of blogging when hysterical conspiracy scenarios about the 2004 election: Some of the post election discussions—it was stolen by the Republicans who hacked the election system; the Democrats had a systematic plan through voter registration drives to double-register people, throw away Republican voter registration forms; the exit polls early on Nov 2 showing Kerry way ahead were accurate and the actual votes counted were not so we should do away with elections and just use polls to select the president.

blog (bläg) **n.** [*short for* Web log] **1.** a website that accommodates easy and frequent posting on any topic; **2.** an online platform for personal anecdotes, criticism and discussion, often featuring links to other websites;

Conservative Blogs
http://www.Nationalreview.com
http://Andrewsullivan.com
http://www.Realclearpolitics.com
http://www.Coxandforkum.com

Liberal Blogs
http://www.Salon.com
http://www.Alternet.com
http://www.Slate.com
http://www.thenation.com

Middle-of-the-Road Blogs
http://abcnews.go.com/sections/politics
http://cyberpolitics.blogspot.com/

Editors note about the author of this article which is edited and up-dated version of his original blog: Steffen Schmidt is University Professor of Political Science at Iowa State University and is also Professor of Costal Zone Management and Environment at Nova Southeastern University Oceanographic Center in Ft. Lauderdale, Florida. His weekly radio talk show can be heard at WOI.org streaming live. He is a frequent commentator on CNN en Español, the BBC, Clear Channel station KASI, Radio Francia en Español, and the Arne Arneson Show in New Hampshire. His comments also appear in the *Christian Science Monitor*, *Reuters News*, *the New York Times*, *Chicago Tribune*, *Boston Globe*, *Dallas Morning News*, *Newsweek*, and other major publications.

© 2004, SEAS Consulting. Do not reproduce or reprint without permission.

http://cyberpolitics.blogspot.com/ to post comments on this or other political issues.

Washington, June 29—The Supreme Court on Tuesday rejected Congress's latest effort to curb children's access to sexually explicit material on the Internet. But at the same time it gave the Bush administration a second chance to defend the law as a trial on its constitutionality goes forward in Federal District Court in Philadelphia.

The 5-to-4 majority kept in place an order that the district court issued in 1999, blocking enforcement of the Child Online Protection Act until its validity can be resolved. The six-year-old law, which imposes criminal penalties of as much as $50,000 a day on commercial Internet sites that make pornography available to those younger than 17, has never taken effect.

The decision came on the final day of the Supreme Court's term. Justice Anthony M. Kennedy, writing for the majority, said that the government must now show why the voluntary use of filters to screen out material unsuitable for children would not work as well as the law's criminal penalties. Filters "impose selective restrictions on speech at the receiving end, not universal restrictions at the source," Justice Kennedy wrote.

The opinion, which was joined by Justices John Paul Stevens, David H. Souter, Clarence Thomas and Ruth Bader Ginsburg, suggested strongly that the government would not be able to demonstrate that the penalties were better than filters. Not only are filters less restrictive, but they "also may well be more effective," Justice Kennedy said, because they can block pornography from anywhere in the world, while the statute applies only to pornography posted on the Web from within the United States.

Even so, the court kept open the possibility that the law, know as COPA, might ultimately be upheld.

"This option does not hold that Congress is incapable of enacting any regulation of the Internet designed to prevent minors from gaining access to harmful materials," Justice Kennedy said.

He said the decision "does not foreclose the district court from concluding, upon a proper showing by the government that meets the government's constitutional burden as defined in this opinion, that COPA is the least restrictive alternative available to accomplish Congress's goal."

Under the court's First Amendment precedents, government-imposed restrictions must go no further than necessary to accomplish a "compelling government interest"—in this instance, protecting children from harmful material on the Internet. The government must show that it is using the "least restrictive means" to achieve its goal.

The coalition of Internet publishers and free-speech groups that filed suit to block the law have argued that the existence of filters showed that criminal fines and prison sentences were not the least restrictive approach. A year ago, the Supreme Court upheld a law that required public libraries to install Internet filters as a condition of receiving federal money.

In a dissenting opinion of Tuesday, Justice Antonin Scalia said the majority had subjected the Child Online Protection Act to too searching a constitutional review. He said that because the commercial pornography that is the law's target "could, consistent with the First Amendment, be banned entirely, COPA's lesser restrictions raise no constitutional concern."

The three other dissenters, Justice Stephen G. Breyer and Sandra Day O'Connor along with Chief Justice William H. Rehnquist, took a different approach. They said, in an opinion written by Justice Breyer, that the law should be interpreted to apply only to a narrow category of obscene material and should be upheld on that basis.

"Properly interpreted," Justice Breyer wrote, the law "imposes a burden on protected speech that is no more than modest," reaching only "borderline cases" beyond speech that is obscene and that thus lacks legal protection. Justice Breyer said that while the plaintiffs raised the specter that the law might apply to famous novels or serious discussions of sexuality, this was not the case. "We must interpret the act to save it, not to destroy it," he added.

Further, Justice Breyer said, there was little reason to suppose that filters would achieve the purpose of shielding children. He said the software "lacks precision" and depends for its effect on parents' willingness to pay for it, install it and monitor their children's computer use.

The court and Congress have had a tangled relationship on the question of Internet pornography. In 1997, the court unanimously invalidated Congress's first effort, the Communications Decency Act of 1996. Congress responded quickly by passing the Child Online Protection Act the next year, responding to a number of the court's concerns by defining pornography more precisely and limiting the reach of the statute to commercial Web sites.

The American Civil Liberties Union, which had organized the successful challenge to the first law, sued to block the new law as well, and won in both the federal district court and the United States Court of Appeals for the Third Circuit, in Philadelphia. The Third Circuit found then that the law's reference to "contemporary community standards" would give "the most puritan of communities" an effective veto over Internet content.

The Supreme Court, in a 2002 decision, disagreed with that analysis and sent the case back to the Third Circuit. This time, the appeals court ruled that the law did not meet the First Amendment's "least restrictive means" test. The Bush administration then appealed that ruling to the Supreme Court, leading to the decision Tuesday. Ashcroft v. American Civil Liberties Union, No 03-218.

Mark Corallo, a spokesman for the Justice Department, expressed the administration's dismay with the ruling. "Congress has repeatedly attempted to address this serious need, and the court yet again opposed these common-sense measures to protect America's children," he said.

Senator Patrick J. Leahy, Democrat of Vermont, who was the only member of the Senate to vote against the law, said he had warned that the law would not withstand a constitutional challenge. "Technology has continued to produce better solutions than this law offers," he said.

Ann Beeson, associate legal director of the A.C.L.U., who argued the case at the court, said she was confident that the law would eventually be struck down. "We urge John Ashcroft to stop wasting taxpayer dollars in defending this unconstitutional law," she said.

There was some evidence that the outcome of the case shifted during the nearly four months that the court had it under consideration. It is likely that Justice Breyer initially had the assignment but lost the case to Justice Kennedy as the result of a change of heart by another justice, perhaps Justice Thomas. The result left Justice Breyer without a majority opinion from among the dozen cases the court heard in March, while Justice Kennedy had two majority opinions.

Chapter 21
Questions

1.   Have you used blogs for political discussions? Whether you have or have not done so, what main political purposes do you believe can be served by blogs?

2.   What limitations, if any, do you believe there should be on what you or anyone else can do on the Internet?